AGAINST THE ODDS

THE INDIGENOUS RIGHTS CASES OF

THOMAS R. BERGER

AGAINST THE ODDS

THE INDIGENOUS RIGHTS CASES OF
THOMAS R. BERGER

Drew Ann Wake, *author and editor*
Thomas R. Berger QC OC OBC, *author*
Michael Jackson KC, *author and photographer*
Dalee Sambo Dorough PhD, *author*
Jean Teillet LLM, *author*
Linda MacCannell MFA, *photographer*

Foreword by Hamar Foster, KC
Afterword by Shaznay Waugh

DURVILE &
UpRoute

DURVILE IMPRINT OF DURVILE & UPROUTE BOOKS
CALGARY, ALBERTA, CANADA
DURVILE.COM

DURVILE & UpRoute

Durvile Publications Ltd.

DURVILE IMPRINT OF DURVILE AND UPROUTE BOOKS
CALGARY, ALBERTA, CANADA
WWW.DURVILE.COM

Anthology © Durvile Publications
Individual Chapters © the Authors

LIBRARY AND ARCHIVES CATALOGUING IN PUBLICATIONS DATA

Against the Odds : The Indigenous Rights Cases of Thomas R. Berger

Wake, Drew Ann: Author
Berger, Thomas R.: Author
Sambo Dorough, Dalee: Author
Jean Teillet, Author
Jackson, Michael: Author and Photographer
Foster, Hamar: Foreword
Waugh, Shaznay: Afterword
MacCannell, Linda: Photographer

1. Indigenous Justice | 2. Northwest Territories | 3. First Nations
4. Truth & Reconciliation | 5. British Columbia | 6. Alaska
Book 11 in the Durvile True Cases Series | Series Editor, Lorene Shyba MFA PhD
ISBN: 978-1-990735-48-6 (pbk)
978-1-990735-28-8 (audio) | 978-1-990735-67-7 (epub)

Cover photo of Thomas R. Berger and Jim Antoine: Peter Gorrie
Cover design: Austin Andrews

Printed in Canada | First edition, first printing. 2024

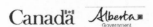

Durvile Publications acknowledges the financial support of the Government of Canada through
Canadian Heritage, Canada Book Fund and the Government of Alberta, Alberta Media Fund.

With gratitude, we acknowledge the traditional land of the Treaty 7 Peoples of Southern Alberta: the
Siksika, Piikani, and Kainai of the Niisitapi (Blackfoot) Confederacy; the Dene Tsuut'ina;
and the Chiniki, Bearspaw, and Wesley Stoney Nakoda First Nations.
We also acknowledge the Homeland of the Otipemisiwak Métis Government of the Métis Nation within Alberta.

Durvile & UpRoute is committed to protecting our natural environment. This book is made of material from
well-managed FSC®-certified forests and other controlled sources.

Against the Odds was written
in honour of the Indigenous leaders
who joined Tom Berger
in seeking paths to
justice and equity in Canada.
We have learned so much from you.

CONTENTS

~⌒

CONTENTS

FOREWORD

Hamar Foster KC

~⌒

I AM HONOURED to have been asked to write the Introduction to Drew Ann Wake's quite wonderful book *Against the Odds*. I appeared as counsel before Tom Berger on two occasions when he was Mr. Justice Berger of the Supreme Court of British Columbia, worked on couple of projects with him when he returned to the practice of law, and came to regard him as a friend. So it is a pleasure to see his career, and the Indigenous people who inspired him and played such a central role in everything from his first case to his last (and so many of the highlights in between), set out so effectively in one volume. But *Against the Odds* is about more than this.

Section 35 of the *Constitution Act*, 1982, states that the "existing aboriginal and treaty rights of the aboriginal peoples of Canada are hereby recognized and affirmed." Since then, a host of developments, notably the Supreme Court of Canada's decisions in the Delgamuukw and Tsilhqot'in cases, have fleshed out what those words mean.

Against the Odds is mainly about what it was like before those words were enacted into law.

Indigenous Peoples have been asserting their rights in this country from the beginning. However, as their populations decreased due to epidemics of smallpox, measles, and other illnesses, and as their roles as traders and military allies diminished, they were gradually marginalized in the consciousness of most non-Indigenous people. Czech novelist Milan Kundera aptly noted, "The first step in liquidating a people … is to erase its memory…. Before long a nation will begin to forget what it is and what it was…. The world around it will forget even faster."

As this book documents, however, there were remarkable people who did not forget. Even before the events described here, there were many such people. In British Columbia, for example, delegations were sent and petitions addressed to the colonial authorities within a few years of the colony's founding in 1858. And after the turn of the last century, these initiatives included delegations to Rome, Ottawa, and London, England. The Cowichan lodged their petition with the Imperial Privy Council in 1909, followed by the Nisga'a petition in 1913. Citing the Royal Proclamation of 1763 and other legal authorities, organizations such as the Indian Rights Association, the Interior Tribes, and the Allied Indian Tribes of British Columbia maintained pressure on provincial, federal, and imperial governments for three decades.

But there were political, legal, and financial obstacles that stood in the way. Then, in 1927, Parliament not only made it effectively illegal to raise funds to assist tribes or bands making claims against the government, but also had a committee of the Senate and House of Commons dismiss the Allied Tribes' request to have their claim referred to the courts. So, this sort of effort had to go underground, and the world largely forgot.

However, when the ban on fundraising and other restrictions were lifted in 1951, the campaign for rights was revived. *Against the Odds* is the story of a hugely important part of that revival. It is the story of so many remarkable Indigenous people: the hunters in the White and Bob case, the Nisga'a tribal leaders in the Calder case, the Dene, Métis, and Inuvialuit of the Mackenzie Valley Pipeline Inquiry, the Alaskans in *Village Journey* (the report of the Alaska Native Review Commission), the people at the heart of the Supreme Court of Canada's decisions in the *Manitoba Métis Federation v. Canada* and *Nacho Nyäk Dun et al v. Yukon,* among others.

It is also the story of a remarkable non-Indigenous man, Tom Berger.

I wonder whether young people today understand how novel it was in 1964 for a lawyer to seek to overturn the convictions of two Indigenous men for illegal hunting, citing a treaty that, until then, almost no one had heard of.

At the time of the White and Bob case, aboriginal rights or title were not being taught in law schools. Certainly Tom had never heard them mentioned in his law student days.

It was also unusual to hold the sort of inquiry that Tom presided over in the Northwest Territories in the 1970s, and to conduct it the way he did. Not content to stay in the south, requiring people to come to him, he travelled throughout the North, visiting every community, bringing the inquiry to them. As Berger told a documentary maker:

What the people of the North are forcing us to do is re-examine the economic religion of our time, that there should be an ever-expanding cycle of growth and consumption, that material well-being is the most important thing in life. They don't share those goals with us. They've made that clear to me. And that makes us uneasy.

Uneasy or not, he listened, he heard what was being said, and he recommended that no pipeline be built until land claims were settled.

George Manuel, a founder of the World Council of Indigenous Peoples and a giant in his own right, said that Tom's Mackenzie Valley Pipeline Report was "the best statement on Indian rights to come from any government since the Europeans first came to Canada."

In December of 2020, Tom Berger argued his last case, representing the Peter Ballantyne Cree Nation in the Saskatchewan Court of Appeal—by video link. Tom died four months later, on April 28th, a month after celebrating his 88th birthday. But he, and those he listened to and worked with, live on in this book.

—*Hamar Foster KC,*
Victoria BC, 2024

OPPORTUNITY OF A LIFETIME

Drew Ann Wake

~⌒

O N THE AFTERNOON of May 7, 1976, I walked into the Vancouver office of Justice Thomas Berger. It was just days before the first southern hearing of the Mackenzie Valley Pipeline Inquiry and the office was alive with speculation. Was the issue of a pipeline corridor along the distant Mackenzie Valley of interest to urban dwellers? Or would the hearing room sit empty?

Although I was a novice reporter, the judge was not a stranger to me. I had spent the previous six months covering the Inquiry hearings in Dene and Inuvialuit communities in the Northwest Territories. I had filed reports to "Our Native Land", a weekly radio program from the CBC, designed to communicate news of interest to First Nations across Canada. I was a junior member of the news corps that covered the Inquiry, but I was happy—deliriously happy—that I had been given the opportunity to cover an important and divisive national debate.

In general, the Inquiry did not encourage members of the media to interview Judge Berger. With a few key exceptions, reporters were asked to cover the testimony given at the hearings. The Judge's views, we were often reminded, would be made public when he issued his final report.

But when I visited the Judge's office in June of 1976, he startled me by asking whether I would be interested in interviewing him. I said "No, thank you." I thought the real issues at the inquiry were being raised by the Dene and Inuvialuit who spoke at the community hearings in the North. They described with great insight how the construction of the pipeline would damage their land, the wildlife on which they depended, and their hopes for a just land claim settlement. As I spoke I became increasingly enthusiastic: I wanted my radio reports to show how Indigenous and environmental organizations were making their voices heard through the inquiry.

Suddenly I realized that I was turning down an invitation that any reporter in the country would be delighted to accept. I fell silent. Tom, gracious as always, said I should continue my work from my preferred perspective.

Thus we began a forty-five-year conversation about balancing the impact of lawyers and political activists on Indigenous rights in Canada. How did those two approaches intertwine? How did they differ?

In the last months of Tom's life, I was reminded of that early conversation as we sat and combed through his boxes of correspondence and speeches. Once again Tom surprised me. He handed me the chapters of an unfinished book with a note: "Do with these what you will."

Issues of Justice

I decided to revisit the conversation we had explored that day forty-five years before, when I visited him in his office. In this book, *Against the Odds* I have attempted to weave together Tom's passion for the role the legal system can play in gaining justice for First Nations with my own conviction that the courage and determination of Indigenous families, leaders and communities have forced Canadians to address these issues. Over the last half century, First Nations leaders and their legal advocates have collaborated on strategies to transform the way Canadians understand issues of justice toward First Nations. I hope this book captures some of the remarkable moments in that transformation.

Acknowledgements
I am deeply grateful to many colleagues and friends who have assisted with this volume. The Berger family has provided crates of speeches, newspaper clippings and correspondence so that I could follow the twists and turns in Tom Berger's legal career.

I also wish to thank more than a hundred First Nations families who have shared their memories. In British Columbia I am thankful for the time that the White family of the Snuneymuxw First Nation and the Nyce family of the Nisga'a First Nation have spent describing the challenges of those two landmark legal cases.

In the Northwest Territories, I am grateful to Martina Norwegian and Terry and Brian Jaffray for their invitation to share my audio recordings from the Berger Inquiry with students in schools in the Dehcho region. Our tour of the communities illustrated the passion that northerners have for their languages and history, passions that continue to the present generation. I have enjoyed a decade-long collaboration with Sharon Snowshoe and Arlyn Charlie at the Gwich'in Tribal Council Department of Culture and Heritage who continue to inspire fresh ways of encouraging young people to incorporate past and present.

I must also thank my colleagues in the south. Professor Michael Jackson KC, Special Counsel for the Berger Inquiry, has shared his photographs from the Mackenzie Valley Pipeline Inquiry. Linda MacCannell, photographer and friend, travelled the length of the Mackenzie River with me, capturing images of the once-youthful activists who have become distinguished Elders and leaders.

In Vancouver, my friends at Theatre of Fire have pushed for creative ways to tell these stories. In 2008, Daniel Séguin initially volunteered to digitize dozens of historic audio interviews, photographs and music. That turned into a sixteen-year task that has enabled us to recapture hundreds of interviews recorded over the last fifty years. Daniel and Markus Radtke have transformed audio and images into short videos that allow us to re-experience the speeches that captured key moments in the Aboriginal rights debate.

It has been a great pleasure to work with Dr. Lorene Shyba at Durvile & UpRoute. Her guiding hand, and her commitment to Indigenous rights issues, are remarkable. Thank you to the author of the foreword, Hamar Foster KC who was the first person to ask me, when we were teenagers: "Would you like to be a journalist?" I guess the answer is: "Yes."

A heartfelt thank you to young Dene scholar Shaznay Waugh for the thoughtful afterword to this book. I hope that, like Shaznay, other young people—future community organizers, future lawyers—will be inspired by the commitment and determination of their predecessors who overcame great challenges to achieve the advances detailed in these pages

—*Drew Ann Wake*
Vancouver, British Columbia, 2024

PART I

THE EARLY YEARS

"It was the first shot fired by the Aboriginal people of Canada
in their campaign to reclaim Aboriginal and treaty rights."

CHAPTER ONE

THE WHITE AND BOB CASE

Drew Ann Wake

~

WHEN 15-YEAR-OLD LEONARD WHITE rolled out of bed before dawn on the morning of July 6, 1963, he was thinking only of the hunting trip that lay ahead. He had no idea that the events of the day would plunge his family into a landmark legal case that would alter the rights of Indigenous Peoples in Canada.

The White family's farm nestled in the forest on traditional Snuneymuxw land south of Nanaimo, British Columbia. There, Leonard's parents, Clifford and Audrey White, raised their nine children on food from the farm and the forest. It wasn't an easy life. When the children were young, Audrey would bundle them up, take them to the barn and lay them on the hay with their bottles. Then, she would milk the cows and clean the stalls while keeping an eye on the sheep. She joked that her children grew up in the hay stalls.

As the children grew older, they took on some of the farm labour. They helped milk the cows and feed the chickens. They took milk cans down to the river and hauled them back up the hill filled with drinking water. In the summer, they tended a large garden and helped their mother can enough fruit and vegetables to last through the winter.

The White family set nets across the Nanaimo River just below the house, fishing for salmon. Leonard's sister, Jackie, remembers that her father would ask the children to carry the salmon up to the house. "In those days I wasn't very tall, so I'd drag the salmon up the hill for our dinner."

Clifford White, like most men in the Snuneymuxw community, worked as a logger and a fisherman. He would be away for days at a time. When he returned, he would hunt for deer to sustain the family. His wife made pots of venison stew and ladled it into jars for the coming weeks. "We hunted deer because we needed to," says Leonard. "One deer would last us a week. The jobs weren't great so if it wasn't for the deer and salmon, where would we be?"

But Clifford didn't just hunt for his own family. Leonard recalls: "We had friends across the river and old people down the hill who couldn't get out anymore. We'd give them deer and they loved us for that." Leonard had learned to shoot when he was six, so by the age of fifteen he was making a contribution to iceboxes across the community.

On July 6, 1963, when his father and David Bob decided to go hunting, Leonard and a friend, Gerry Thomas, jumped in the back of the car. Together, they headed up a back road behind Mount Benson, which crossed traditional Snuneymuxw land. Over the next few hours, the hunters shot six deer. They cleaned the carcasses and packed the meat into the car. Then they headed home. But as they approached the farm, the local conservation officer, Franklin Greenfield, was waiting for them. Leonard's sister, Jackie, remembers: "The conservation officer went up to my dad's vehicle and said: 'Cliffy, Cliffy, Cliffy.'"

Dad said: "What?" The officer said: "I see you're at it again." My Dad said: "I hunt for my family. I have to feed nine kids." But his argument fell on deaf ears. Clifford White and David Bob were ordered to appear in court the next day.

All evening, Clifford and Audrey White discussed what to do. One option was that Clifford could base his defence on an oral history that had been passed down through generations of Elders for more than a century. This history held that in 1854, James Douglas, the Factor of the Hudson's Bay Company and the Governor of Vancouver Island, had negotiated a treaty with the Snuneymuxw people, ensuring their right to hunt and fish on unoccupied lands. The other option was that Clifford could plead guilty and face a fine that the family could not possibly pay. He would be sent to prison. Audrey would be left to find food for herself and nine children.

The younger children huddled around their parents as they debated. Heather White remembers: "We clung onto my mother. She was a tiny spitfire. She was shaking her finger, saying: 'You can't let them put you in jail. You go and fight, Clifford.' You knew there was trouble if she called him Clifford instead of Cliff."

By the time morning came, they had settled on a plan: the hunters would ask their lawyers to defend them in Magistrate's Court based on what was sure to be regarded as a fragile legal argument: an agreement made more than a hundred years before.

Court Case in Nanaimo

When White and Bob met their lawyers to plan their strategy, they encountered a serious setback. The lawyers had never heard of the Treaty document that Clifford White and David Bob wanted to use as the foundation of their defence. When the case opened in court, their lawyer Mr. J. Wilson, asked Judge Lionel Beevor-Potts for an adjournment. He explained that the defendants had "a special interest" and the lawyers were having trouble obtaining instructions from their clients.

Judge Beevor-Potts noted that it had been more than two months since the two men had been caught with the deer, enough time to have assembled their case. Wilson countered that Snuneymuxw families had been away from their homes during the summer months, gathering food for the winter. But the prosecutor, Don Cunliffe, was emphatic: "I do not think that the Indian Race are entitled to special privileges in our Law Courts."

When Judge Beevor-Potts ruled against an adjournment, Wilson asked to withdraw from the case. Clifford White and David Bob were left to defend themselves. Judge Beevor-Potts gave the men a three-sentence description of the legal process, and the hearing began.

The first witness was the conservation officer, Franklin Greenfield, who described encountering David Bob and Clifford White on the road a few miles outside Nanaimo. Two teenagers, Leonard White and Gerry Thomas, were in the back seat of the car. At their feet were three rifles, covered by an old blanket. When Greenfield opened the trunk, he found six black-tailed deer, still warm to the touch.

In response to a question from Cunliffe, Greenfield said that Clifford White's permit had expired in March. But Clifford White interrupted, saying that his last permit had been issued a year before, in 1962. He said it was very rare for Greenfield to issue a permit to a member of the Snuneymuxw community. Usually, when they went in to ask for a permit, Greenfield refused. "He said no, it is just for needy Indians. Who is Mr. Greenfield to decide who is a needy Indian and who is not?"

Clifford White told the court that he had visited Greenfield's office in 1963, trying to get a permit. Greenfield countered that he had sent a permit by mail: perhaps someone else had picked it up? The exchange ended in an impasse.

The second witness was James Dewar, a conservation officer who had stored the six deer in a freezer. He had brought the deer to Nanaimo for the hearing. Judge Beevor-Potts decided that the six cardboard boxes of deer meat should be brought into the courtroom and entered as exhibits.

Leonard White and his friend, Gerry Thomas, were sitting in the balcony. The teenagers had never been in a courtroom before and they found the arcane dress and language of the lawyers entertaining. But their amusement turned to shock when the conservation officer carried in six boxes of deer meat. "I was upset to see those deer carcasses lying there, rotting away," Leonard recalls. "They could have been on somebody's table."

Both Clifford White and David Bob declined to testify. The Indian agent for the Nanaimo band, Mr. Samson, had been expected to appear at the hearing, but he sent word that he had to travel to Victoria. Judge Beevor-Potts agreed that the hearing would be adjourned for a few days until he could appear. This gave Clifford White and David Bob valuable time to prepare a case based on the Treaty documents signed more than a century before. They contacted Joseph Elliott, who had collected and reviewed historical documents for the neighbouring Cowichan Union band. He agreed to testify.

When the hearing resumed, the Indian agent once again failed to appear. He sent a message that he was "disinterested in the case". Clifford White took the opportunity to ask the court to hear from their witness. Historian Joseph Elliott from Cowichan had brought a photostatic copy of *Papers Connected with The Indian Land Question 1850-1875*. He read aloud a clause stating that traditional lands were to be kept for the use of the Indigenous people, not only for the current generation but for the generations to come. Moreover, the Treaty contained a sentence that was directly applicable to the White and Bob case. "We are at liberty to hunt on unoccupied land for game and fish and carry on as formerly." On that note, the hearing came to a close.

Within minutes, Judge Beevor-Potts announced his decision. "I hold that the alleged Treaty as read by Mr. Elliott does not apply to this case. You are both found guilty as charged." Then he added insult to injury, with a direct rebuke to the defendants: "It is on the face pure piggishness. You could have had permits for a reasonable amount."

The rejection of the Treaty incensed Clifford White and he rose to defend the document. "Would that pact be called a liar?" But the judge was unmoved, ordering each of the men to pay a $100 fine or spend forty days in jail. David Bob found the money to pay the fine. Clifford White asked for a month to raise the money but the judge gave him two weeks. Unable to meet the terms, he was incarcerated in Oakalla, a prison on the mainland with a grim reputation.

In their coverage of the case, the Nanaimo newspapers used language borrowed from the cowboy movies that were popular at the time. An early article blazed with a headline: "Two Indians Challenge Powers of White Man". By the end of the trial, the headlines had not gained much subtlety: "Pair Learn in Court: Old Treaty Worthless to Indians".

The conviction left the White family in dire straits. Audrey White was left with no income and nine children to feed. The family was shaken by the loss of Clifford, the breadwinner. Heather remembers that her mother often felt so alone that she would scrub the floors, just to take her mind off her worries. She also recalls that the conservation officers would sit farther up the road with binoculars, watching. "If they spotted someone hunting or fishing, they would swoop onto our homeland."

While his father was away, fifteen-year-old Leonard assumed some of the responsibility for putting food on the table. One morning before school started, he jumped into his father's boat and headed out to check his nets. But the conservation officers were on watch. Leonard was picked up and the boat and nets were seized.

In a letter, his mother, Audrey, described what happened.

It was a Mr. Arnold Epps from Ladysmith (Fish Warden) that took the net and boat off of Leonard. Our son, Richard, saw him when he was taking the nets off of Lenny. So I went down and got after him. I told him he had no right doing that. I told Lenny to come back across to our side of the river on the boat. And Mr. Epps said that he couldn't touch it. That he was taking it. So I told him that he had better bring him home. Which he did. I then asked him what he was going to do with the net and boat. He said they usually get rid of them. He took it to Ladysmith.

A week later Clifford White passed on news from Nanaimo: conservation officers had caught a group of non-Indigenous hunters with an elk shot out of season. They were let off with a reprimand.

The Nanaimo Appeal

The case had sparked the interest of First Nations across British Columbia. Guy Williams, the leader of the Native Brotherhood of BC, recognized that the White and Bob case represented a serious challenge. Clearly, a case in the legal sphere was moving into the realm of the political.

Guy Williams was determined that the White and Bob case should be appealed. So he asked Maisie Hurley, the editor of the Brotherhood's newspaper, *The Native Voice*, to search for a lawyer who could mount an effective appeal of the White and Bob case. Maisie said she knew just the man.

The man Maisie Hurley had in mind was Thomas Berger, who had opened a one-man law practice in Vancouver a short time before. He often sought the advice of Maisie's husband, Tom Hurley, who was widely admired as a defence lawyer. "[Tom Hurley] was very generous with his time," Tom Berger recalled. "He would sit down with me and we'd go over my cases. I learned a lot, just soaking up his knowledge."

Many of Tom Hurley's cases involved Indigenous defendants, making him one of the few British Columbia lawyers with experience in the knotty dilemmas emerging at the time. Maisie Hurley had built her own remarkable career as the editor of *The Native Voice* by championing the First Nations of British Columbia. She made sure that the White and Bob case received extensive coverage.

The stories measured the impact that the case would have, not only on the defendants but on First Nations across British

Columbia. By the time the White and Bob case concluded in Nanaimo, Tom Hurley had passed away so Maisie Hurley sailed into Tom Berger's office, determined to recruit him for the appeal.

"[Maisie Hurley] was a formidable woman," Tom recalled. "She was dressed all in black, with horn-rimmed glasses, and she had a cane. She said, without any preamble: 'Now Tommy, you must defend the Indians.' And I had no choice in the matter."

When Maisie Hurley brought the White and Bob case to his attention, Tom Berger headed over to Nanaimo to meet his clients. The Snuneymuxw First Nation held a meeting so that Berger could gather a range of information about the history of the community.

"I talked to some of the Elders and they said: 'We have a treaty that allows us to hunt at any time of the year.' I'd never heard of the Treaty. I'd been to law school, and nobody there ever discussed any treaties on Vancouver Island. In fact, we never discussed the rights of Indigenous people at all."

Across British Columbia, First Nations began to organize in support of Clifford White and David Bob. In October 1963, leaders from the South Vancouver Island Allied Tribes set up a fund to meet the legal expenses of an appeal. The money was raised through donations, many from individuals who committed a few dollars. It was a fragile financial base to contest a landmark legal case.

In the two months that followed, Tom Berger worked feverishly to organize the argument that he would put before the appeal judge in December. First, he wrote the provincial archivist, Willard Ireland, to ask if the archives held any historical materials related to the treaty that Joseph Elliott had read aloud during the September hearing. Ireland wrote back to say the Provincial Archives had a Register with the Treaty materials published in 1875 under the title *Papers relating to the Indian Land Question*. He noted that in most of these documents, the terms of the treaties were fully described, followed by the signatures of members of the band in the form of a long row of X marks.

But Ireland had found a problem. In the case of the Saalequun purchase, the inscribed wording outlining the terms of the Treaty was missing. This blank space was followed by a line of x marks representing the signatures of 159 members of the band. But there was hope. A note, written in pencil, was pinned to the page. The note read: 'A similar conveyance of country extending from Commercial Inlet, 12 miles up the Nanaimo River.' This geographic designation matched the traditional lands of the Snuneymuxw people. Was it wise to submit this document, with its empty space, as evidence? Tom Berger felt that it could be submitted if the Provincial archivist was willing to appear as a witness and to bring the *Register of Land Purchases* with him. He added that the archivist might prefer to be summoned by subpoena, so he wouldn't appear to be partial. Willard Ireland agreed.

Berger also elicited the assistance of an anthropologist from the provincial museum, Wilson Duff. In a letter, Duff pointed to a way that the case might be strengthened. "My impression is that your present conception of native title is based on usufruct, the right to use the products of the land. My conception is that native title is based on clear-cut Indian concepts of ownership of the land." He pointed out that the case had been made in that way before the US Court of Claims. He suggested the framework could apply equally to the northern coast of British Columbia. At Berger's request, Duff also agreed to testify.

Early in November, Tom Berger wrote to Clifford White and David Bob, asking them to travel to Vancouver on November 23, to discuss the case. Neither man appeared. Days later, letters arrived from each of the men, apologizing that they had not had the ferry fare. "I was not able to get a hold of any money," wrote Clifford White. "I have been out of work for a while now." In light of the straitened finances of the appeal, Tom Berger arranged to meet with White and Bob, and two representatives of the Southern Vancouver Island Allied Tribes, in Nanaimo on the evening before the trial was to begin. This gave them only a few hours to meet face-to-face before the hearing began.

The appeal captured the attention of reporters, who continued to treat the case as a media spectacle. On opening day, the *Nanaimo Daily Press* reported that "Indians formed the majority of the spectators in the courtroom today where the hatchet buried nearly 112 years ago was not only dug up but was sharpened, ready for battle."

Crown prosecutor Don Cunliffe took the position that James Douglas had been acting in his role as Chief Factor of the Hudson's Bay Company when he signed the agreements. "I do not think that Mr. Douglas was empowered to enter into any treaties with the Indians," he said. "The land sale conveyances were a furtherance of company policy which he carried out in the capacity of Chief Factor, not as Governor. I think the defendants are after the best of both worlds."

In his final argument, which lasted·three hours, Berger took a position that came from his initial conversations with Elders of the Snuneymuxw First Nation. The Elders had told him that they had Aboriginal title. That enabled Berger to make a double-barrelled argument. "When we appealed I said: We've got this treaty. But if you say we don't have a treaty then we have Aboriginal title. Which is it going to be?"

In March of 1964, Judge A.H.J. Swencisky's concluded:

> ...the vested rights of the Indians have never been taken away. I hold that the agreement between Vancouver Island Indians and the Crown was a solemn document with all the status of a settlement or contract.

The White family celebrated by going out hunting. The men shot an elk which provided enough meat for the many relatives and friends who stopped by with congratulations.

The Provincial Appeal

Shortly thereafter, the Crown announced an appeal to the British Columbia Court of Appeal. Five judges reviewed the arguments and as 1964 drew to a close, their ruling was made public.

Judge Shepphard wrote for the two judges who dissented. He stated that the Royal Proclamation of 1763 did not apply to Vancouver Island because the Island and its Indigenous population were unknown to the Crown until Captain Cook arrived in Nootka Sound fifteen years later. He also noted that the terms of the agreement with the Indigenous people in the Nanaimo area had not been written into the document. He concluded that the document submitted as Exhibit 8 "is neither in form nor in substance a treaty."

Judge Davey wrote for the majority:

> Considering the relationship between the Crown and the Hudson's Bay Company in the colonization of this country... I cannot regard Exhibit 8 (the Treaty) as the mere agreement for the sale of land made between a private vendor and a private purchaser. The right of the two Indians to hunt the lands in question are preserved by *The Indian Act* and remain unimpaired by *The Game Act*.

He concluded that White and Bob were rightfully in possession of the deer carcasses.

Justice Thomas Norris was the third judge to weigh in. He submitted a carefully researched, 52-page judgment, calling on Indigenous rights documents going back as far as the British explorers Drake and Cook. As well, he cited legal cases from the United States, Nigeria, and India. He pointed out that the Douglas agreements were necessary to ensure that settlement took place peacefully. In the 1850s there were about a thousand settlers on Vancouver Island, moving onto lands that had supported some 30,000 Indigenous people for centuries. "The treaties were no mere scraps of paper," he argued. They provided the newcomers with the assurance of an orderly and peaceful settlement.

Judge Norris did not dismiss the document that James Douglas had given to the Snuneymuxw people to sign, despite the fact that the terms of the agreement were missing. "The unusual (by the standards of legal draftsmen) nature and form of the document, considered in the light of circumstances on Vancouver Island in 1854, does not detract from it being a treaty."

But he went further, stating a strong opinion in support of the Indigenous right to gain food from the land.

> This is not a case merely of making the law applicable to native Indians as to white persons so that there may be equality of treatment under the law, but of depriving Indians of rights vested in them from time immemorial, which white persons have not had, *viz.,* the right to hunt out of season on unoccupied land for food for themselves and their families.

Thus, in the 52 pages of his Reasons for Judgment, Justice Norris framed in legal terms the argument that Clifford White and David Bob had brought before Judge Beevor-Potts almost eighteen months before. The Sununeumuxw history, which had been passed orally through three generations, was vindicated.

Following the judgment, Tom Berger wrote a hopeful letter to Guy Williams of the Native Brotherhood of BC. "I think that Mr. Justice Norris' judgment is the most important judicial announcement we have ever had in this province relating to the Aboriginal rights of native Indian people," he wrote. If upheld in the Supreme Court of Canada, "it will mean that Indians in all parts of BC (except on Treaty 8 lands) will be able to assert their Aboriginal right to hunt and fish. If the federal and provincial governments want to extinguish these rights, they will have to make treaties, with compensation."

The ruling did not ease the immediate concerns of the Snuneymuxw people. In the spring of 1965, an article appeared in the Nanaimo newspaper, announcing that the Fisheries Department had closed all fishing until September to protect the declining fish stocks. Tom Berger wrote a letter to the Indigenous leaders in Nanaimo, outlining the favourable rulings they had won in court. He suggested that fishermen carry a copy of the letter with them as they headed off in their boats.

The Supreme Court of Canada

The decision was greeted with elation among British Columbia First Nations. But the leadership recognized that the case would almost inevitably be appealed to the Supreme Court. Mounting a strong case in Ottawa would be a formidable challenge.

Guy Williams of the Native Brotherhood of BC organized a meeting of chiefs from across the province, to raise money for the appeal. At the meeting, chiefs and councillors stood up, one by one, to make contributions on behalf of their people. Sechelt band councillor Clarence Joe framed their position succinctly: "This case does not only concern two members of a village, but all the Indians of Canada. If Vancouver Island loses this case, we will all lose our rights."

Seven judges heard the case in the Supreme Court. T.G. Bowen-Colhurst argued the case for the Crown. The judges had reviewed the arguments beforehand and, after Bowen-Colhurst completed his statement, they informed Tom Berger that he did not have to reiterate his case. Without leaving the bench, the judges dismissed the appeal. The following day, newspaper headlines registered the surprise felt by many Canadians. An editorial in one Vancouver newspaper had the headline: "Indian Rights Restored... Forcing Whites to Bargain... From Weak Position."

The writer of the editorial had interviewed fish and wildlife officers to gather their opinions.

Provincial conservation officers are frightened. They foresee chaos in game and fish management ... if the Indian privilege is abused. They are appalled to see one ethnic group, as they put it, to be permitted to harvest indiscriminately two resources of such consequence to the province as a whole....

If anything is certain, as a consequence of the Supreme Court decision, it is that we are in for a lively season of wheeling-dealing between Indian and government with, for the first time, the Indians holding the whip hand."

The news travelled across the First Nations of British Columbia at lightning speed. Against the odds, the case that Clifford White and David Bob had defended alone in a magistrate's court in Nanaimo had found success in the highest court in the land. In Nanaimo, Snuneymuxw Chief Douglas White immediately began planning a potlatch to celebrate. He invited representatives of the British Columbia First Nations who had backed the appeal to the Supreme Court, recognizing that this was victory and would have ramifications for Indigenous hunters and fishers across the province.

⌒𝓸

A CONVERSATION WITH DOUGLAS WHITE III, LAWYER

While growing up, Douglas White III often heard about his family's involvement in the White and Bob legal case. Over time, he became a lawyer, a leader of the Snuneymuxw First Nation and the chair of the First Nations Justice Council. In 2023, British Columbia Premier David Eby appointed Douglas White III to be Special Counsel on Indigenous Reconciliation.

"Clifford White was my grandfather's first cousin. I've talked with him about the history of the White and Bob case over the years. He shared with me that there was a cat-and-mouse game with the conservation officer, who had a reputation for chasing down the Aboriginal guys hunting out of season.

So July 7, 1963 was a day that had been many months in the works, Clifford White and David Bob knew they were being chased by the conservation officer and it happened to be that day when he caught them. They were charged with hunting out of season and the next day they had to answer the charge in court in front of Magistrate Beevor-Potts.

Clifford White had to advocate for himself because the lawyers for the Canadian legal system abandoned him and David Bob in the trial. The lawyers asked for permission to step back from representation because they didn't want to have to talk about treaty rights when they didn't know what this crazy Indian was talking about.

This was the end of a long struggle for Indigenous rights—by the Allied Indian Tribes of BC, the great Squamish leader, Andy Paull, the great Haida leader, Peter Kelly—they were the great advocates in the early years of the twentieth century. That culminated, unfortunately, in the effective criminalization of advocacy. *The Indian Act* was amended and modified to prohibit anyone from seeking to raise money to hire a lawyer to advance a land claims issue. So all of that legal knowledge was suppressed. It was only maintained through the Native Brotherhood of BC and Maisie Hurley's newspaper, *The Native Voice*.

What gave Clifford White the courage and the strength to stand up in the courtroom and talk about a treaty history that at that point had been denied for 110 years? When representing himself, Clifford White put forward his own oral history about the Treaty relationship. He also asked an Indigenous historian, Joe Elliott, to come forward to share the Treaty history as well. So in a remarkable way, that oral history of the Elders was there at the very outset. Unfortunately, that trial ended in a conviction.

Tom Berger called this the first shot fired by the Aboriginal peoples of Canada in their quest to re-establish recognition and respect for their Aboriginal and treaty rights. This was an important moment at the outset of fifty hard years of fighting in the courts to give shape to basic issues: what an Aboriginal right is, what Aboriginal title is, what treaty rights are.

I asked Tom: Where did that come from? Because in the fall of 1963, he had no precedents to follow. He said: "I was asked to sit down with the Elders and I heard what they had to say about the Treaty and the relationship to their territory. That became the foundation for his arguments in White and Bob.

When we finally won, it was a remarkable thing to look at the newspapers. At the outset, they said things like 'Indian versus White Man in Court'. It was novel. Everyone was amazed that this fight was emerging in a Canadian courtroom. When the Snuneymuxw were ultimately victorious, there was a lot of celebration. This was a vindication of a very long process of advocacy. ""

CHAPTER TWO

A MEETING AT PORT EDWARD

Thomas R. Berger

~

In 1966, a provincial election was held in British Columbia. Tom Berger ran for the New Democratic Party and won. In the legislature, he came to know the Nisga'a leader, Frank Calder, who had represented the Atlin riding in northern British Columbia since 1949. Frank used to visit the Berger home from time to time. The two men would sit in Tom's home office to talk about Frank's dream of securing Nisga'a rights in law.

In October of that year, the Nisga'a Tribal Council held its annual conference at Port Edward, a village on the northern coast of British Columbia. Frank Calder invited Tom Berger to address the gathered Nisga'a leaders. But the Nisga'a Tribal Council also invited two men who would have considerable sway over the way their claim would be handled by the federal government. One was the Minister of Indian and Northern Affairs, Arthur Laing. The other was W. R. Hourston, Director of Fisheries for the Pacific region. As Tom Berger rose to speak, he was throwing down the gauntlet.

THE TAKING of First Nations lands was the first and greatest of the many injustices to which the Indigenous people of this province have been subjected. In the years before the white people began to colonize British Columbia, when the main interest that the white people had on the North Pacific coast of

North America was the fur trade, the rights of the Indigenous people were recognized and respected. But when the colonization of Vancouver Island and the mainland got under way a century ago, the settlers, aided and abetted by the government of the colony, appropriated the lands that had been occupied for centuries by the First Nations people.

There is one honourable exception: James Douglas, who governed Vancouver Island and the mainland between 1851 and 1864, made every effort to see that treaties were made with the First Nations, that they were compensated for their tribal territory, and that their hunting and fishing rights, essential to their way of life, were guaranteed.

Governor Douglas had spent all of his adult life with the Indigenous people and had married a woman of Cree heritage. He understood the people and their culture and treated them fairly. The same could not be said of those who governed British Columbia after Douglas' retirement. It should not be forgotten that the First Nations of the North Pacific coast had developed a century ago a culture that surpassed any other Indigenous culture in North America. They had no written language, but each tribe recognized the rights of all of the other tribes to their tribal territories.

The Indigenous people were hunters and fishermen, but the use they made of the resources of the lands they occupied went farther than that: they used the trees for houses and canoes. They used surface deposits of iron and copper to manufacture implements. They hunted throughout their territories and fished in the lakes and rivers and on the coast.

As settlement proceeded westward across North America in the 18th and 19th centuries, treaties were made with the Indigenous people. They surrendered their land, peacefully by and large in Canada, only after prolonged warfare in the United States. But it was acknowledged that the land was theirs, and treaties were made which guaranteed their rights against further incursions by white settlers.

In fact, throughout the English-speaking world, the Aboriginal title of Indigenous people was acknowledged; everywhere, that is, except in British Columbia. The North Pacific coast was in fact the last part of the world to which the white people came. If you look at the old maps, you will see that the world's only uncharted coast, as late as the 17th century, was the North Pacific coast.

When at last the white people came, they were not prepared to acknowledge that the Indigenous people of the North Pacific coast had any rights at all—they believed that the white European civilization they represented had no obligation to acknowledge the culture of the Indigenous peoples.

The history of the Indigenous people for the last century has been the history of the impingement of white civilization upon the First Nations. The Indigenous people were virtually powerless to resist the white civilization: the white community of British Columbia adopted a policy of apartheid. This, of course, had already been done in Eastern Canada and on the Prairies, but the apartheid policy adopted in British Columbia was of a peculiarly cruel and degrading kind. They began by taking Indigenous land without any surrender and without their consent. Then they herded the Indigenous people onto reserves. This was nothing more nor less than apartheid, and that is what it still is today.

British Columbia's reserves were established in the 1860s. They were smaller in size than the reserves on the Prairies. When the reserves were established on the Prairies, 120 acres were allotted for each Indigenous family. In British Columbia the government of the province, once British Columbia had entered Confederation, was prepared to allow only ten acres for each family.

But after the federal government, on one of the infrequent occasions when it roused itself and came to the defence of the Indigenous people, had remonstrated, this was eventually fixed at 20 acres for each family—one-sixth of the allotment on the Prairies.

But even then, the requirements of white settlement were not satisfied. By the turn of the century, the government of British Columbia was insisting that the First Nations did not require all of the land on the reserves. As a result, the McKenna-McBride Commission was established to redistribute the reserves. The Commission decided to 'cut off' much of the valuable lands held by the Indigenous people, and substituted for the 'cut-off' land that was in many cases virtually worthless. This process was completed by 1923. We proved in British Columbia that apartheid is not only immoral and wrongheaded; we also proved that it does not work.

In British Columbia, apartheid had resulted in a century of degradation and neglect. When the white man came to British Columbia there were 80,000 Indigenous people living here, a proud race leading a communal way of life; they believed each man was his brother's keeper. They were a society of hunters and fishermen it is true, but their society was sophisticated in the complexity of its social and ceremonial ritual and it was adorned by works of art that have endured for a century.

The white man's diseases and the white man's refusal to provide Indigenous people with the opportunity to pursue their ancient way of life, and the white man's failure to provide medical care, decimated the Indigenous people, and by the turn of the century there were only 15,000 Indigenous people in British Columbia. Apartheid could have led to the destruction of the race had it not been for the capacity of the Indigenous people to endure and to survive. Even today the Indigenous population of British Columbia is only 43,000, little more than half what it was a hundred years ago.

Apartheid is still with us today, and the plight of the Indigenous people is as wretched as it ever was. The Indian Affairs Branch reported to the Conference on Poverty held last December in Ottawa that the life span of the Indigenous people in Canada is 30 years, while that of the white man is 60 years. Indigenous people die of colds and pneumonia, owing to the wretched housing on our reserves, while the white man dies of heart disease.

There are virtually no Indigenous people in law or medicine. They have been excluded from white-collar occupations. In fact, until recent years only a few of them were employed in the Indian Affairs Branch itself. It is my view that the disregard of the Indigenous people's right to their land led directly to the disregard of their culture and their right to an equal place in the community. Once their right to their land had been denied, it followed that their right to hunt and to fish were denied. Having thus destroyed the Indigenous people's way of making a living, it by no means followed that they should be given a place in the white community. How could they? They had been banished to the reserve. While their own culture was slowly eroded, they were overwhelmed by the acquisitive society of the white man.

Today we must make a start to redress the wrongs done to the Indigenous people. Where to begin? I suggest that we should begin with the British Columbia land question. The Government of Canada and the Government of British Columbia ought to acknowledge Aboriginal title and negotiate a settlement with the Indigenous peoples. After all, just a year ago, in the White and Bob case Mr. Justice Norris of the British Columbia Court of Appeal ruled that Aboriginal title in British Columbia remained unextinguished today. But any settlement of the Indigenous land question would have to be a twentieth century settlement. To begin with, generous compensation would have to be paid for the surrender of the Aboriginal title. If this were done the funds that were made available could be used to build new homes.

Recently the Cowichans asked that nineteen new homes be built on their reserve, but the Indian Affairs Branch said it had only budgeted for two on the Cowichan Reserve. It is not a question of squandering public money. It is a question of paying to the Indigenous people the money that is coming to them, to enable them to bring their families up in decent homes. It is more than that, it is a question of life or death: Are Indigenous people going to live as long as the rest of us, or must they die thirty years before any of us do?

There must be ironclad guarantees to protect the hunting and fishing rights of the Indigenous people. In some parts of British Columbia, it is still necessary for Indigenous people to hunt and fish during the closed season in order to survive. Their right to hunt and to fish cannot be taken for granted. The recent judgments of the Supreme Court of Canada in the Sikyea case and the George case show how federal statutes can take away long-established rights. There is no reason why Indigenous people should not be given the right to hunt and fish for food at all times of the year. Conservation would not be endangered. First Nations practiced conservation long before the white man ever heard about it.

I believe that Indigenous people should no longer be second-class citizens in British Columbia. They were given the right to vote in provincial elections in 1949. But political enfranchisement has not been followed by social and economic enfranchisement. The full benefit of provincial social welfare and health services should be extended to Indigenous people in British Columbia.

Some people say it is a matter of transferring Indigenous people from federal to provincial jurisdiction under the *British North America Act*. Indigenous people are not cattle or a commodity to be shifted about from one governmental authority to another, they are citizens entitled to the same right to enjoy the benefits that are provided by governmental action, whether it be on the federal or the provincial level.

Steps have already been taken to integrate Indigenous children into our public school system. But the alarming failure rate of children in Grade 1 reveals how inadequately we have comprehended the difficulties that a child from a reserve faces when he enters the public school system. As the failure that the children experience in their early years at school makes itself felt, the result is that many of them, a far greater proportion than exists among white children, drop out. It is too much to expect a six-year-old to be able to bridge the gap from one culture to another. We should be providing nursery schools and kindergartens for Indigenous children—an Operation Headstart for these children—to enable them to adjust to the disciplinary requirements of the school system and to acquire the verbal skills that are taken for granted in Grade 1.

We are going to have to retain the reserves. Many know no other way of life, they have no other home except the reserve. But surely we ought to help them to become thriving communities. The reserves ought to be eligible for grants in aid from the provincial government in the same way as the municipalities are. It will be said that to do these things will be to confer special privileges upon the First Nations.

I disagree. It is rather a question of recognizing that they have special rights. We acknowledge in Canada that many groups have special rights. The people of Quebec have special rights in Canada, based largely on the fact that the French established New France before the conquest in 1763, that is, rights based on the fact that they were here first. Why should Indigenous people not have special rights for the same reason? After all, they were here before the French or the English. And the purpose is the same, to enable the First Nations to retain and develop their distinctive culture, just as we allow French-speaking Canadians to do. All of these things will cost money, a lot more money than the federal government is spending on Indian Affairs, and a lot more than the government of British Columbia is spending on Indian Affairs.

But surely we can afford to redeem the promises that were made to Indigenous people. Surely we can afford to demonstrate our goodwill. Surely we can afford to render simple justice to Indigenous people. Justice is an expensive commodity, but it is worth paying for. If we used the same ingenuity today to bring justice to First Nations that we used hundreds of years ago to take their land away from them, it would not take very long to give them a place in our society equal to the white man.

But in the final analysis, you cannot repeal a century of injustice by passing a law. You can spend all the money you want and the extent to which Indigenous people are restored to their rightful place will depend on the extent to which the white community is willing to allow them to occupy that place.

Indigenous people will have to assert their rights. They will have to insist upon their rights, and when they do, they will find that they have many friends and allies.

~

CONVERSATION WITH SIM'OOGIT HLEEK, CHIEF HARRY NYCE, NISGA'A NATION

The Nisga'a Nation has a centuries-long tradition of collective action. With the decision to take their case to the courts, they began to organize for the long battle ahead. One of the first actions was to expand the ranks of the leadership by bringing back young Nisga'a who had taken up residence in other regions of the province.

"I went to residential school in Edmonton from 1955 to 1959 with my brother, Ron, and my late sister, May. Those times were very difficult. It seemed there were no rules, what those people did. But I survived.

I moved back to British Columbia. My mom was at Noah Bay. She had tuberculosis. In those times, the early sixties, with tuberculosis it wasn't safe, so they sent me to Port Alberni residential school. There I met Deanna. After a year and a half in Port Alberni we said: "This is not good. We've got to change the picture." Getting into Grade 12, we decided to get married.

I was a commercial fisher and had experience with longshoring. I had a number I kept for life. I could go anywhere along the British Columbia coast, enter a longshoreman's hall and present my number and I'd be working. That's how we were going to make our life in Prince Rupert. I would fish commercially in the summer and in the winter I would be a longshore-man. It worked out perfectly.

Our grandparents came to visit us in Prince Rupert where we were liv-ing after we got married. Logging in the Nass Valley was very busy at that time. The communities were not developing as our grandparents thought they should be. They got worried because all the young people were work-ing for the logging companies. My grandparents thought that because there was so much logging activity and disruption of the environment, something needed to be done. We had to rebuild our communities with the amenities that everyone else had: electricity, running water, schools, health care.

I hesitated to move because there were no services in the Nass Valley. It was a very rough place: no running water, no electricity, no roads. We came in here with our eyes wide open. This was 1969 and we moved just as everything was developing.

It seemed like some of our people in the valley weren't safeguarding these cultural things that we needed to hold on to. I relearned the lan-guage, I am fluent now. The Elders of the day, they spoke right to the point: safeguarding our fish, our rivers and our lakes, and our mountains around us. All of that was for the Nisga'a economy: fishing, drying fish, smoking fish, salting fish, hunting moose, picking berries. That was the economy of the day. In the Elder's time, that was all they had. That sustained them. The concern was: what's happening in the valley is so much industry, all at once.

Our families were fishing families. They set up canneries at the mouth of the Nass River and they moved south towards Prince Rupert and the mouth of the Skeena. We were fishing next to our neighbouring tribes—the Haida, the Gitxsan, the Tsimshian, the Haisla—intermin-gling with them in the fishing business. The leadership took positions with those companies. Frank Calder worked at Sunnyside Cannery. When the fish arrived at the cannery, they had to be weighed, recorded. James Gosnell, he was a commercial fisher, Red Robinson, Bill McKay, they were a fishing group.

On our fishing ground, late at night, when things were calm and we weren't fishing—between one and four in the morning—they'd have a chat on the radio phone. They'd switch over to a different channel and they'd chat about what they thought was going to happen in the fall, the business of the tribe.

They had harbour days when they were able to encourage the work. It wasn't an issue that could be left, they had to speak about it. They did that in the summers when they were gainfully employed in the fishing industry. Then in the fall they'd get together in the communities to deliberate on ideas they had about taking the white man to court. 'Those who stole the land', that's how they talked in those days.

Formally, administratively, they set up the Nisga'a Tribal Council. Frank Calder and the boys went and sought out Tom Berger in Vancouver: James Gosnell, Red Robinson and my father, Maurice Nyce. They went to see him to ask if he could help with taking the government to task. They thought if they lost their grip on the land, the titles and the names, all would be lost. The White and Bob case was the light at the end of the tunnel. They wanted the same. They thought: this guy Tom has the right stuff to take on this case.">

CHAPTER THREE

THE COMMON BOWL

Drew Ann Wake

⌒

NISGA'A LEADER Mitchell Stevens shared this story during an interview I conducted with him about the initial battle in his Nation's prolonged struggle for their traditional land in the remote Nass Valley of northern British Columbia.

> When the first surveyors were sent by the government, they said: 'We're here to give you land.' A hereditary chief by the name of Israel Sgat'iin walked down to the surveyor, put a rifle on his chest and said: 'How can you give what is not yours to give? This land already belongs to me. You're to leave this land.'

The confrontation that Mitchell described marked the beginning of a century-long struggle for Nisga'a land and rights. In 1887, only twenty years after Confederation, a Nisga'a delegation travelled to Victoria to assert their ownership of their traditional lands to Premier William Smithe. However, they were turned away at the steps of the Legislature.

Another attempt to reach an agreement took place 26 years later when the Nisga'a hired a London law firm to draw up a petition that was delivered to His Majesty's Privy Council, asserting the Nisga'a ownership of their traditional lands. The Privy Council determined that the matter would have to be dealt with first by the Canadian courts. In Ottawa, Prime

Minister Robert Borden responded that his government would treat the issue "with utmost liberality." But nothing was done.

Nisga'a leader Mitchell Stevens further emphasized that in 1923, that the Nisga'a people were searching for a way to resolve the land question without resorting to conflict, saying:

> We're not opposed to the coming of the white man. We merely want a tract of land to be set aside for ourselves, that we can use for the benefit of our people. We want to be out of the (control) of the federal *Indian Act*. We want to govern ourselves, to have ownership, true title to our land. And we want to pay our own way.

Stevens noted that in that statement to His Majesty's Privy Council, the Nisga'a stated that the other issues could be left to be deliberated between the province and the Nisga'a people. "Back then they were saying: 'We know we won't get it all. We're willing to sit down and come to a fair and equitable decision.'"

Over many years, the Nisga'a had tried to reach a compromise by different routes: proposing negotiations at the regional, provincial and national levels. All had failed. It was time for a new approach.

Voices from the Nass

In 1949, Nisga'a leader Frank Calder ran for a seat in the British Columbia Legislature. His ebullient personality and his determination to bring government services to Northern British Columbia won over voters. He became the first Indigenous person to sit in a legislature anywhere in the British Commonwealth.

Almost at once, Calder began to use his new position to speak out about issues that were roiling Northern communities: the decline of the fish stocks, the impact of logging on the land, poverty and increasing the supply of housing in Indigenous communities. His success in raising the profile of these issues ensured that he remained visible in the political life of the province.

The Nisga'a leaders had watched with great interest as the White and Bob case wound its way through the courts. Mitchell Stevens recalled:

> When the case was successful, they made the decision to engage Mr. Thomas Berger as our general counsel to bring Canada and British Columbia to task over the question of our land. They knew they had to engage a lawyer who had the integrity that they saw in themselves, so they chose Mr. Berger.

But a legal challenge costs money and the Nisga'a were not wealthy, so they used an ancient Nisga'a law: the common bowl.

> The women took their jewellery, their gold, their silver earrings, and put them in a bowl. Those who had currency put it in the bowl. When they came down to see Mr. Berger, they carried it in a pillowcase.

Years later, Tom Berger recalled the arrival of four Nisga'a leaders at his office on Hastings Street in Vancouver:

> My office was very small, I don't think there were enough chairs for all of them. Frank Calder said: 'We want you to take our case to the Supreme Court of Canada to establish that we, the Nisga'a, have Aboriginal title to our ancient tribal territory.'

Berger concluded: "That was a tall order."

The Nisga'a gave Berger a history of the efforts they had made to resolve the situation in 1887 and 1913. When they finished, Tom Berger agreed to take the case. Mitchell Stevens described the firm agreement:

> [The Nisga'a] knew: if we stand together, no one will beat us. But if we take Canada and British Columbia to court as individual houses and chiefs, we will be defeated. So

they decided to put all their holdings in a bowl and they went with one voice.

The Nisga'a Tribal Council met yearly, discussing how to come up with a firm plan for moving forward with their claim. At the tenth annual convention of the Nisga'a Tribal Council, the issue came to a head. The leaders sat around a table and debated whether to take their claim to court. James Gosnell was adamant: the Council had held ten conventions without significant progress. "No result. No action, no action. Waiting... We want to get a settlement once and for all. Now, not a hundred years from now."

He urged his fellow leaders to look around at the damage the logging industry was causing on their traditional lands. He ended on a personal note, describing a trip he had made the year before to his family's traditional trapping ground. He had found the land stripped of its once majestic forest. "Not a tree left," he concluded. "It hurts me deeply."

Frank Calder rose to put the proposed legal action into context. "The Nisga'a Tribal Council is not on trial," he said, his arm sweeping across the audience gathered around him. "The Nisga'a people are not on trial in this issue. British justice is on trial." The convention ended with a determination to take their case to court.

The decision to move forward with a legal claim had implications for Indigenous people across British Columbia, so the Nisga'a approached other First Nations to support them to carry the case forward. But leaders feared that a loss in court would put an end to future claims based on Aboriginal title. "You can count on one hand the number of Aboriginal leaders who stood in support of us," said Chief Nyce. "There are 204 First Nations in British Columbia, but to our dismay the comment was: 'Why should we get on board a sinking ship?'"

The Nisga'a leaders were not deterred; they were more determined than ever to move forward.

Preparing the Case

At the time the Nisga'a case moved toward the courts, a young law student named Don Rosenbloom approached Tom Berger about articling at his law firm. In an interview, Don recounted, "I was fascinated by the First Nations issues in British Columbia. If, as Tom argued, Aboriginal title had not been extinguished, British Columbia would be in a unique position. I was intrigued by that."

Securing a position at Berger's firm proved challenging. "Tom had never taken on an articling student. He hesitated and hesitated. I was interviewed and interviewed. I went down to the office at least three times." Don explained that if he hadn't been offered the position, he would have packed his bag into his Volkswagen Beetle and returned to his career as a reporter in Ontario.

During this time, Tom Berger was preparing a case, *Jones v. Bennett,* which he was taking to the Supreme Court of Canada. Jones had been the purchasing agent for the government of British Columbia in Victoria. He had been fired. When reporters met with Premier W.A.C. Bennett, they raised the question of why Jones had been fired. The Premier responded: "I could tell you a lot about that Jones boy, but I'm not going to." Tom Berger brought a suit against the Premier, saying that his comment implied wrongdoing on Jones' part.

When Tom Berger was about to leave for his appearance at the Supreme Court in Ottawa, he startled Don Rosenbloom by handing him the legal appeal book. Tom said:

Why don't you read this over tonight and come back tomorrow to tell me how you'd handle the case? I was just an articling student—and he was asking me how I'd handle the case! I read the appeal book overnight and went back the next day, but I don't remember a word of what I told him. I'm sure it was worthless in terms of the case, but I will never forget the experience.

This was one of many times that Tom Berger would test a young person by giving them a challenging, but confidence-building, assignment.

Don Rosenbloom began articling at the law firm in 1968, but almost immediately things took an unexpected turn. Tom Berger decided to run for the leadership of the New Democratic Party of British Columbia against Dave Barrett, who came out of the labour movement. It was a bitter campaign, made more so when the labour movement backed Berger. Don's background as a newspaper reporter came in handy for writing press releases as Tom Berger crossed the province seeking support. He won, but his tenure at the head of the party was brief. Nine months later, Premier W.A.C. Bennett called an election and Tom Berger lost his seat. Rosenbloom remembered:

> We left the realm of the political and leapt back into the world of legal strategy. Tom was working full-throttle on preparing the Nisga'a case. A prime responsibility was anthropological. To prove Aboriginal title, we had to prove that the Nisga'a had occupied their lands 'from time immemorial'. I was sent into libraries to research early contact with explorers in the Nass Valley.

During his research, Don found some unique materials that gave a significant boost to the Nisga'a case.

> There were some explorers from Japan who came down the Aleutian chain and wrote diaries in Japanese that were published in Japan in that early period. My wife was Japanese and she was very instrumental in helping me with this because the diaries had not been translated into English. The explorers speak of laying their nets at the mouth of the Nass River. A group of Nisga'a came out and told them they had to leave; those lands belonged to them.

The discovery of the diaries, along with other historical

materials, led the Attorney General of British Columbia to agree that he would not contest the Nisga'a claim that they had lived in the Nass Valley from time immemorial. The critical issue remaining to be contested in court was that of Aboriginal title.

On January 7, 1969, Tom Berger filed the writ in the British Columbia Supreme Court. Don Rosenbloom recalled that it was received "with hilarity" by the legal profession.

> Berger had the audacity to claim that British Columbia was owned by people who were not white and Anglo-Saxon—but First Nations. Nobody had a clue that Aboriginal title had not been extinguished.

The counsel representing the Attorney General of British Columbia, Douglas McK. Brown, took the position that there was never Aboriginal title to be extinguished. But if there had been Aboriginal title, then it had been extinguished between 1858, when the mainland colony of British Columbia was established, and 1871 when British Columbia joined Confederation. In either case, Brown argued that the Nisga'a could not claim to have Aboriginal title to their traditional lands.

The Nisga'a, on the other hand, claimed they did have Aboriginal title to the land and it was communal. That proved to be a difficult aspect of the case. Don Rosenbloom explained:

> We had to persuade lawyers who had practiced law with the land registry for forty or fifty years. They believed the only way you could prove title was by going to the registry. Tom was presenting a completely different structure of ownership and he had to get over the biases that the judges had. That was challenging.

Years later, Tom Berger described the issue this way.

> Our profession has too often demonstrated an incapacity to understand the fact that Indigenous peoples had

well-defined and sophisticated concepts of legal relations and legal rights. Indigenous ideas of land ownership, though quite different than those of the common
law, have in the past been rejected because judges and
lawyers simply could not appreciate the fact that people without a written language may, nevertheless, have
well-developed legal concepts."

To confront this challenge, Tom Berger made use of a skill
that would be the backbone of his legal work throughout his
career: he built bridges between his Indigenous clients and the
lawyers and judges who were steeped in Canadian law but had
little understanding of other ways of seeing the world.

In the Calder case, his witnesses included a Nisga'a leader
from each of the four villages along the Nass River. Berger
hoped they could help the legal community to see the Nass
Valley from a Nisga'a perspective. Frank Calder testified that
the Nisga'a did not roam indiscriminately across their traditional lands. There were boundaries that had been observed for
centuries, between villages, between families, just as there were
between settler families.

We still hunt within those lands, and fish in the waters,
streams and rivers, we still do, as in times past, have our
campsites in these areas, and we go there periodically,
seasonally, according to the game and fishing season...

Calder concluded with a point that defined the strong connection between the Nisga'a and their land: "We bury our dead
within the territory so defined."

The second aspect of Berger's legal approach was fairly
unusual for the time: he invited the testimony of an anthropologist, Professor Wilson Duff from the University of British
Columbia. Berger asked Duff to prepare a map of Nisga'a traditional land, a device to help the judge understand the territory. The Nisga'a leaders who appeared in court described

the features of their land from memory—the mountain peaks, the flow of the rivers—but Berger realized that non-Indigenous lawyers and judges would need a paper map to help their understanding of the issues.

Duff had a deep respect for Nisga'a history. He described the First Nations of British Columbia as "one of the world's most distinctive peoples" with cultural achievements that surpassed any Indigenous people north of Mexico. He connected the land to cultural achievements, describing how immense logs were used to make the long houses, canoes, and totem poles.

Duff had an unusual gift: he was able to place, side-by-side, the ways that the Nisga'a and settlers understood the land. This allowed the judge and lawyers to compare their own legal notions of land ownership with the Nisga'a concept of land. Wilson Duff explained:

> Even if the Nisga'a didn't subdivide and cultivate the land, they did recognize ownership of plots used for village sites, fishing places, berry and root patches and similar purposes. Even if they didn't subject the forests to wholesale logging, they did establish ownership of tracts used for hunting, trapping, and food gathering. Even if they didn't sink mine shafts into the mountains, they did own peaks and valleys for mountain goat hunting and as sources of raw materials.

Over five days, Tom Berger constructed a bridge between the Nisga'a understanding of their land and the way lawyers had traditionally understood land ownership. But the carefully reasoned arguments did not meet with success. Justice Jay Gould dismissed the Nisga'a case, declining to decide whether Aboriginal title existed in British Columbia at the time when settlement began. But he did acknowledge the scholarship of Wilson Duff and expressed his view that in all likelihood the case would be appealed.

And it was appealed. But all three judges at the British Columbia Court of Appeal rejected the idea of the concept of Aboriginal title under Canadian law. They added that if Aboriginal title had once existed, it had been extinguished by statutes passed in pre-Confederation times.

How did the loss impact Tom Berger? Don Rosenbloom believed that Tom had set out with a step-by-step strategy that accepted losses along the way.

> He recognized that this area of law had to be developed in incremental stages. The first step in the ladder was the White and Bob case where he argued for the recognition of the Treaty signed by Governor Douglas. He wanted recognition of that before he went into the next step at the Supreme Court of British Columbia. I don't know how many lawyers would have had the wherewithal to think on that level. Most lawyers would say: I have this case and I'll fight it. But they wouldn't plan the next steps. Tom had a game plan that went beyond the case that was at the bar at that moment. So as we headed for the Supreme Court of Canada our state of mind was not: this case is a loser. We assumed we had a fighting chance.

To the Supreme Court of Canada

The Nisga'a, too, wanted to take the case to the highest court in the land. Chief Harry Nyce recalled: "The first two times we went to court, it didn't go in our favour. The decision to go to the Supreme Court was made very early on. We were determined to carry on until such a time as we got it right."

Initially, the Nisga'a Tribal Council did not have the funds to sustain the legal battle, so they did what their ancestors had done for generations: they passed the common bowl. Each family contributed what it could and, with a gift from the Anglican

Church, they raised $25,000 to pay the costs of taking the case to the Supreme Court of Canada. Harry Nyce remembers that his father, Chief Maurice Nyce, carried the cash to Ottawa in a sports bag with a chain on the handle. "He hugged it for his life. In Ottawa they went to President James Gosnell's hotel room and laid the money on the double bed, flat out, to make sure they had the right amount."

On the flight to Ottawa, a surprise awaited Tom Berger and Don Rosenbloom. The lawyer for the British Columbia government, Douglas McK. Brown, was travelling on the same flight. He walked back from his seat in first class to chat with Berger and Rosenbloom, who were travelling in economy. His news: it appeared that Justice Emmett Hall was about to retire and would not be sitting on the case.

The news put the success of the Nisga'a case in jeopardy. As a lawyer, Emmett Hall had taken on some unpopular cases, notably in 1935, when he represented some of the On-to-Ottawa trekkers who had been arrested after riots in Regina. Although many in the legal community believed the trekkers were violent leftists, Hall had succeeded in getting many of the charges quashed. As a judge, he had chaired the Royal Commission on Health Services, which led to the founding of Canada's universal healthcare system. This history suggested that Justice Hall might be open to the reasoning of the Nisga'a case.

Tom Berger spent the weekend before the trial in Toronto, testing the ideas behind the case with a group of sympathetic law professors. When Berger mentioned that Justice Hall might not be sitting, one of the professors went to call a student who was clerking for Hall. The professor returned with a smile on his face: Justice Hall had postponed his retirement so that he could hear the Nisga'a case.

A second phone call that weekend took Tom Berger by surprise. John Turner, the Attorney General of Canada, invited him to become a judge in the Supreme Court of British

Columbia. Don Rosenbloom remembers that Berger struggled with the decision of whether he should go to the bench or not.

> I was opposed to it because I thought he was walking away from important work. I was proven wrong. Had he not been a judge, he would not have been appointed to lead the Mackenzie Valley Pipeline Inquiry.

When the court convened in Ottawa, a delegation of Nisga'a leaders was present in the courtroom. They listened as Tom Berger made the case that there were errors in the reasoning of the lower courts, reasserting that the Nisga'a had retained title. Frank Calder described their mood as determined and confident. Tom Berger observed that: "they showed the firmness of spirit that has characterized the Nisga'a over their long history."

The Nisga'a had to wait thirteen months for the judgment of the Supreme Court. In late January of 1973, the court released a split decision. Three judges decided that the appeal should be dismissed. In a decision written by Justice Judson, they concluded that the Nisga'a had Aboriginal title before the arrival of Europeans, but that title had been extinguished by the pre-Confederation enactments of the Colony of British Columbia.

Justice Emmett Hall, writing for Justices Spence and Laskin, acknowledged that the appeal raised issues of vital importance to the First Nations of northern British Columbia, particularly the Nisga'a People. He gave careful consideration to the ideas raised both by the Nisga'a leaders and Wilson Duff and concluded that Aboriginal title continued to exist for the Nisga'a People. Justice Hall had crossed the bridge that Tom Berger and the Nisga'a people had constructed: he was able to see Aboriginal title from the perspective of Indigenous Canadians.

The seventh member of the court, Judge Louis-Philippe Pigeon, ruled on a technicality that the Nisga'a had not sought the approval of the Attorney General of British Columbia to bring the case to the Supreme Court.

The case was lost. Or was it? Frank Calder explained that a 3-3 judgment suited him perfectly. After almost a century of struggle, the ruling had put the Nisga'a and the government on an even footing. Moving forward, they could negotiate as equals.

Tom Berger noted that the case persuaded the legal community that Aboriginal title was an issue that had to be faced in Canada.

> Mr. Justice Emmett Hall wrote the leading judgment in which he said the Aboriginal peoples of the West Coast had their own concepts of legal rights, ownership of property, ownership of fishery locations. He said there was a well-developed system of law and it was based on the fact that the Nisga'a were the first people who used and occupied the land, and that means they had Aboriginal title. And he said they still have it today.

Although the court was divided on the issue, Prime Minster Pierre Elliott Trudeau was advised by the Department of Justice that the questions should be settled. The federal government decided to negotiate the outstanding claims in Canada, claims that amounted to almost half of the vast land mass of the nation. Chief Harry Nyce said:

> In 1969, Prime Minister Pierre Trudeau refused to consider Aboriginal title, calling it 'a historical might-have-been.' But after the Supreme Court decision in 1973, to his credit, he said: 'You do have rights and title that this country has to deal with.' Despite all the pressure from his party, he made the decision. That decision strengthened Treaties 1 to 8, which had already been established. It also had a positive impact on the forty percent of the country that had not settled treaties yet. That was now open for negotiations.

On August 8, 1973, Indian Affairs Minister Jean Chrétien held a press conference to announce that the federal government was prepared to open land claims negotiations with First Nations across Canada. Asked for a response, Nisga'a leader Frank Calder joked: "It's high time."

Mitchell Stevens concluded: "Calder opened the door. The case opened the door for Aboriginal rights and title. Now the rest of the Indigenous people can do their negotiations."

A CONVERSATION WITH BEVERLEY BERGER

Beverley Crosby met Tom Berger in 1953 when they were both students at the University of British Columbia. They were introduced by a friend who had met Tom during a snowstorm while students were coasting down a hill on cafeteria trays. Bev recalls, "In March, Tom appeared at my dorm and invited me for a walk in the gardens. We walked together for the next sixty-six years."

"Tom grew up in a financially tight situation. His family had a tough time: four children in a small home. His parents even resorted to eating salt and pepper sandwiches at one point. Despite this, they were determined to ensure their sons continued their education. Both parents were stoic but valued education above all else.

Tom's older brother, Ted Berger, was particularly concerned about the family's finances. He would overhear his parents discussing whether they could afford things. As boys, Tom and Ted each received an allowance. Tom would spend his on comic books, while Ted saved his money and read Tom's comics. At university, Tom got a summer job on a 'green chain' at a sawmill, where lumber was graded and sorted. Later, this experience helped him represent the International Woodworkers of America.

When we started dating, I visited Tom's parents for the first time. They lived in a simple house that looked like a garage. Tom's parents were non-judgmental and seemed to approve of me. Tom had a rowboat and would row me to an island off Deep Cove for a picnic, with Old Gold orange juice and peanut butter sandwiches packed by his mother. When we first married, we lived in a small basement suite for $56 a month. I earned $200 a month as a teacher in Burnaby. When we bought a table and chairs, I cried over the bill, but Tom reassured me, saying, 'Don't worry. We'll figure out how to manage.' He always had a positive outlook.

At university, Tom considered becoming a history teacher but saw injustices that he wanted to change through law and eventually politics. He joined the Canadian Commonwealth Federation (CCF), which later became the New Democratic Party. Despite his parents' concerns that he should first establish himself in law, Tom decided to run in Vancouver Centre. Without a chief of staff, Tom's campaign was assisted by an English bobby. They would go to English Bay, where the bobby would gather a crowd, and Tom would jump up on a wall and give a speech.

In the next federal election, Tom ran against John Taylor, the son of the famous hockey player Hurricane Taylor, in Vancouver Burrard. Tom won by 97 votes and went to Ottawa. There, he worked with political leaders like Tommy Douglas and David Lewis. He worked tirelessly, often until midnight, building a network.

A year later, after losing his federal seat, Tom started his own law office with just a desk and one chair. When guests visited, they would sit in the chair while Tom leaned against his desk. Looking back, it was a modest start to a long and successful legal career.

Tom was always quietly optimistic about his cases. He never allowed himself to become over enthusiastic or unduly depressed. He knew the Calder case would be long and drawn out, waiting for a decision.

In 1971, John Turner appointed Tom to the bench and he agreed. On the day he was to be sworn in, he came home in a taxi and went upstairs to think about it. He was considering changing his mind. He was still waiting for a decision on the Nisga'a case. He didn't think he could leave them and go to the bench. He was torn. But ultimately, the decision in the Supreme Court pointed to a victory.

Tom said that his years in politics helped him with his work as a lawyer, because he learned how governments operated, how bureaucrats worked. When he was appointed to lead the Mackenzie Valley Pipeline Inquiry, he went to Ottawa and he knew it would take a while to get through to the hierarchy. But in his years as a politician, he had learned how to approach the governments, both federally and provincially. He knew how to express his views.

The longer he did it, the better he got at it. He was at home with speaking to people, and he could bring humour to the conversations. But after he ran both federally and provincially, he lost his taste for politics. He said: 'I can accomplish more of what I want to achieve in the courts rather than in politics.''

PART II

THE MACKENZIE VALLEY
PIPELINE INQUIRY

"We are embarking on a consideration of
the future of a great river valley and its people."

CHAPTER FOUR

THE CAVEAT CHALLENGE

Drew Ann Wake

~◦

IN 1956, Prime Minister Louis St. Laurent made a wry comment on the Canadian government's lack of interest in the
North. "Apparently," he said, "we have administered these vast
territories in an almost continuing state of absence of mind."
That was to change in the era from 1968-78.

With the discovery of oil in the Arctic, both government
and industry focused their attention on drawing the Northern
territories into the fold. One initiative, the Mackenzie Valley
Pipeline Inquiry, was to play a fundamental role in transforming the North from a neglected hinterland to the centre of
Canada's economic plan for the future.

Oil in Alaska

Just before Christmas in 1967, petroleum geologist Tom
Marshall boarded a plane that would take him from Fairbanks,
across the Alaskan tundra to a remote location on Prudhoe
Bay. For years, Marshall had been promoting the hypothesis
that the frozen plain between the Brooks Range and the Arctic
Ocean covered a massive reserve of oil and natural gas. But
time and again, test wells had come up dry. Now only one oil
rig remained in that remote region, drilling the last test well
at Prudhoe Bay before the industry moved to locations with
greater promise.

Marshall remained optimistic, but he knew that he was the butt of jokes. It had taken years to persuade Alaska's first Governor, Bill Egan, that the state should stake its claim to the remote region. "Doesn't he know it's frozen?" the Governor asked. One of Marshall's colleagues had even scrawled "Marshall's Folly" in large letters across an office map of Prudhoe Bay.

But in the winter of 1967, when the drilling crew opened a valve to test the well, a torrent of natural gas burst from the pipe. When it was lit, a fiery needle of flame shot into the air.

It was the first well in what would become the largest oil-field in North America. In Anchorage, oil industry executives began to grapple with the challenge of moving the oil from its remote location on the Arctic coast to the southern United States. The major oil companies, BP, ARCO, and Exxon, developed a proposal for a 800-mile pipeline that would carry oil from Prudhoe Bay across Alaska to the port at Valdez, where it could be loaded onto tankers for the journey south.

But what could be done about the natural gas that surged out of the remote wells? Although it was possible to liquify natural gas and send it by tanker to West Coast ports, the natural gas would still be distant from its principal markets in the US mid-west. So the oil companies proposed a pipeline that would carry natural gas across the north coast of Alaska and the Yukon to the Mackenzie Delta in the Northwest Territories. If more reserves were discovered in the delta, Canadian natural gas might augment the supply. From there, the pipeline would turn southward, travelling along the Mackenzie Valley until it merged with the pipeline network in Alberta, which had been carrying oil to the central United States for decades.

The plan seemed straightforward. Little did they know.

On to Ottawa

On January 10, 1973, the newly elected Member of Parliament for the Northwest Territories, Wally Firth, rose in the House to make his maiden speech. Wally was the first Indigenous MP from the North, and only the second Indigenous MP in Canadian history, so the other politicians were curious to hear his response to the Speech from the Throne.

Wally introduced himself by presenting a unique family story. His grandfather on his mother's side was Dinji Cho, a leader from Arctic Village in Alaska who helped to resolve disputes when the boundary was being drawn between Alaska, Yukon, and the Northwest Territories.

Wally's other grandfather, John Firth, was a Scotsman who travelled from the Orkney Islands to the remote Hudson's Bay post in Fort McPherson in 1872. John Firth managed the post for 52 years, while acting as Justice of the Peace and an honourary constable. When Wally reached this moment in his speech, he brandished his grandfather's handcuffs. He received a chuckle from his new Parliamentary colleagues.

Wally's maiden speech raised the issue of the oil discovery in Alaska and the possibility of a natural gas pipeline that would cross the traditional territory of the Gwich'in people.

> I think we should find out, for once and for all, if we do have a storehouse of oil, gas, and minerals in that part of the world, to be developed by Canadians for Canadians. I think it might be wise at this time to take a more careful look at the situation and abandon the idea of building a large pipeline, maybe two pipelines, without talking to the people in that area. I think the people in that part of the country should be consulted.

But he went further, as is recorded in *Hansard* on January 10, 1973 : "Of course, Mr. Speaker, this would all be done after the settlement of Aboriginal rights and the native land claims up there."

Wally was uniquely positioned to take on the task of representing the Dene and Inuvialuit communities of the North. In an interview, he shared that he was raised in Fort McPherson and, as a boy, often ventured into the land.

> I guess you could say we were poor but we didn't know it. We didn't have any money from September to March. Then when the muskrat season came, we'd get a few dollars from trapping. Otherwise, we lived from the land, fishing and hunting. We worked hard and we played hard. As kids, there was no such thing as boredom. We entertained ourselves by going out on the land to snare rabbits. We all had guns and we were good shots. I don't know how many hundreds of thousands of bullets we shot but we became good because we did that. That's how we made our living."

Initially, Wally followed in the footsteps of his father and grandfather, working for the Hudson's Bay Company in the Mackenzie Delta, where he conducted business in the Gwich'in language. Later, he was sent to manage the post in Wrigley where he was in charge of trading, medicine, the post office, welfare, and plane tickets. He remembered:

> I loved the people and they loved me. They had a good name for me: 'mek'aadhi nezi' or 'the good Hudson's Bay man'. Slowly, I learned the Dene Zhatié language so I could do trade. The people got to know me, and when it was time to leave I was bawling.

When Wally was young, he wanted to learn to fly an airplane so he could take trappers out to their cabins. But it seemed like an impossible dream. The training would cost thousands of dollars. But when Wally reached his thirties, he realized he couldn't postpone the dream any longer. He took a bus from Yellowknife to Edmonton where he trained to be a pilot. By 1966, he was walking down Jasper Avenue, staring at the pilot's licence in his hand, oblivious to the traffic around him.

Four years before, Wally had opened the Yellowknife office of the Indian Eskimo Association of Canada, an organization dedicated to creating Indigenous organizations that would give Dene, Métis, and Inuit people a voice in national affairs. On his return to Yellowknife, Wally started a campaign to buy an airplane for the organization.

"I was successful in getting a brand new Cessna 185 on floats," Wally recalled. The plane enabled him to ferry Indigenous leaders to communities across the North. Together, they founded an organization to represent the Métis and non-status people of the NWT. They also conducted research that led to the creation of the Indian Brotherhood of the NWT. Both organizations would give Indigenous Northerners a voice in their own future.

One day in 1972, Wally received a phone call from the New Democratic Party (NDP) in Ottawa. Would he be interested in running for Parliament? Wally hesitated, pointing out that he was working as a pilot, a job he had dreamed of since boyhood. But after the call, Wally considered the offer. In his work for the Indian Eskimo Association, he had found it difficult to reach politicians with his message. In Parliament, as the sole representative of the Northwest Territories, he would be able to carry his views to the politicians who were showing so little regard for the interests of Indigenous Northerners. The next day, the NDP called again and Wally agreed to run for Parliament.

The election was held in October, 1972. Wally won and almost immediately he began to field calls from the North.

The day after I was elected as a Member of Parliament, I got a call from some people in Tuktoyaktuk. They said, 'There's a plan for the oil industry to do some seismic blasting in the caribou calving grounds. We don't want that to happen.' So I called the Minister of Indian Affairs, Jean Chrétien and he said: 'It's cancelled.'

On the first day of his new job, Wally was learning the ropes. Still, there were lessons to be learned and protocols to be observed.

> In Parliament, you have to have a tie. I didn't know that. Our House leader, Stanley Knowles, told me: 'You have to have a tie or the Speaker won't recognize you.' So I asked my secretary, Bunny, to go out and buy me a tie. She came back with a red, Liberal tie. That's what I had to wear for a while.

Wally began to meet experienced politicians who would give him advice and encouragement.

> When I gave my first speech in the House of Commons, old man Diefenbaker came over and said: 'I've been here many a year and I've heard many a maiden speech, and yours has got to be the best.' Three times that day he came to congratulate me. The last time he said: 'A word of advice: Don't get up too often'.

With the election of an Indigenous Northerner to Parliament, one key policy was about to change. Wally sponsored the private member's bill that created a new territory for the Inuit people of the eastern Arctic: Nunavut. The NDP party would back the creation of old age pensions and a national oil company, PetroCanada. But perhaps most importantly, Wally and the NDP would play a role in the decision to appoint Judge Thomas R. Berger to lead an inquiry into a pipeline from Alaska, along the Mackenzie Valley, to markets in the south.

The Caveat Case

In October of 1969, the Indian Brotherhood of the Northwest Territories began planning a challenge to the pipeline proposal. The Brotherhood invited a dozen Dene chiefs and Elders to a gathering in Fort Smith, to formalize an organization that would represent their joint interests. The first step was to examine Treaties 8 and 11, which had been signed by Dene chiefs in 1899 and 1921. When Treaty Commissioner Henry Conroy travelled along the Mackenzie River to negotiate the treaty, he had discussed the terms of the agreement verbally. Fifty years later, for the first time, the chiefs read the terms that had been written into the formal treaty.

Ted Blondin, a reporter for *The Native Press*, remembers:

> What they read when they were 70 years old was totally different from what they heard fifty years earlier when they were teenagers. In 1921, they heard all the promises that were made by Commissioner Conroy who represented the federal government. But what was written in the documents was totally different.

The greatest discrepancy between the written agreement and the memories of the Elders was the issue of the land. The Treaty stated that the Dene had surrendered the Aboriginal title to their traditional territory. But the leaders remembered that they had argued, sometimes for days, against a surrender. They had only agreed to sign the treaty when Commissioner Conroy assured them that it represented a peace agreement between the Northern Dene and the government in Ottawa. Now, before them, sat a document that misrepresented the dialogue that had taken place in 1921.

Charlie Barnaby of Fort Good Hope remembered that in the 1960s the Indian Brotherhood tried to resolve the discrepancy by meeting with government representatives.

> When the Dene wanted to straighten it out by meeting with the government people from Ottawa, the government kept sending different officials to every meeting. It was their way not to deal with it. The Elders knew that. I remember a meeting at Fort Simpson one time. Three people from the government showed up.

The chiefs demanded to speak with the same officials that had spoken with us on the issue previously. They ended up kicking out the three government officials. It was like the government had sent the officials not to be truthful. The chiefs wanted to talk to officials who knew about the land. But they only knew papers.

Dene leaders agreed that their new organization should hire a lawyer to begin gathering the recollections of the Elders who had been present at the signing of Treaty 11, so their memories could be brought forward as testimony in court. The lawyer they hired was Gerald Sutton. He recommended filing a caveat that would freeze any further development on Dene traditional land until the outstanding issues were resolved. The leadership studied the treaty book from 1921 to ascertain the amount of land in the Northwest Territories that was identified under the treaties. They concluded that they could assert their Aboriginal right to 425,000 square miles of land—almost a million square kilometres.

In April of 1973, the Dene applied to file a caveat at the Land Titles Office in Yellowknife. The claim was markedly different from the usual caveats, as it put most of the land in the Northwest Territories in question. This worried the registrar at the Land Titles office, so he referred the case to the court, asking for a judgment on whether the caveat could be filed. In Yellowknife, Justice William Morrow was to hear the case.

Ted Blondin remembered that the Elders worried as the hearing drew near.

Going to court was foreign to us because in the past going to court meant you had to go to jail. It was a huge gamble. They were bringing in a judge who wasn't Dene. It would be his decision. All the chiefs discussed the pros and cons at an annual gathering. Francois Paulette from Fort Smith made a motion to go to court and the motion passed.

Then, just as Judge Morrow was preparing to begin the hearings, the federal government moved to have the case taken from his jurisdiction. Morrow was deeply disturbed because he feared that an issue that was fundamental to the future of the North would not be handled by a judge who lived in the North and was acquainted with the issues. In his autobiography, *Northern Justice*, Judge Morrow described the sleepless nights he spent trying to think of a way to keep the case in the North. Finally, he found a strategy to circumvent the roadblock: he wrote a strongly worded rebuke and released it to the media just before the case got underway.

Newspapers in the south covered the story, albeit with a tongue-in-cheek reference to the Northern judge. *The Globe and Mail* stated that "the pistol-packing judge from the NWT is once again battling Ottawa". A Northern newspaper, *The Yellowknifer*, criticized the federal government, saying: "Political pressure is not to be tolerated." *The Native Press* accused the federal government of "trying to stop our case for political reasons." Judge Morrow sat at home while a decision was reached: the case would remain in his hands.

Judge Morrow was now at liberty to run the case using a Northern legal tradition: a circuit. The court would travel along the valley to take the evidence from each of the Elders who had been present during the treaty negotiations. Gerald Sutton points out that,

> Judge Morrow was used to going around to communities in the North, that's how courts operated in the Northwest Territories. But usually it was for criminal matters. This was unique because people, many of whom hadn't been to court before—old people, very old people—came forth and told their stories. They gave evidence as to the meaning of the treaties to the Dene people and to what actually took place. The purpose was to establish that Aboriginal rights had not

been surrendered by those treaties and therefore people could make a claim for Aboriginal rights. It was an historic experience. We were examining history in a way that had not happened before.

A Circuit of the Communities

In Yellowknife, the staff at *The Native Press* prepared to cover the hearings. Their weekly newspaper had been established to keep leaders in the far-flung band offices aware of political issues that might impact the Dene people. Bundles of newspapers were sent out weekly to each of the communities. To reach non-Dene readers, copies were placed on newsstands in larger towns. The Indian Brotherhood was not shy about sharing its views with the territorial and federal administrators; copies were shipped to the offices of the Department of Indian Affairs in Yellowknife and Ottawa.

Producing the weekly newspaper was an antiquated process by today's standards. The reporters wrote their articles on clunky manual typewriters. Then they cut out the articles and and pasted them onto large squares of paper. The photographers processed the film in a darkroom, producing the photographs on paper and then pasting them onto the pages of the newspaper.

Patricia Anderson, a reporter for the *Native Press* recalls:

We worked until three in the morning each week to get the edition out. We'd send it off in a plane to Edmonton in the morning and we'd be excited to see the finished newspaper come back a few days later. There was optimism in the Indian Brotherhood offices because everyone knew we were involved in something very important. We were challenging the status quo. There was an air of excitement to be in the forefront."

The *Native Press* asked Patricia to travel with the court and cover the caveat case. She remembers that Justice Morrow showed a lot of respect for the witnesses.

> In those days, some courts didn't give credence to oral evidence, but he did. He showed a lot of quiet respect for the people who came before him to testify. Again and again, the Elders testified that the treaties represented a shared understanding between Canada and the Dene, but it was not a ceding of land.

The court heard from sixteen witnesses in communities along the valley. Gerald Sutton recalled the unusual approach to the hearings.

> In Fort Resolution we went into the home of an elderly man. He was in bed. His brother was looking after him so they had him dressed up. We went into his house, a very small house, and took the evidence at his bed. Later, in Colville Lake, the judicial party was having problems finding a hall where they could hold the hearing. It was a beautiful day, so the hearing was held outside and the evidence was taken in the open air."

A key witness was Julien Yendo, an Elder from Wrigley who was one of the signatories to Treaty 11 in 1921. He described in detail the day when Commissioner Conroy arrived in Wrigley. He had gone down to check his fish nets and when he brought his catch back he was told that the treaty party had arrived. He hurried to the meeting without stopping to eat. Strangers were sitting at a table, including the Commissioner, an RCMP officer and the Bishop. One by one, the Dene men in attendance were asked whether they would take the role of chief. One by one, they declined. Finally, Julien Yendo agreed.

Fifty years later, when he appeared before Judge Morrow, Julien Yendo was asked to examine the syllabics and the elegant script that was purported to be his signature. Using a phrase used by the treaty party, he stated that he "had not put his hand to the pen." He added: "I don't think I did that at the time of the treaty because I didn't know how to write."

Throughout the hearings, evidence mounted that the treaty had not represented a meeting of minds between the Dene and the treaty commission from Ottawa. On September 6, Judge Morrow released his judgment, concluding that the Indian Brotherhood of the Northwest Territories had the right to ask the registrar of land titles to file a caveat to protect Dene traditional territory. That week, under the headline "First Step to Victory" *The Native Press* celebrated the ruling.

> Tension was high when word came that Judge William Morrow was ready to read his decision on the Indian caveat. After his first few conclusions were read out, smiles broke out on the faces of the Indian people in the Yellowknife courtroom. Judge Morrow recognized that the Indian chiefs and their people are the descendants of the first owners of the land and concluded that the Indian people have never given up their rights to this land.

The case moved on slowly to the Supreme Court of Canada, where the justices ruled against the caveat in December of 1976 on the technical ground that a caveat could not be registered against unpatented lands. But by then, the case had had a significant impact on the young Dene activists at the Indian Brotherhood and *The Native Press*. They had come to believe that they could influence the future by joining forces and speaking out.

Ted Blondin believes that the caveat case had an impact on bureaucrats in Ottawa as well.

> When the judgment came down, it woke up the federal government. They said: 'The Dene are serious. We

better consider the possibility of settling land claims with them.' That was the first time the federal government considered a comprehensive land claim being settled in the Northwest Territories.

Choosing a Judge

In 1973, the Liberal government of Prime Minister Pierre Trudeau found itself in an unenviable position. A federal election the previous year had given their Liberal party a narrow win over the Conservatives, so they had to rely on the support of the New Democratic Party to pass legislation.

As they re-assumed power in May of 1973, the Liberals were facing two critical dilemmas. The first concerned energy policy. Tom Axworthy, the principal secretary to Prime Minister Pierre Elliott Trudeau, recalls the sudden rise in oil prices in 1973:

> After OPEC restricted oil production, prices were doubling and tripling; $4 oil became $20 oil and then $70 dollar oil. Suddenly we had a major economic crisis that was having an impact on inflation and job creation.... There were debates about how much Canada's oil and gas should be reserved for Canadian citizens, as opposed to exporting it to foreign customers. So energy sustainability quickly emerged as a huge issue.

In that context, the proposed pipeline bringing natural gas from Alaska to the Mackenzie Delta and southern provinces had clear benefits.

The second issue that the Liberal government faced was Indigenous rights. Two key rulings in quick succession—the Nisga'a case and the caveat case—had dramatically changed the future of Indigenous law in Canada. Clearly, a legal framework for Indigenous rights was forming.

The government began to consider solutions that would resolve these two issues, but they had to be solutions that would win the support of the New Democratic Party. Ed Broadbent, then a Member of Parliament for the NDP, remembers that it was a very exciting time in the history of Canada and of the New Democratic Party:

> We realized that for a small party we had a lot of power in terms of potentially influencing Mr. Trudeau's government in the direction it would go. This was very positive. You go into politics because you want to do something, not just make speeches. But it was also a time of great tension because at any time the government could come down on a vote of confidence, triggered by ourselves.

Instead of charting a path between two contentious issues, the politicians followed a common Canadian route: they decided to appoint a commission to explore the idea of a Mackenzie Valley Pipeline. This meant that the two thorny issues of energy policy and Indigenous rights would be left to an outsider whose advice could be accepted or ignored, depending on how the political circumstances evolved. But who would the government choose to lead the Inquiry?

Positioned in the middle of this debate was Wally Firth, the new Member of Parliament for the Northwest Territories. Wally had more experience with the Northern pipeline issue than anyone else in Parliament. His hometown of Fort McPherson sits in the Mackenzie Delta where the oil industry was cutting seismic lines across the Delta. During his election campaign his future constituents raised repeatedly the impact that the oil industry's seismic tests were having on their land and waters that they relied on for food and fur. By sending to Ottawa a man who had seen the destruction with his own eyes, Northerners hoped that action would be taken to protect their land and livelihood.

Wally Firth's understanding of the North enriched the discussions within the NDP, as the party sought to recommend a commissioner for the pipeline inquiry. "Our party leader, David Lewis had the mandate to speak for the Northwest Territories because I had a good plurality of the vote, over 40 percent," Wally recalls. "That gave us some power, so David was able to talk to Trudeau."

The NDP recommended Justice Thomas R. Berger as the commissioner. They pointed out that he had political experience: he had represented the New Democratic Party, both in the British Columbia legislature and in Parliament. Moreover, Berger had brought the issue of Indigenous rights to national attention through the White and Bob and Calder cases.

The Liberals did not disagree. Tom Axworthy believed that Trudeau had developed an admiration for Berger's work in the Nisga'a case:

> Mr. Trudeau was a lawyer and had been Minister of Justice and there were few areas that interested him more than Supreme Court decisions. He looked carefully at Mr. Berger's arguments in the Calder case because he was a legal scholar of some renown himself.

Jean Chrétien, as Minister of Indian Affairs and Northern Development, phoned Judge Berger and asked him to lead an inquiry into the proposed Mackenzie Valley pipeline. Years later, Tom Berger remembered the phone call clearly.

> When Mr. Chrétien phoned me, I don't think either of us had any conception of what it would involve because, as the Inquiry unfolded, it became apparent that there had never been an inquiry quite like this one. We talked about how long it would take and we thought perhaps six months should do it, to hold some hearings, perhaps in Yellowknife, to hear from the experts and the industry, and write my report.

It was an assessment that vastly underestimated the work that lay ahead. Berger also reflected on a key issue that was not raised in that phone call: if the commission would decide whether the pipeline would be approved. Berger recalled that he wasn't given the job of saying to the government whether the pipeline should be built or not.

> I don't think I regarded that as important at the time, because in those days the idea of progress involved pipelines, dams, pulp mills. So the idea that someone would say 'no' to the pipeline hadn't really entered into the equation.

With that conversation, the die was cast. Justice Thomas R. Berger would embark on an investigation of the engineering, environmental, and social consequences of what was, at the time, the largest construction project in the world.

A CONVERSATION WITH TOM AXWORTHY, LIBERAL PARTY STRATEGIST

Tom Axworthy began his career in politics at a challenging moment in the history of the Liberal Party of Canada. In an election at the end of 1972, the Liberals lost 38 seats, leaving them with only two more seats than the Conservatives. When Axworthy arrived in Ottawa a year later, the government of Prime Minister Pierre Elliott Trudeau was seeking new ways to address a multitude of contentious issues. One of them was Indigenous rights.

"When the Liberal Party initially turned to Aboriginal affairs, they came out with their White Paper, which would have gotten rid of the *Indian Act*. The desire was that no longer should the federal government be the warden of native citizens. That desire is felt deeply across every Indigenous person I've spoken to. The government initially wanted to get out of that protective, quasi-colonial position that Canada had for a hundred years.

But their proposed solution was opposed by virtually every important native organization. That opposition was important because it galvanized a generation of leadership around Indigenous leaders. They came together to oppose an idea...the proposed solution went against their collective and group traditions. We needed a better solution to the issue of removing the *Indian Act*.

This was a time of turmoil, of intellectual searching for the best solution. The Berger Inquiry has to be considered in that context because it was an important milestone for political, economic and social development in the Yukon and Northwest Territories. This was a time of reflection, consideration, when old assumptions were being questioned and new ideas were being probed but not necessarily accepted. But then we had the Calder Case, the Berger Inquiry, a whole host of new developments of which the judiciary and the Indigenous leadership brought to the courts. This was a time of fertile development.

Fast forward to the end of Mr. Trudeau's career in government. By about 1983 the concept of self-government with First Nations became the predominant view. Now just think of that. It's a huge intellectual change in a decade or so. From 'we will treat you as an individual citizen' to 'we will recognize your right to self-government in your territory'. The whole context shifted. That is a huge intellectual shift and the Berger Commission moved that along.

A second sea of change occurred at the same time: the price of oil. After OPEC restricted oil production and the Israeli Gaza War, prices doubled or tripled. Suddenly you had a major economic factor, important for inflation and job creation. Mr. Trudeau's government created PetroCanada, Canada's own oil company, because no one wanted to put our future in multinationals. There were debates about how much Canada's oil and gas should be reserved for Canadian citizens, as opposed to exporting it to foreign customers. So energy sustainability quickly emerged as a huge issue, as did the price of energy since that had an impact on inflation.

The Berger Commission was appointed in the midst of these tremendous changes: in the assumptions about the role of Aboriginal people and the price of oil when suddenly it went to $20 and then $70, heights that hadn't been considered.

So Berger came in the midst of two paradigm-changing events. One is usually enough, but he was doing his inquiry with two.”

CONVERSATION WITH ED BROADBENT,
NDP MEMBER OF PARLIAMENT

In the federal election of 1972, the New Democratic Party, under its new leader David Lewis, won nine more seats than it had held in the House of Commons the year before. In the view of NDP Member of Parliament Ed Broadbent, this may have been one reason why Prime Minister Pierre Trudeau appointed Judge Berger to lead the Mackenzie Valley Pipeline Inquiry.

"Tom Berger had been a federal Member of Parliament in Ottawa. David Lewis was in a leadership position in the party at that time so I would not be surprised if Lewis and Pierre Trudeau discussed the possibility of Tom Berger leading the Inquiry.

We were positive about it. We thought it followed a remarkable process of public hearings, so that the people of the North had an input into the final document, a major input. Also, the communications system that was set up during these hearings by Mr. Berger, the people in the North were able to listen to each other over CBC radio. That played a major role.

It was a remarkable period of creative politics and minority government. We showed what could be done with the right kind of collaboration. But the crucial point is having power to do it, not just making the right speeches. We had the votes, Mr. Trudeau knew that.

Mr. Trudeau had a well-earned reputation for being rather stubborn. But less well-understood was the flexibility that Mr. Trudeau could show when power politics was at play. He did that in the 1972-74 minority government period. He accepted wording and ideas that he would not have had otherwise. He responded to the power that other parties had in a democratic way."

CHAPTER FIVE

THE INQUIRY MANDATE

Thomas R. Berger

~⌒~

ON FEBRUARY 23, 1974, Jean Chrétien, Minister of Indian Affairs and Northern Development, telephoned to ask me to conduct an inquiry into a proposal to build a pipeline along the Mackenzie Valley. The Mackenzie Valley Pipeline Inquiry was to be unique in Canadian experience: for the first time we sought to determine the impact of a large-scale frontier project before and not after the fact.

It is only in recent years that we have realized that the advance of science and technology—especially large-scale technology—may entail social, economic and environmental costs which must be reckoned with.

That pace of change, and the costs that it entails, are only now beginning to be understood in the industrial world. In North America the metropolis' requirements for energy and resources—energy and resources now being sought at the frontier—are bringing industrial activity to communities which may not be prepared to cope with the impact.

When the oil and gas industry proposed building a gas pipeline from the Arctic to the mid-continent, running from Alaska through Canada along the Mackenzie Valley to the Lower 48, the Government of Canada appointed a commission of inquiry to examine the social, economic, and environmental impacts of the proposed pipeline.

The Mackenzie Valley Pipeline Inquiry provided a focus

for consideration of the consequences of the advance of the industrial system to Canada's last frontier and beyond, the necessity for the preservation of the Northern environment and, above all, the rights of the Indigenous Peoples living on the frontier. The Inquiry had to weigh the value of establishing large-scale extractive industry in the midst of native communities trying to preserve traditional values and to re-establish local self-sufficiency. In the end, after twenty-one months of hearings, I wrote a report that, when it was published in 1977, aroused intense controversy.

Framework
The Arctic Gas pipeline project would be the greatest project, in terms of capital expenditure, ever undertaken by private enterprise, anywhere.

Although the Inquiry was established to recommend the terms and conditions to be attached to any grant of a right-of-way, the project would entail much more than a right-of-way. It would be a major construction project across our Northern territories, across a land that is cold and dark in winter, a land largely inaccessible by rail or road, where it would be necessary to construct wharves, warehouses, storage sites, airstrips—a huge infrastructure—just to build the pipeline. There would have to be a network of hundreds of miles of roads built over the snow and ice. The capacity of the fleet of tugs and barges on the Mackenzie River would have to be doubled. There would be 6,000 construction workers required north of 60 to build the pipelines, and 1,200 more to build the gas plants and gathering systems in the Mackenzie Delta. There would be, in addition, thousands of immigrants seeking jobs and opportunities. There would be 130 gravel mining operations. There would be 600 river and stream crossings. There would be pipe, trucks, heavy equipment, tractors, and aircraft.

We were told that if a gas pipeline were built, it would result in enhancing oil and gas exploration activity all along the route of the pipeline throughout the Mackenzie Valley and the western Arctic.

My terms of reference were to recommend terms and conditions for a right-of-way for a gas pipeline. This was to be, therefore, an inquiry of unprecedented magnitude. I was to examine the social, economic, and environmental impact on the North of the proposed pipeline and energy corridor. The merit in such a comprehensive mandate is plain. The consequences of a large-scale frontier project inevitably combine social, economic, and environmental factors.

Funding Intervenors
So there was to be a public inquiry. The issues were to be canvassed in public. But how could the public participate effectively in the work of the Inquiry? After all, the Mackenzie Valley and the Western Arctic constitute a region as large as Western Europe. Though it is sparsely settled, it is inhabited by four races of people: White, Dene, Inuit, and Métis speaking six languages—English, Slavey, Gwich'in, Dogrib, Chipewyan and Inuvialuktun. They were all entitled to be heard.

Governments have lots of money. So does the oil and gas industry. So do the pipeline companies. But how were the Indigenous people going to be able to participate? How was the environmental interest to be represented? If the inquiry was to be fair and complete, all of these interests had to be represented.

Soon after I was appointed, it became apparent that there was no precedent for the task I had been given. How to go about it? How to decide what the future should hold for a great river valley? I decided to hold preliminary hearings, that is, to invite all those concerned: the pipeline companies, the oil and gas industry, the environmental organizations and the Indigenous organizations to tell me how they thought I should proceed.

The pipeline companies wished to proceed with the inquiry at once. So did the Government of Canada and the

Government of the Northwest Territories. All assumed, so did I, that the pipeline ought to be built. All that was required was to work out the conditions to be imposed to maximize the benefits and to minimize the adverse effects to Northerners. The pipeline companies had already spent $50 million on engineering and environmental research.

They were ready to present their evidence. Indeed, on March 23rd, 1974 they had filed ten volumes of material with the Minister of Indian and Northern Affairs, much of it technical, in support of their application for a right-of-way. The Indigenous organizations and the environmental organizations said, "How are we to digest this material and respond intelligently? Without qualified researchers of our own, without time to consider the material and without money to hire counsel, our participation will be a sham."

There was much to be said for this. I therefore decided to go to the government to ask that funds be made available. But how should the right to funding be determined? On my flight to Ottawa to see Mr. Chrétien, I wrote out five principles on the back of an envelope:

1.　There should be a clearly certainable interest that ought to be represented at the Inquiry.
2.　It should be clear that separate and adequate representation of that interest will make a necessary and substantial contribution to the Inquiry.
3.　Those seeking funds should have an established record of concern for, and should have demonstrated their own commitment to, the interest they seek to represent.
4.　It should be shown that those seeking funds do not have sufficient financial resources to enable them adequately to represent that interest, and will require funds to do so.
5.　Those seeking funds should have a clearly delineated proposal as to the use they intend to make of the funds, and should be sufficiently well-organized to account for them.

Mr. Chrétien was, I think, impressed, especially with the back-of-the-envelope submission, and went to the Treasury Board to obtain funding.

The pipeline companies said that the impact of the pipeline would on the whole be beneficial to the North. That might or might not be true. The funding program was established for those who had an interest that ought to be represented, but whose means would not enable them to participate. On my recommendation, funding was provided to the Indigenous organizations, the environmental groups, the Northwest Territories Association of Municipalities, and the Northwest Territories Chamber of Commerce, to enable them to participate in the hearing on an equal footing (so far as that was possible) with the pipeline companies. This was to enable them to support, challenge, or seek to modify the project.

These groups are sometimes called public interest groups. I suppose that is because they represent interests that the public believes ought to be considered before a decision is made. They represent identifiable interests that should not be ignored, that, indeed, it is essential that they be heard. These groups did not represent the public interest, but it was in the public interest that they should participate in the inquiry.

If the inquiry were to be fair and complete, all of those interests had to be represented. A funding program was established. These groups received $1,773,918. The cost of the Inquiry altogether came to $5.3 million.

In funding these groups, I took the view that there was no substitute for letting them have the money and decide for themselves how to spend it, independently of the Government and of the Inquiry. If they were to be independent, and to make their own decisions and present the evidence that they thought vital, they had to be provided with the funds and there could be no strings attached. They had, however, to account to the Inquiry for the money spent. All this they did.

I can illustrate the rationale for this by referring to the environment. It is true that Arctic Gas had carried out extensive environmental studies, which cost a great deal of money. But they had an interest: they wanted to build the pipeline. This was a perfectly legitimate interest, but not one that could necessarily be reconciled with the environmental interest. There had to be representation by a group with a special interest in the Northern environment, a group without any other interest that might deflect it from the presentation of the case for the environment.

Funds were provided to an umbrella organization, the Northern Assessment Group, that was established by the environmental groups to enable them to carry out their own research and hire staff, and to ensure that they could participate in the Inquiry as advocates on behalf of the environment. In this way, the environmental interest was made a part of the whole hearing process. The same applied to the other interests that were represented at the hearing. The result was that witnesses were examined and then cross-examined not simply to determine whether the pipeline project was feasible from an engineering point of view, but to make sure that such things as the impact of an influx of construction workers on communities, the impact of pipeline construction and corridor development on the hunting, trapping, and fishing economy of the Indigenous people, and the impact on Northern municipalities and Northern business, were all taken into account.

The usefulness of the funding that was provided was amply demonstrated. All concerned showed an awareness of the magnitude of the task. The funds supplied to the intervenors, although substantial, should be considered in light of the estimated cost of the project itself, and of the amount expended, approximately 50 million dollars, by the pipeline companies, in assembling their own evidence.

Formal Hearings

The formal hearings were held at Yellowknife, the capital of the Northwest Territories. At these formal hearings expert witnesses for all parties could be heard and cross-examined. The proceedings resembled, in many ways, a trial in a courtroom. It was at Yellowknife that we heard the evidence of the experts: the scientists, the engineers, the biologists, the anthropologists, the economists—people from a multitude of disciplines who had studied the Northern environment, Northern conditions and Northern peoples. Three hundred expert witnesses testified at the formal hearings.

At the formal hearings, all the parties were represented: the pipeline companies, the oil and gas industry, the Indigenous organizations, the environmental groups, the Northwest Territories Association of Municipalities and the Northwest Territories Chamber of Commerce. All were given a chance to question and challenge the things that the experts said, and all were entitled to call expert witnesses of their own.

The Government of Canada had carried out a multitude of studies on the North. These studies had cost $15 million. The oil and gas industry had carried out studies on the pipeline that we were told cost something like $50 million. Our universities had been carrying on constant research on Northern problems and Northern conditions. It would have been no good to let all these studies and reports just sit on the shelves. Where these reports contained evidence that was vital to the work of the Inquiry, they were examined in public, so that any conflicts could be disclosed, and where parties at the Inquiry wished to challenge them they had an opportunity to do so. It meant that opinions could be challenged and tested in public.

Community Hearings

At the same time, community hearings were held in each city and town, settlement and village in the Mackenzie Valley and the Western Arctic. There is a tendency for visitors to the Mackenzie

Valley to call at Yellowknife, the centre of government, and at Inuvik, the centre of the oil and gas play in the 1970s. They see very little else. But there are 35 communities in the region. And the majority of these communities are Indigenous communities. In fact, the native people constitute the majority of the permanent residents. I held hearings at all of these communities. At these hearings the people living in the communities were given the opportunity to tell the Inquiry, in their own languages and in their own way, what their lives and their experience led them to believe the impact of a pipeline and an energy corridor would be.

This is how it came about that, when the formal hearings at Yellowknife adjourned from time to time, I went to hold hearings in the Dene and Inuvialuit communities, travelling by aircraft, in pickup trucks, and sometimes by freighter canoe. It was these visits to remote Indigenous villages that aroused the interest of the media. But the fact that I was travelling to Old Crow, Fort Good Hope, and Paulutuk would not have kept the attention of the media. Rather, it was the testimony of the inhabitants of those villages that riveted the reporters who travelled with us.

In this way we had the best of the experience of both worlds: at the community hearings, where most witnesses spend their lives, and, at the formal hearings, the world of the professionals, the specialists and the academics. In order to give people —not just the spokesmen for Indigenous organizations and for the white community, but all people—an opportunity to speak their minds, the Inquiry remained in each community as long as was necessary for every person who wanted to speak to do so. In many villages, a large proportion of the adult population addressed the Inquiry. Not that participation was limited to adults; some of the most perceptive presentations were given by young people, concerned no less than their parents about their lands and their future.

I found that people with the experience of life in the North had a great deal to contribute. I heard from almost one thousand witnesses at the community hearings—in English (and occasionally in French), in Gwich'in, Slavey, Dogrib, Chipewyan and in the Inuvialuit language of the Western Arctic. They used direct speech. They seldom had written briefs. Their thoughts were not filtered through a screen of jargon. They were talking about their innermost concerns and fears.

What can Northern people tell the planners and the policymakers in government and in industry? The conventional wisdom is that a decision like this should only be made by professionals in government and industry: they have the knowledge, they have the facts, they have the experience. Well, the hearings showed that the conventional wisdom is wrong. I found that people who lived in the region had a great deal that was worthwhile to say. We discovered what should have been obvious all along: that the judgment of the planners and policymakers at their desks in Ottawa and Yellowknife might not always be right.

The contributions of Northern people were important in the assessment of even the most technical subjects. For example, I based my findings on the biological vulnerability of the Beaufort Sea not only on the evidence of the biologists who testified at the formal hearings, but also on the view of the Inuit hunters who spoke at the community hearings. The same is true of ice scour on the seabed, and of oil spills: they are complex, technical subjects but our understanding of them was nonetheless enriched by testimony from people who live in the region.

When North America's most renowned caribou biologists testified at the Inquiry, they described the life cycle, habitat dependencies and migration of the Porcupine caribou herd. Expert evidence from anthropologists, sociologists and geographers described the Indigenous Peoples' dependency on caribou from a number of different perspectives. Doctors testified about the nutritional value of country food such as caribou, and about the consequences of a change of diet. Then the Indigenous people spoke for themselves at the community hearings about the caribou herd as a link with their past, as a present-day source of food and as security for the future. Only in this way could the whole picture be put together.

The testimony of the people at the community hearings was of even greater importance in connection with the assessment of social and economic impact. The issue of Indigenous claims was linked to all of these subjects. At the formal hearings, land use and occupancy evidence was presented in support of Indigenous claims through prepared testimony and map exhibits. There the evidence was scrutinized and witnesses for the Indigenous organizations were cross-examined by counsel for the other participants. By contrast, at the community hearings, people spoke spontaneously and at length of both their traditional and their present-day use of the land and its resources. Their testimony was often painstakingly detailed and richly illustrated with anecdotes.

The most important contribution of the community hearings was, I think, the insight it gave us into the true nature of Indigenous claims. No academic treatise or discussion, no formal presentation of the claims of Indigenous people by their organizations and their leaders, could offer as compelling and vivid a picture of the goals and aspirations of Indigenous people as their own testimony did. In no other way could we have discovered the depth of feeling regarding past wrongs and future hopes, and the determination of Indigenous people to assert their collective identity today and in years to come.

An Inquiry Without Walls

The Inquiry faced, at an early stage, the problem of enabling the people in the far-flung settlements of the Mackenzie Valley and the Western Arctic to participate in the work of the Inquiry. When you are consulting local people, the consultation should not be perfunctory. But when you have such a vast area, when you have people of four races, speaking six languages, how do you enable them to participate? How do you keep them informed? We wished to create an 'inquiry without walls'. We sought, therefore, to use technology to make the Inquiry truly public, to extend the walls of the hearing room to encompass the entire North. We tried to bring the Inquiry to the people. That meant that it was the Inquiry and the representatives of the media accompanying it, not the people of the North, who were obliged to travel.

I wrote to M. Laurent Picard, the President of the Canadian Broadcasting Corporation, urging that there be broadcasts from the Inquiry for the purpose of keeping Northerners, Indigenous and non-Indigenous, informed. I suggested this should be an inquiry without walls and that, using technology, we could encompass the entire North, making the North itself a hearing room. M. Laurent and CBC responded magnificently. The Canadian Broadcasting Corporation's Northern Service provided a crew of reporters who broadcast across the North on radio and on television highlights of each day's testimony at the Inquiry. Every day that there were hearings, they broadcast both in English and in the Indigenous languages from wherever the Inquiry was sitting. In this way, the people in communities throughout of North were given a daily report, in their own languages, on the evidence that had been given at both the formal hearings and the community hearings.

The broadcasts meant that when we went into the communities, the people living there understood something of what had been said by the experts at the formal hearings, and by people in the communities that we had already visited. The broadcasters were, of course, entirely independent of the Inquiry.

The media in a way served as the eyes and ears of all Northerners, indeed of all Canadians, especially when the Inquiry visited places that few Canadians had ever seen. The Inquiry had a high profile in the media. As a result, there was public interest and concern in the work of the Inquiry throughout Canada. When the report of the Inquiry, entitled *Northern Frontier, Northern Homeland,* was made public on May 9, 1977, it became the largest selling volume ever published by the Government of Canada, and even found its way onto Canada's bestseller lists.

A CONVERSATION WITH
DIANA CROSBIE, MEDIA RELATIONS

The Mackenzie Valley Pipeline Inquiry unfolded in an era when the Canadian news media was situated in cities, primarily in Ontario and Quebec. That posed a challenge. How would southern Canadians hear about the scientific and socio-economic evidence being presented at the formal hearings in Yellowknife? Would the passionate voices from the community hearings be heard beyond the North? Those questions were addressed by Diana Crosbie, the Inquiry's media relations specialist.

"I was working for *Time* magazine. Out of the blue, Judge Berger invited me to lunch at the University Club in Toronto. Women had to enter by the back door in those days. The Judge asked: 'How can I ensure every Canadian has the chance to hear what Northerners have to say?' At that time, it was unusual for news outlets to send reporters to the North, I only knew one who had worked there. Coverage was very limited. I accepted the job, but honestly, I couldn't imagine that the Berger Inquiry would explode into an international story.

Whit Fraser, the senior newsman at the CBC in Yellowknife, wanted communities across the NWT to follow the Inquiry in their own languages. He reasoned that if Northerners heard evidence from the formal hearings in Yellowknife, they would be able to participate fully when the Judge arrived in the communities.

Whit spent more than six months writing eloquent memos to head office and every station across the North, trying to convince the CBC executives to fund the team. He argued that it would be catastrophic if the CBC failed to inform Northerners about the critical issues before the Inquiry.

The Indigenous news team paved the way for reporters from the south. When reporters began to arrive from Montreal, Toronto, and Vancouver, it was quite possible they would just report on what was said in the hearings. But the Indigenous news team introduced them to people, provided language assistance—they were a conduit into the communities.

In Yellowknife, I sent out daily transcripts of the hearings to more than a hundred reporters across Canada. This gave reporters a record of the exact words that were spoken at the hearings, so they didn't have to visit the North to get their stories. Geoff Stevens, the editorial writer of the *Globe and Mail*, commented wryly: 'This is not light weekend reading.'

The large newspaper chains did send reporters to the North. It was an expensive trip, and the editors wanted to get the most impact, so they sent their top reporters. They also wired the stories to hundreds of smaller newspapers across the country. So the word spread, connecting north and south. "

A CONVERSATION WITH WHIT FRASER, REPORTER, CBC

The Canadian Broadcasting Corporation was in a unique position to carry news from the Berger Inquiry across the North. The CBC had studios in Yellowknife, Inuvik, and Whitehorse; all were broadcasting in English and the Indigenous languages. But the national radio and television network, prodded by newsman Whit Fraser, went beyond expectations, ensuring that news from the Inquiry would reach remote fish camps and trappers cabins all across the North.

"I'd been working in the newsroom in Yellowknife for three or four years as the senior reporter when Mr. Berger was appointed. And all hell broke loose. We knew it was going to be a big story. I couldn't see us covering it with a single reporter.

I was called to the manager's office and introduced for the first time to Andrew Cowan, the Director of the CBC Northern Service. He had been a World War Two reporter, a tremendous broadcaster. We feared him: stern features, fierce eyes, mutton chop side-burns. He asked: 'How do you think we should cover the Inquiry, Whit?'

I said: 'We just can't do it with me running up in the middle of the afternoon and grabbing a clip and coming back. We have to cover this unlike anything we have done before, because there hasn't been anything like this before. We need to do it in all of the Indigenous languages, we have to be with the Inquiry the whole time, we have to go into every community, we have to maintain our independence.'

He listened and he began to ask me some questions, looking to pick holes in my idea, and I said: 'Mr. Cowan, you asked me how I think we should cover it. I told you. It's three o'clock in the afternoon. I have a newscast at 5:30. I haven't got ten words written yet. I have a deadline.' He said: 'Forgive me, forgive me.' And we became colleagues and friends.

I wrote up a plan that we should hire reporters for all the Aboriginal languages. They should not translate what I said, but should have their own take on the story according to their region. Cowan said: 'I want you to be ready to come with me to Ottawa the day after tomorrow.' We flew over there, presented our idea, and we got the money.

I knew I had one if the best broadcasters right there in the Yellowknife station, Joe Tobie. I didn't select him, he selected me. He was working for Health Canada as a field worker and a translator. He would come over to the CBC once or twice a week to do a programme on good health and he'd play country music. He was very respected. Joe covered two languages: Dogrib and Chipwyan.

Joe and I got on a plane and we flew down to Fort Norman to see John Blondin. Joe knew him so he broke the ice and did the introductions. I talked to John and he agreed to join the team. I did notice his son, a young guy about twenty, terribly crippled with arthritis and on crutches, listening with interest from the sidelines. I was introduced to him, Louie.

So Monday morning I was waiting for John Blondin in the Inuvik newsroom and the door opens and the first thing I see are a pair of crutches and Louie swings in. I was looking behind him and I said: 'Hi, nice to see you again. Where's your dad?

'Oh, he's not coming,' he said. 'He sent me.'

I said: 'He sent you?'

'Yeah,' he said. 'He thinks it's going to be too much for him, but he sent me.

Here's this young guy, he doesn't weigh 110 lb. He's standing on crutches, paralysed from the waist down. I said: 'Can you do this?' He looked me straight in the eye and he said: 'Yeah, I can do this.' And boy, could he do it. He could do it better than any of us.

I knew a big Inuk, Abe Okpik, who had, just a few years earlier, completed one of the most remarkable initiatives in Canada, Project Surname. He went across the Arctic and got rid of the despised disc numbers that had been given to the Inuit. He interviewed all the families and recorded their family names. He presented them to the Supreme Court in Yellowknife and in one fell swoop the disc number was gone and people had their identity back. Abe spoke two languages and he was always looking for a challenge. So I called Abe and he said he was in.

Patrick Scott came to us as a rookie cameraman, with a bag of old 16 mm film equipment. He captured the heart of the Inquiry visually. If you see old footage of that era, it's a safe bet that the weathered and wise faces of the Dene and Inuit Elders in the smoky community halls are Patrick's pictures.

When I went up to the Delta, Nellie Cournoyea of the CBC had suggested a man who was seventy at the time, Jim Edwards Sittichinli. He was an Anglican minister, preacher, terrific presence and command of his own language, Gwich'in. These guys had to be as versed in English as anybody because the entire hearing was going to be in very complicated English terms.

They were all gifted in their own languages and they all had a great grasp of the English language. But beyond that, they had a deep knowledge of their own environment: the terrain, the rivers, and streams. So when a biologist talked about the pipeline crossing a river, they knew where the fish spawned and they knew who depended on the fish. And if they didn't know, they could find out with one phone call. There was more than one time that they caused PhDs to sit back and say: 'Holy smokes!'

For example, the Inquiry went through weeks of hearings about how to put the pipeline with the gas from Alaska across Mackenzie Bay. The wildlife biologist, a nice guy, Dick Webb, said that the pipeline construction that they would do in the summer would cause havoc, chase the whales away so they couldn't have their calves in the warmer waters where the calves needed to be born. The marine biologist said: 'Mr. Berger, we've been researching this for the last couple of years. We've spent a million bucks on it. The company will give you the commitment that we will continue the research until we get the answer. We will not do construction in the area when the whales are having their young. But first we have to find out exactly where they have their young.'

Jim Sittichinli said to me, 'I know that. Most people know that.' He gave me a map of Mackenzie Bay and he said: 'Right there in that little harbour and usually on the second of July.'

Then Berger called a break. I spoke to Dick and said he should talk to Jim. So he went over and got two cups of coffee and I can see those two heads together yet, Jim with the map. Then the fifteen minutes were up and the hearing resumed. To Dick Webb's great credit, he said: 'Mr. Berger, back to the issue of when the whales have their young. Over the coffee break, Mr. Sittichinli from the CBC was good enough to spend some time with me. He tells me that the whales are born in this bay and usually in the second of July. So I think we've got the answer.'

I believe that's the only piece of scientific evidence that went into that Inquiry that was not challenged by anyone."

CHAPTER SIX

LAYING THE FOUNDATION

Michael Jackson KC

~

The Community hearings for the Berger Inquiry were organized by a young lawyer from England, Michael Jackson. He had arrived in Canada only a few years before to teach in the law school at the University of British Columbia (UBC). It might seem odd that the lawyer who was to play a key role as emissary to Dene and Inuvialuit communities in the Arctic had been raised in London. Michael is aware of the irony.

WHEN I WAS growing up in post-Second World War England, food rationing was still in effect. My mom received packages from an uncle in Philadelphia which contained canned food, chocolates, chewing gum, silk nylons, and clothes not easily available in England, which my mom would distribute among families in the neighbourhood.

Among those packages was a cowboy outfit with a Stetson cowboy hat, satin shirts and neckties, and a leather holster set with two silver replica Colt 45s with silver bullets in the holster belt. In the 1950s every Saturday morning, the older kids in our neighbourhood would take the younger kids to the movies. We would watch Disney cartoons, and the main feature would usually be a Western with stereotyped white heroes like Roy Rogers, Hopalong Cassidy, and the Lone Ranger. So as a nine-year-old boy my first images of Indians were those projected by

Hollywood as the implacable foes of good white pioneers and the legitimate target of cowboys' Winchester rifles.

So it was an unusual rite of passage that a nine-year-old English boy, after studying law at Kings College, London and becoming a lawyer working for a large law corporate firm in London, exchanged the cultural baggage of replica Colt 45s, holstered over top of a satin Roy Rogers cowboy shirt, for the black silk robes of a Canadian Kings Counsel and the armoury of a law professor and lawyer's arguments for Indigenous self-determination.

I was the only Jewish kid in my school. There was a group of boys, three or four years older than I was, who took it upon themselves to follow me home from school. They never attacked me but they were very intimidating. They would call me hateful expressions.

I didn't tell my mom about it for a long time. Then one day I was crying and she wanted to know what was the matter. So I told her. The next day she came to the school. We had an assembly every morning, all the students, and that day my mother walked in. Without saying anything to the headmistress, she went onto the stage and made a speech in which she explained what was happening to me. She said: "Your fathers and your uncles went to war to stop this hatred. You should be ashamed." And she walked out. That was the end of the bullying.

That early childhood experience and understanding of racism was broadened when I completed graduate work at Yale Law School in the 1960s. The time I spent at the Yale Law School was at the height of the US civil rights movement. I was struck by Dr. Martin Luther King's quote, "The arc of the moral universe is long, but it bends towards justice," and in my studies at Yale I recognized that lawyers and the legal profession had a broader social and professional responsibility in that struggle for justice.

When I moved to Canada in 1970 after being hired as a young law professor at the UBC Faculty of Law, I very quickly realized that in the Canadian context, Indigenous Peoples occupied little space in the moral and legal universe and had bended towards injustice. That realization, and discovering the groundbreaking efforts of Tom Berger in his professional struggle for achieving justice for Indigenous peoples in British Columbia, brought me into his orbit and my work as special counsel for the community hearings in the Mackenzie Valley Pipeline Inquiry.

In the summer of 1971, I was invited by two of my first-year law students, who had obtained a federal Opportunities for Youth grant, to study the need for legal services in an Indigenous reserve community. I spent a week on the Nimpkish Indian Reserve (now the Namgis First Nation), which is part of the Kwakwaka'wakw Nation. The reserve is located in Alert Bay, a small island off Northern Vancouver Island, about 200 miles from Vancouver. One half of the island is home to a settler population dating back to the late nineteenth century, while the other half is inhabited by the Namgis First Nation, who have occupied this area of British Columbia for millennia.

While attending court proceedings, what my students saw bore little resemblance to the model of criminal justice they had learned about in my lectures in their first-year criminal law class. Representing half of the island's population, Indians were the overwhelming majority of the accused in the prisoners' dock. The judge was white as were all the court officials. The prosecutor was an RCMP officer, a senior member of the same police detachment who had arrested the accused.

The week I spent on the Nimpkish reserve was a revelation, but only many years later did I fully appreciate the extent to which what I saw and heard that week represented the full spectrum of the colonial experience, not just of the Namgis First Nation, but of Aboriginal peoples throughout British Columbia. As I got off the ferry I was met by a two-fingered signpost. One finger pointed to "Indian Land," referring to the Nimpkish reserve, and the other to "Stolen Indian Land," denoting the village of Alert Bay. This terse but accurate statement reflects the history along the coast of British Columbia, where extensive Indigenous territories have been reduced to postage stamp-sized reserves over the course of a hundred years.

On my return to UBC, I approached my Dean, George Curtis, and urged that the new curriculum the Law School was building should include space for a course on Native People and the Law (the terms Aboriginal Peoples, First Nations and Indigenous Peoples had not yet entered the language of either legal or popular discourse). For over a century Canadian law had attempted to reshape the lives of the Namgis and other Indigenous Peoples, creating separate legal regimes and giving rise to a host of other legal issues relating to the interpretation of Indian Treaties and land claims where no treaties were signed. Surely the Law School had an obligation to teach this body of law so that lawyers could address the issues that I had encountered in my short stay at Alert Bay and represent the interests of Indigenous peoples. Dean Curtis, ever a legal visionary, welcomed this initiative.

However, as I searched for guidance in preparing an outline of course materials, I discovered that no law school in Canada had ever offered a course of this type. This perfectly, though unconscionably, reflected the manner in which Indigenous people had been pushed to the margins of Canadian social, economic, legal, and political life.

As I began my research for course materials I discovered that while far removed from the contemporary legal landscape of 1971, the rights of Indigenous People had a deep and impressive footprint in the diplomatic and jurisprudential record of the British Colonial era, the United States, Canada and other parts of the British Commonwealth. I learned that the issue had come before the US Supreme Court in the first part of the nineteenth century, the highest court in New Zealand in 1849 and featured in a series of cases in the late nineteenth and early twentieth centuries before the Canadian Supreme Court and the English Privy Council (which until 1949 heard appeals from the Canadian Supreme Court). Building upon the British Colonial practice of treaty making, I also read the history of Canadian treaty making in the post-confederation era in the so-called Numbered Treaties, which according to their English text surrendered Aboriginal title in Manitoba, Saskatchewan, Alberta, and the eastern part of British Columbia and the Western Arctic.

I also discovered that, as a lawyer, Tom Berger had dug deep into this thesaurus in his representation of the hunters in the 1964 White and Bob case again in initiating in 1969 the Calder case on behalf of the Nisga'a Nation, a case that was destined not only to re-introduce into the lexicon of the common law the concept of Aboriginal title, but fundamentally change the politics of recognition.

I also discovered that, as a lawyer, Tom Berger had extensively drawn from this rich legal history in his representation of the hunters in the 1964 White and Bob case, and again in 1969 when he initiated the Calder case on behalf of the Nisga'a Nation. The Calder case was destined not only to reintroduce the concept of Aboriginal title into the lexicon of common law but also to fundamentally change the politics of recognition.

So it was to Tom Berger that I turned in 1971, after his appointment to the Supreme Court of British Columbia, in search of materials and guidance for my new course on Native People and the Law. Tom gave me access to his old files and to his personal copies of his legal arguments in both White and Bob and Calder. These cases became the fulcrum of the course in its inaugural year in 1972. The Supreme Court of Canada handed down its judgment in Calder a year later, and the legal and political landscape was changed. The rights of Indigenous Peoples became centre stage, and the moral and legal universe of Canada began bending towards justice.

Based upon my research and teaching in the field of Indigenous rights, in 1974 Tom Berger invited me to become a member of his legal team with the role as Special Counsel for the community hearings.

Preliminary Hearings

Early in 1974, when the Inquiry began, Judge Berger decided to hold a set of preliminary hearings to get input about how the pipeline inquiry should be organized. One of the most important of those hearings was held at the conference centre in Ottawa, across the street from the Parliament Buildings. The Indian Brotherhood of the NWT sent a representative to the hearing, Chief George Kodakin from the remote community of Fort Franklin, now Deline, on Great Bear Lake.

Chief Kodakin arrived with a translator, Addy Tobac. Speaking in his own Dene K'e language, he suggested that the judge should spend a year in Fort Franklin before the hearings began. He offered to teach the judge about the importance of the land to sustain the Dene way of life. After that, he felt, the judge would be in a better position to lead the inquiry.

Judge Berger considered the idea. Then, at the coffee break, he called me over and said: "That's a good idea." But Judge Berger couldn't take the time away from his duties as Commissioner. He had already planned to visit a number of communities across the North over the summer, to get a broader picture of how the pipeline might impact different regions of the North. But he suggested that my young family and I might accept the chief's offer.

I invited Chief Kodakin and Addy Tobac to join me for lunch at the Chateau Laurier, the elegant castle-like hotel across the street from the conference centre in Ottawa. The three of us stood at the door, waiting for a table. After some time it became clear that the restaurant staff had no intention of seating us. Then, Bora Laskin, who had been named Chief Justice of the Supreme Court, entered the restaurant. He recognized me because we had met at a conference. We shook hands and chatted for a moment. Suddenly, the restaurant staff were able to find a table for me and my Northern guests.

By the end of lunch, Chief Kodakin and I had come up with a plan: the Jackson family would visit Fort Franklin to experience the Dene way of life and plan the community hearings.

Fort Franklin (Deline)

The day after our family arrived in Fort Franklin, there was a feast in the village. After a winter on the land, the Dene were gathering to share a meal of moose meat and fish and swap stories with relatives and friends. We were in our little wood cabin and we heard drums beating, an accelerating crescendo. The accompaniment, which I had never heard before, was dogs howling. At that time, almost every family in the community had a dog team, so we heard a mixture of vibrant drumming and dogs howling. I was aware that this was a very different world.

The next day I woke up and pondered how to proceed. If I had been preparing for a southern hearing I would have spoken with the people who were going to be witnesses, to schedule their appearance at the hearing. But in the North, I would have to explain the Berger Inquiry and its purpose before the planning could begin.

I sat at home in the cabin and I waited. Nobody showed up. So I went to the chief's house and reintroduced myself. Chief Kodakin welcomed me and we had a cup of tea. When I went back to the cabin, I found my wife Marcie and my son Shane surrounded by children from the village. The children played with Shane and asked questions. Who were we? Why had we come to Fort Franklin? The children taught Marcie how to carry Shane on her back, in a blanket, the way the Dene did. After that, when we walked around the village, people realized we were open to education.

One of the many challenges facing the Inquiry was to convey the message that the community hearings would follow a different protocol than that which characterized previous 'consultation' with federal and territorial government officials. From my base in Deline I observed how meetings were held within the village, both amongst the people themselves on such issues as organizing the community caribou hunt and those which the chief and council regularly had with government officials.

There was a stark contrast between the two kinds of meetings. The meetings with government officials typically dealt with agendas predetermined by the government upon which the chief and council were being 'consulted'. Government officials would fly into Deline (the only other access was by boat) and, while their planes waited on the runway or lake, the meetings, attended only by the chief and a few councillors, would be hurriedly conducted in a small room in the village office.

By contrast, meetings held by the Dene themselves dealt with agendas of their own making and were carried out in conformity with the traditional pattern of decision-making which operates by consensus. Issues are discussed by heads of families and others who are respected for their skills and knowledge and eventually a position or decision would emerge to which everyone could subscribe. Issues are not necessarily settled at a single sitting. There is much informal discussion within the community to ensure that all members of the community are involved. The formal meetings were held not in the village office but in the large log community hall which is also used for traditional dances and other community events. Meetings on important issues were often preceded by a community feast and followed by a community drum dance.

It was clear from my discussions with Chief Kodakin and other people in Deline that they assumed that the community hearings on the impact of the Mackenzie Valley Pipeline would follow the government model. Their expectation was that Judge Berger would fly in with his entourage, spend a few hours speaking with the chief and council, and leave. Such was the cumulative experience of the Dene, Métis, and Inuit with the process of government consultation that it was a major task to persuade them that, in this inquiry, things would be done differently. I encouraged the community leaders to help fashion a procedure which would ensure that their traditional model of holding meetings would be respected by the Mackenzie Valley Pipeline Inquiry, consistent with the carrying out of its mandate.

Part of my continuing education in understanding the scope of the community hearings, and why community members wanted Judge Berger to fully understand the importance of their land and waters to their way of life and cultural and spiritual values, was to participate and observe Dene life on the land.

That winter, I was invited by Charlie Neyelle, a highly respected and productive hunter and trapper who, at 31, was the same age as I was, to accompany him on a five-day hunting and trapping trip deep into his territory. But, accustomed to Vancouver winters, I didn't have suitable clothing for minus 40 degrees. In Deline the men wore parkas made of navy-blue stroud wool, beautifully embroidered. The fur encircling the hood was wolverine which would not freeze to the face, even on the coldest days of winter. Charlie was concerned about taking me into the bush without proper warm clothing, so the night before my first foray onto the land, the women of Fort Franklin formed a sewing circle. By morning, I had a wonderful wool parka.

Travelling by snowmobile, breaking trail through deep snow drifts, setting traps, cutting trees for the fire that needed to be kept going while sleeping in a tent where at night the temperature plunged to almost 50 below, Charlie told the stories of other hunting and trapping trips. The skills he demonstrated helped me learn, bit by bit, what it means to be Dene. That learning path also included participating in community fishing trips around Great Bear Lake and observing the community caribou hunt on the North Shore of the Lake. These experiences shaped my understanding of how we should hold community hearings that were respectful both of Indigenous protocol and the rhythms of the Dene and the Inuvialuit relationships to their lands and waters.

One of those lessons learned was that the timing of community hearings had to accommodate the periods where members of the community were away from the community in their seasonal harvesting. Thus the scheduling of hearings was not just dependent on the availability of charter flights, avoiding conflict with the formal hearings in Yellowknife, but also fitting in with the rhythms of Dene and Inuvialuit harvesting. In several cases, hunters and fishers who were identified by their communities as important witnesses for the hearings were out on the land and ice. In one such case, the inquiry travelled to a Dene fish camp at Willow Lake where the hearing was held in a tepee. On another occasion the Inquiry travelled over the sea ice to an Inuvialuit hunters' camp at North Star Harbour on the Arctic Ocean.

The timing of the hearings was not only dependent on the Indigenous rhythms of the year but also on the appropriate time of the day and night to conduct important business. In contrast to the typical ten-to-four schedule of judicial and formal inquiry hearings, the communities advised me to begin the hearings in the afternoon and continue into the evening. Often, after the day's hearing concluded, the appropriate protocol was to hold a drum or tea dance, inviting Judge Berger, the inquiry staff, pipeline company representatives, and CBC reporters and other media accompanying the Inquiry to participate.

The result was that instead of the typical government consultation which might last a few hours, many of the hearings in the larger communities took place over three days and went on late into the night. On one occasion, the Inquiry traveled by float plane to Willow Lake. After the hearing concluded, Judge Berger and the inquiry team journeyed by canoe downriver to Tulita, arriving well after midnight. Despite the late arrival, they began the hearing in Tulita the following afternoon. At the end of that hearing, Judge Berger reminded me: "It has been a very long day."

Fort McPherson

In the summer of 1974, Judge Berger and I had planned to visit several communities to get an overview of the land and the people before the hearings started. We chose the community of Fort McPherson for one of their first visits. There we were introduced to Chief Johnny Charlie and his wife, Jane. Chief Charlie showed the judge a magnificent home-tanned moose hide. Jane had scraped it with tools made of moose bone and then tanned it over an open fire. The hide would be used to make a jacket, gloves and moccasins for the winter.

Chief Charlie then took us on a trip on the Peel River, the lifeline that carries people to their hunting and fishing camps upriver as far as the Richardson Mountains. During the journey, Johnny Charlie used for the first time a phrase that the Inquiry was to hear many times in the future: "The land is my bank."

His wife, Jane Charlie explained that the phrase is not only a metaphor; the economy of the Gwich'in people is entwined with the land.

> We fish in the summer, lots of fish. Johnny would make big bales of dryfish. I remember one time he made fifteen bales. We'd take it to the store and trade it for flour and sugar. In the spring we'd go down to the Husky River and hunt muskrats, lots of muskrats. I remember I used to skin two hundred a night. We'd make drymeat and eat that. Johnny would go to town with a big bag of muskrat skins, about five hundred muskrat skins, that's what he'd take to the store. We didn't have debts. We'd get all we need from the land.

From our first home base in Fort Franklin (Deline), my family and I moved to Fort McPherson. I was welcomed with

Dene hospitality and my months there became part of my continuing education in Aboriginal rights.

On that first visit Judge Berger and I had been introduced to Sarah Simon, who I learned was one of the most informed historians of Fort McPherson. On my return I spent many evenings with Mrs. Simon and she showed me a remarkable collection of photographs of village life, some black-and-white from before the Second World War but many others dating from the 1950s, recorded on early Kodachrome. It was not a coincidence that Mrs. Simon was among the first Northern residents to use the then new technology of colour photography.

I discovered that historically, Fort McPherson had a long tradition of keeping an open window to developments in the South. During the days of the Klondike Gold Rush in the late 1890s, men from Fort McPherson had journeyed south to Dawson City, which, with a population of over 30,000, was the largest city in Canada west of Winnipeg. They worked in various capacities, providing caribou meat to the mining camps (where the price of meat was fantastically inflated), as stevedores and deckhands on river steamboats, and scow pilots.

A number of these men ventured further south to San Francisco and when they returned to Fort McPherson they brought back with them not only great stories but a knowledge of Yankee technology and frontier culture. With that knowledge came a healthy appreciation of the hazards of the frontier situation. They became known as the 'Dawson Boys'. Sarah Simon represented the contemporary incarnation of that spirit of embracing new technology that enhanced but did not overwhelm Dene values and traditions.

I asked Sarah Simon if she would present a slide show of her photographs at the community hearing, which she graciously agreed to do. This not only gave Judge Berger a sense of the community's history, but opened a photographic window of the personalities who had animated the community through images that many of the young people had not seen before.

Field Workers

Over the next few months, I began to visit villages along the river to tell people about the community hearings that would be held the next year. One of the challenges I faced was to get people to talk to me with any degree of trust. Their experience with southerners coming into the communities was with people who had power over them. So when I told people that I was a lawyer working with Judge Berger, coming to organize the community hearings, people doubted me. With my shoulder-length hair, I didn't look like a lawyer. Instead of wearing a suit, I was wearing an Indigenous Cowichan vest.

In Deline and Fort McPherson, I had been able to overcome that concern because Chief Kodakin and Chief Johnny Charlie accompanied me. But in other communities I didn't have that entree. So I began to introduce myself to the young men and women who were field workers for the Dene Nation. We were working along parallel lines because our purpose was to ensure that we had a plan for the hearings. We worked together. The community hearings were a combination of our collective efforts.

~

A CONVERSATION WITH JOHN T'SELEIE, FIELDWORKER

In order to determine the vast area of land that could be claimed by the Dene, the Indian Brotherhood of the NWT began work on a Land Use and Occupancy Study. The study gave Dene young people, returning to their communities after years in residential school, the opportunity to immerse themselves in the history of their people

"There's an old fish camp, that's where I was born. In the summer, people used to go to fish camps. They would make dryfish all summer and store enough fish for dog feed for the winter.

In the fall they would head out to trapping areas from October to

Christmas. They might not stay in one place the whole time. They would move around, the men trapping and hunting moose. In those days, nobody stayed in the village in the winter.

My parents were traditional. My step-father didn't speak English, he was unilingual. My mom went to residential school. She could speak English and French. But they lived a traditional Dene life so that's all I was exposed to. In the summertime, we went to fish camp with them. We'd haul wood, fish and water, do all kinds of chores. That's how I grew up. You can't take that out of me.

I never remember seeing much money. I only learned about money after I became a teenager. We never really had any use for it when I was growing up. We might have five or ten cents, enough for a pop at the Hudson's Bay store. I remember one year trapping squirrels, selling fourteen. I got seven dollars, which was a lot of money in those days. I had candies for quite a while after that.

I went on a barge with my older sister. At first I wanted to get on the barge for a ride, that was all that was in my head. But once it left, I knew it was going to be for a long time. There's a big bend and I remember looking back and seeing the community disappear and feeling sad. The other kids in the barge, they were looking back and crying. Still today I feel sad.

Two or three days passed and we made it to the school in Aklavik, a strange environment. We had to get washed up, our hair cut. We had to turn in all our clothes. We slept in one big dorm, heated by wood. The food was not very good. Some of that time I can't remember. I think my memory wiped it out.

Years later, when I came back from university, Georges Erasmus was working for the Indian Brotherhood, now the Dene Nation. He hired me for the community development program. The Indian Brotherhood was still a very young organization. It had just started in 1969 so it was four years old, a group of about twenty people, maybe twenty-five. Some of the non-Dene staff had expertise in activism and social change, so we learned a lot from working with them.

When I worked for the Indian Brotherhood I had some really good experiences. They assigned me to do land use research, about how the Dene people used the land. I got to talk to a lot of Elders in the Sahtu. I'm happy that I had a chance to meet up with those respected Elders: Paul Baton, Chief

George Kodakin. They talked to me about everything. I remember an Elder whose name was Albert Menicoche. I went to see him at his house with maps and a tape recorder and explained to him what we were doing, what it was for. I pulled a map out and he said: "What's that?" I told him: "It's a map of Great Bear Lake."

He said: "I don't know anything about maps but I can tell you about the lake." He talked for half an hour, explaining the shape of Great Bear Lake and he described it exactly as it was on the map. He drew it with his hands. Really detailed knowledge.

When we put all the maps together, it showed the Dene were using a huge area of the land. That didn't surprise me. The idea was to illustrate visually what we all knew. Many of those routes are still there. You can see one of the trails on Google Earth. They are not big but they are stamped into the earth. But you have to know where to look. I've walked those trails myself, so I knew where to find them.

Part of my work was to prepare Fort Good Hope for the Berger hearings. It was my job to go out and tell people about the hearings, in their own language. We talked about what a pipeline could do. We identified Elders who could contribute. People would say: 'That person is knowledgeable.'

This is where we come from as Dene people. The Mackenzie River is our homeland. I think Indigenous people have much to offer Canadians: how we view the land and environment, how we want to take care of it. We have a spiritual way of looking at land, water, animals. We have respect. Today, when we look at the impact of climate change, that can help."

~

A CONVERSATION WITH ELIZABETH HARDISTY

"In the summer months, when there was no school, I would go to my parents' camp at Rabbitskin. My mother would take me and my brothers and sisters on the Mackenzie River, the Dehcho. We would go by canoe farther up the river, and set nets and go berry picking.

My parents lived in town for a while but they decided to go back trapping. It was hard to make a living in the wage economy. In those days the kids were put in residential schools so we learned to be educated, but we didn't learn about hunting and trapping. We just spoke English. We lost our language so we couldn't communicate with our parents who spoke Dene. So there was a breakdown in communication. Parents were grief-stricken. They lost their children.

I went away to college in the 1970s, and when I came back, Georges Erasmus offered jobs to young people who had finished high school, as fieldworkers and community development workers. I worked for the Dene Nation, doing Land Use mapping for the Dehcho region. There was a workshop for a month for the Mackenzie Valley. All the fieldworkers were trained how to map and how to ask questions.

It was exciting going to the communities and talking to the Elders, interviewing them in our language, encouraging them to share their stories. We went and visited the hunters. We had the maps of the area and asked them where they had trapped and what land area they used. We coded the maps accordingly: what kind of animals they hunted. Then we drew the lines where they trapped and travelled. The areas that people used the most would be dark. It was like the spokes on a wheel.

The hunters and trappers told us stories about where they were raised, the cabins they used, where they found game and fish. In summer they travelled on the rivers and sometimes they portaged. Some people travelled quite a distance. William Antoine was raised across the river, about 90 miles away. When they walked back to town it took two days.

The Dene Nation used those Land Use maps at the Berger Inquiry to verify how vastly the land was used by the Dene. When we went to the hearing in Yellowknife, we put the map on the wall. Once you put it all together it was like a huge net.

The Land Use mapping was worthwhile because it gave some breathing room to the Dene. More people in the communities could get on board for a land claims settlement.

The maps were a bridge from the older generation to my generation. We were a conduit for the knowledge of the Elders. "

CHAPTER SEVEN

UNDER CROSS-EXAMINATION

Drew Ann Wake

~

IN EARLY 1974, lawyer Ian Waddell received a call from Judge Berger, asking him to drop by the judge's chambers at the Vancouver courthouse. Ian assumed Tom wanted to wrap up some final details of the Family Law Commission which had recently concluded. But when he arrived, the judge had a surprise. Berger showed him a stack of boxes and said: "I've just been appointed by Prime Minister Pierre Trudeau to be Commissioner of the Mackenzie Valley Pipeline Inquiry."

The boxes sitting in the office contained the application from Canadian Arctic Gas Pipelines (CAGPL) to build a pipeline to bring Alaskan natural gas across the Arctic coast to the Mackenzie Delta, then south to the US Midwest. "We pulled the boxes open and saw a great pile of reports and papers." Ian remembered that it looked daunting. "Then, Tom asked me to work with him, so I guess I was the Inquiry's first employee."

Ian Waddell pointed out that they didn't really know much about the North. But Berger said: "Well, when we started working on the Family Law Commission we didn't know much about unified courts. We'll learn." When Ian asked how they were going to start, Berger replied: "I want you to go up to Yellowknife and get us some offices. How about tomorrow?"

Ian Waddell flew to Yellowknife and began his search for office space. By luck he met a man who worked for the

Department of Indian Affairs and Northern Development. He said: "There's an old building owned by DIAND over there. Check it out." Ian found the building, an old wooden structure a few blocks from the main street. It was empty so he arranged for it to become the office for the new inquiry.

Many years later, Ian laughed when he recalled that he had quickly found himself in hot water with the federal government. "When I made the letterhead for the Commission it read: Principal Office: Yellowknife, Branch Office: Ottawa."

First Steps
The pipeline companies had submitted an enormous volume of research on every aspect of the proposed pipeline construction. There were engineering studies detailing where and how a pipeline would be constructed across the frozen tundra. Biologists had written twenty-four volumes reviewing potential impacts on the land and wildlife. A three-volume socio-economic study detailed the benefits that would come from the jobs that would be created.

Tom Berger was determined that the Inquiry would put this research under careful review. To do that, he needed a team that would thoroughly examine the pipeline proposal and relentlessly cross-examine the witnesses who appeared before the Inquiry.

The first task was to hire a Commission Counsel to prepare for a demanding set of hearings. Tom Berger felt that the commission should hire a legal firm from Toronto. In those days, Vancouver sat in the fringe of the Canadian legal community; a Toronto law firm would be closer to the seat of economic and political power. Ian Waddell recommended Ian Scott and Stephen Goudge, two bright young lawyers he had known since his university days. "I was relieved when the judge agreed to bring them out for a meeting because I had already bought their plane tickets."

The meeting of the four lawyers went smoothly and Ian Scott was hired as Commission Counsel for the Inquiry. They agreed on an approach: to promote a rigorous examination of the pipeline plans, key stakeholders in the process—the environmental organizations and Indigenous groups—would have to participate fully. These organizations would have to receive funding to hire lawyers, prepare their research and call their own witnesses.

But the Inquiry needed the approval of the federal government to fund intervenors, so Tom Berger and Ian Waddell flew to Ottawa to meet with Jean Chrétien, the Minister of Indian Affairs and Northern Development. Chrétien arrived at the meeting with two Englishmen, his Deputy Minister E. Digby Hunt and the Assistant Deputy Minister.

Ian Waddell remembered that the opening minutes of the meeting did not go well.

Berger said: 'We want funding for environmental groups so they can hire a lawyer.' Hunt replied: 'No. We can't give them money.' Then the assistant Deputy Minister said, out of turn: 'In England they have barristers and solicitors, so we could fund a solicitor for research.' Chrétien said, 'That's what we'll do. Fund the environmental group and call it research.'

After the meeting with the Minister, Tom Berger asked to meet with a group of twenty researchers from various government departments who had been appointed to review the application and determine if there were areas of weakness. They were well along in their assignment when Tom Berger and Ian Waddell asked whether they would be interested in working with the Inquiry. Tom Berger told the researchers what he had discussed with the Minister—the Inquiry would bring a range of witnesses to encourage a thorough examination of the ideas before the Inquiry. "Half of them couldn't handle it. They didn't want to work for the Inquiry," Ian Waddell remembered later.

The other half recognized that an inquiry that encouraged dialogue and debate would give them much more freedom to conduct their research. One of those was Ed Weick, a career civil servant.

> When the pipeline application was made, we were asked to evaluate the proposal, to determine the impacts a pipeline might have, environmentally and socially. We were, of course, being watched quite closely. The government wanted a positive answer. We put together a book called the Mackenzie Valley Assessment. We had to conclude the pipeline was a good idea. We had done a good job for the government but we didn't feel we could say what we wanted to say, think what we wanted to think.

For that reason, Ed Weick was keen to work on the Inquiry: it would offer a broader opportunity for debate. Even then, he felt some pressure from Ottawa.

> What the government didn't understand was: we couldn't build this pipeline without a better understanding of the impact on the environment, on Aboriginal rights to the land. The government didn't want to accept that. But in the end, they had to.

It had taken months of careful negotiation, but the framework for the inquiry was set. This Inquiry would not rubber-stamp the proposal from the pipeline companies. Each aspect of the hearings, covering the engineering, environmental and socio-economic impacts of the pipeline, would be scrutinized. Lawyers would represent groups with markedly different perspectives. The cross-examination promised to draw out key issues that would have to be addressed before plans for a pipeline could move forward.

Setting the Stage

The formal hearings of the Berger Inquiry were held in the ballroom of the Explorer Hotel, a location normally reserved for weddings and the annual New Year's Eve Ball. For the hearings, the judge was seated in front of curtains with a bright blue design. The five legal teams fanned out in front of him, each at its own table. Judge Berger began the first day of the formal hearings with a phrase that was more poetic than legal: "We are embarked on a consideration of the future of a great river valley and its people."

Commission Counsel Ian Scott rose to state that the Inquiry would unfold in phases. First, they would examine the engineering aspects of the pipeline proposal, how it would affect the land and sea. This would be followed by an evaluation of the impact the pipeline would have on the living environment and key wildlife species. Finally, the Inquiry would examine the social and economic impacts of a pipeline. He concluded: "With some trepidation, we are prepared to begin."

Pierre Genest, the lawyer for Canadian Arctic Gas Pipelines Ltd., was the first to address the inquiry. He pointed out that the twenty companies that had joined to form the consortium had spent in excess of $75 million dollars, "to carry out what I can call, without hesitation, the most extensive and thorough preliminary engineering, environmental, and sociological study ever given to any project anywhere." The cost of building the pipeline was estimated to be $7 billion dollars.

The prime route chosen by CAGPL was composed of two pipelines that would carry natural gas a distance of 2,435 miles. One line would travel eastward from Alaska across the North Slope of the Yukon. The other would carry natural gas from the Mackenzie Delta. The two lines would join at Travaillant Lake, to the east of the Mackenzie River, and head south to Alberta.

But, Genest said, if this prime route was ruled out, CAGPL had studied a second possibility. The Interior route ran through more difficult terrain: from the Brooks mountain range of

Alaska, across Yukon border, and through the Richardson mountains to Travaillant Lake. A third possibility had been reviewed: the Cross-Delta route would transport the natural gas from Alaska across the myriad small lakes of Shallow Bay, where the Mackenzie reaches the Beaufort Sea.

By studying three possible pipeline routes, the CAGPL consortium had hedged its bets. Surely the Inquiry would approve one of them.

CAGPL's socio-economic argument could be summed up in a single word: Jobs. Genest framed the impact of the pipeline crisply: "The hard fact is that without some sort of economic development, this land—this Northern land, enormous, beautiful, and awe-inspiring as it is—is not now supporting the population of the Northwest Territories." The consortium was offering a sound and stable economic base. With this brief speech, Genest had laid out the argument that CAGPL would follow for the next eighteen months.

The second lawyer to address the Inquiry was Reg Gibbs, who represented the competing pipeline applicant, Foothills Pipelines. This company had been created a short time before when two leading Canadian transmission companies, Alberta Gas Trunk and Westcoast Transmission, left the CAGPL consortium. Gibbs admitted that Foothills was not yet a formal pipeline applicant but promised that its application would be filed by the end of the month.

Gibbs' opening remarks were filled with nationalist rhetoric. How could Canada's energy needs be met? Not by CAGPL, which had only five Canadian companies among its twenty corporate members. Their primary interest was to meet the American demand for natural gas. Gibbs argued that Canadian needs were better served by a pipeline that would supply natural gas to Canadian consumers. "Why not build—at a quarter of the cost—a smaller line, just far enough to connect with existing systems in Alberta and British Columbia?" he asked.

The environmental organizations from across Canada had joined forces with the Canadian Arctic Resources Committee to make their legal argument. Their lawyer was Russell Anthony who had spent several years trying to get the courts to allow environmental intervenors to appear. "In the early 1970s, getting environmental evidence into hearings was very difficult," he recalled. "The hearings were between government and industry, and the public was not invited to participate." One time Anthony had travelled to Yukon for a hearing on the Asiak dam, which threatened the Asiak Falls and a burial ground of archaeological importance. He made the long road trip, bunked down on the floor of a sympathetic local host and appeared at the hearing the next day. But he was denied the opportunity to speak. Now, only a few years later, the Berger Inquiry was giving him the opportunity to intervene on the most important environmental issue in the country.

Russ Anthony began his opening statement by quoting a recent comment by Prime Minister Trudeau, that Canada was experiencing a loss of faith in government.

> The Prime Minister is surely right to identify this growing cynicism. A review of resource development decisions demonstrates however that his own government must bear a great deal of the responsibility for the creation of this mistrust.... We do not believe that policies should be made behind closed doors and then 'sold' to the public.

As an example, he pointed to news that the Cabinet had recently instructed its ministries not to play a role in the Mackenzie Valley Pipeline Inquiry. Researchers were to stop preparing questions for Commission Counsel to raise in the hearings. Anthony described this as "unthinkable." The next day, the Inquiry team joined him in petitioning the government to reverse that instruction. Two weeks later the Inquiry received a letter from the Minister of the Environment, Jeanne Sauvé in Ottawa. The government acquiesced: the bridge between the Inquiry and government researchers would remain open. At the very beginning of the Inquiry, the environmental movement had found its voice.

Judge Berger had also requested funds so that the Indigenous organizations could be represented at the hearings. He thought they would choose high-profile lawyers, perhaps Queens Counsel. But the organizations wanted to hire lawyers who would understand their point of view. Dene Nation and the Métis Association chose Glen Bell who had worked for the Canadian Civil Liberties Association. Glen Bell said:

> It was a lawyer's dream. It was in-depth work. You could get to understand the topic you were working on, unlike most legal cases where you dealt with an individual problem, closed the file and moved on.

When Bell rose to give his opening remarks at the inquiry, he too criticized a recent statement by the Prime Minister.

> Perhaps you will recall the occasion when Prime Minister Trudeau compared the Mackenzie Valley pipeline favourably to the building of the CPR. What the Prime Minister neglected to mention at the time he made that comparison was the fact that for the Indigenous people of southern Canada, the CPR was a disaster. It meant the loss of their land and the slaughter of the buffalo herd upon which their livelihood depended. It is with a view to avoiding this fate that the Indigenous people of the North will take the position before this inquiry that there should be no pipeline before a land claims settlement.

The organization that represented the Inuvialuit people of the Mackenzie Delta, the Committee for Original Peoples

Entitlement, had chosen a lawyer from Yellowknife, John Bayly, to represent them at the Inquiry. In contrast to the other lawyers, Bayly had moved North permanently and had adopted a Northern lifestyle. He lived with his family in a cabin on the outskirts of Yellowknife and was often seen racing through the forest on a sled pulled by his team of dogs.

Bayly too presented an argument that focused on a land claim. He pointed out that the land that was being considered for the pipeline belonged to the Inuvialuit people. No treaties had been signed, no rights had been given away. Negotiations, he insisted, should come first. "COPE and the Inuit Tapirisat of Canada do not wish to see their people placed in the position of having to negotiate in the shadow of a partially completed mammoth project."

At the end of the first week, five lawyers had spoken and many divergent positions had been staked. No one envied the judge who would have to find a path through the conflicting opinions.

Engineering

A mere two weeks after the formal hearings began, the idea of encouraging rigorous cross-examination underwent its first test. On March 21, CAGPL assembled a panel of engineers to explain their plan to construct a pipeline across the frozen Arctic terrain. The companies planned to bury the pipe, but that raised a contentious issue: natural gas flowing through a buried pipeline would thaw the permafrost in the ground surrounding the pipeline. So the companies proposed to refrigerate the gas. But the permafrost along the pipeline was not continuous: when the chilled gas pipeline passed through areas without permafrost, the cooled temperatures would produce 'frost bulbs' in the surrounding soil. These ice blocks would push the pipeline slowly upward until the steel pipe ruptured, a process called frost heave.

The CAGPL panel of engineers explained the research that had gone into studying frost heave. Dr. William Slusarchuk presented a slide show illustrating the work underway at a research facility in Calgary. A model of the pipeline had been built to observe the process by which the ice bulbs formed. Then experiments had been conducted by burying four 12-metre lengths of pipe at different depths. Gravel was placed over the pipe so the researchers could study the growth of the frost bulbs. The research team also conducted laboratory tests to ascertain how water was drawn into the soil and how ice lenses developed.

They concluded that the problem of frost heave could be resolved. "The results of the field test site, the model box and the laboratory field test clearly show that the rate of heave is significantly reduced as the load in the frost front increases." The researchers concluded that the frost heave could be controlled if the pipe were buried beneath at least six metres of gravel.

When Pierre Genest, the lawyer for Canadian Arctic Gas Pipelines, began to question the witnesses on their evidence, Commission Counsel Ian Scott rose to complain that Genest's questions did not clarify the pipeline engineers' complex evidence. Genest snapped back that the Commission had its own scientific team: they could clarify the information. But Ian Scott interrupted: "It seems to me that there is some obligation for him to attempt to make some of this comprehensible. If not, it is pointless."

Judge Berger stepped in. He reminded the lawyers that the hearings had to be understood by a general audience. He made an analogy to the complex language used by the legal community. "If lawyers here started talking about *res ipsa loquitur* and *caveat emptor*, you and I who believe in putting these things plainly, as plain men, would soon put a stop to it." He asked all of the lawyers to ask questions that would clarify the issues so that the hearing could engage in a meaningful discussion.

This proved to be a key moment in the Inquiry. From then on, the lawyers were careful to examine their witnesses in a way that could be understood, not only by other lawyers but by the reporters who were carrying news from the Inquiry to the Canadian public.

The issue of frost heave was revisited unexpectedly at a hearing many months later. Judge Berger had just suggested a coffee break and lawyers were heading out of the hearing room. Pierre Genest rose from his seat, looking anxious, and asked the judge if he could have a moment of his time. As the two men spoke, an expression of concern spread over Judge Berger's face.

When the lawyers returned to their seats, Berger announced that Canadian Arctic Gas Pipelines had informed him that they had discovered a fault in the equipment that had been used for their experiments on frost heave. The frost heave data from CAGPL could not be relied upon. The room fell silent as the lawyers absorbed the fact that for months the issue of frost heave had been debated based on faulty evidence.

But the hearing process that Judge Berger had insisted on had worked. The evidence had been explored from multiple perspectives, in terms that everyone could understand. Frost heave had become an issue debated not only in a distant hearing room in Yellowknife, but in corporate boardrooms and college classrooms across Canada.

Environmental Hearings

The lawyers were on more familiar footing when the environmental hearings began. Key evidence in this phase dealt with the impact of the proposed pipeline on the Porcupine caribou herd, about 115,000 animals that migrate across a vast terrain between northern Yukon and Alaska. At different times of the year, the herd crossed both of the proposed pipeline routes, so it was vital for CAGPL to show that the herd would not be endangered by the pipeline.

In 1971, CAGPL hired a team of wildlife biologists to begin field studies on the herd. The team leader, Ron Jakimchuk, recalled that when the research began the scientific community had only a fragmentary understanding of the Porcupine caribou herd. The herd's territory was so remote, and its migration was so vast, that most of the information was anecdotal.

The biologists set up a research base in Old Crow, a remote Gwich'in community in northern Yukon. Ron Jakimchuk recalled that 1971 was a rough-and-ready time for biologists. "We were given a notebook, a pencil and a pair of binoculars. We jumped into a helicopter and were transported to a camp. It was: 'See you in ten days.' We were on our own."

From March to October they studied the differences in the behaviour of the caribou, male and female, young and old. They tracked the migration route as the herd left their winter range in the mountains and headed for the calving grounds on the North Slope of Yukon. The goal was to assess how the two pipeline routes, one across the North Slope and the other through the mountains, might impact the herd.

After their first season on the land, the biologists proposed a departure from the usual methodology: they would conduct experimental studies to determine how caribou would react to the noise produced by pipeline compressor stations across the wilderness. These studies, in Jakimchuk's view, were both "innovative and pioneering." They constructed a simulator that emitted all the noise frequencies of a compressor station. The machine was transported to a spot along the migration route and the biologists settled in to observe the reaction of the herd. Jakimchuk recorded that the response to the noise was limited; the caribou remained at a distance of about 200 metres from the simulator.

As Jakimchuk drew closer to the day when he would give evidence before the inquiry, he became increasingly worried. He recalled,

> It was adversarial. There were conservation groups, the
> government, Aboriginal intervenors and the academic

community, all asking questions. And the Commission Counsel. They were pros: lawyers who knew how to cross-examine. You had to be forthright, but you had to be accurate.

In his evidence, Ron Jakimchuk presented a slide show with maps and graphs that illustrated the advantages and disadvantages of the two primary pipeline routes. He stated a clear preference for the pipeline route along the north coast of Alaska and Yukon. He pointed out that construction would take place in winter, so the pipeline companies could access the construction sites by driving on ice roads instead of on the tundra. He admitted that the coastal route would go through the calving grounds, but noted that pipeline construction was scheduled for completion by May 1, prior to the time that calving and migration would take place. The plan mandated that compressor stations would be built in summer, every seventy kilometres along the pipeline route, but he recommended that strict measures be put in place to control vehicular traffic, aircraft flights, and construction activities.

Jakimchuk also provided a list of disadvantages of the Interior route: it crossed the path of the spring and fall migrations, as well as the winter range in Alaska and the Richardson Mountains. The Interior route would also pass through the Old Crow Flats, a critical hunting and fishing area for the Gwich'in people.

He concluded that an Arctic Gas pipeline along the North Slope route posed few risks to the Porcupine herd. "It is in fact my expectation that actual losses or effects attributable to the pipeline, both short and long-term, will be negligible."

Jakimchuk's evidence disturbed the Canadian Arctic Resources Committee. Their lawyer, Russ Anthony described the Porcupine caribou herd as "an international treasure." He worried that in the summer months, even a minor disruption could have a catastrophic impact on the herd. To make his case, he invited George Calef to testify. Calef, too, had just completed a three-year caribou research study and had reached very different conclusions from those of Jakimchuk and his team.

Calef gives an amusing interpretation of his decision to become a wildlife biologist. "I had the misfortune to grow up in Chicago, and by the time I was six years old, I knew I was in the wrong place. All I wanted was to be a mountain man, a hunter and a fisherman, as far from Chicago as I could get." He trained to become an oceanographer at the University of British Columbia, with a focus on zooplankton. His doctoral thesis was written on frogs and salamanders. But when a job came up doing caribou research for the Environmental Protection Agency in the Arctic, he was intrigued. "I didn't know much about aerial surveys, so I had to kind of fake it."

Two weeks after getting the job he was in Whitehorse, getting on a helicopter to fly to Inuvik.

> In the whole 550-mile flight, we only crossed one road. The electrical generator in the helicopter went out so we had to cut everything off, including the heater. When we got to Inuvik, it was 49 below zero - on April 1. I thought it was a great adventure.

Calef's job was to monitor the caribou migrations, to understand which routes they followed in their journey from Alaska across the Yukon, as far east as the Mackenzie Delta. The researchers used aircraft to follow the herd, ski planes in winter, floats in summer. They camped out on the land. He was enthralled.

> Caribou are one of the most beautiful hooved animals and they make the greatest land migration in the world. The distances they travel are on the scale of bird migrations. And the numbers! There are herds estimated at a million animals.

Calef also created a list of the advantages and disadvantages of the two pipeline routes, but his conclusions were opposite to those of Jakimchuk's team. He emphasized the disadvantages of the coastal pipeline route. He estimated the summer calving ground to be an area of 4,000 square kilometres, while the land in the interior that the caribou used for wintering and migration comprised some 150,000 square kilometres. On the coastal route, the animals would be in contact with the pipeline and attendant noise for two months. On the Interior route, they would be surrounded by noise for two weeks.

Calef concluded that the coastal pipeline route should be rejected. Years later, he summed up his conclusions:

> The pipeline companies favoured the coastal route because it was shorter. But the coastal plain is small, especially the cotton grass plain along the coast of the Yukon, and it's much richer. You have marine mammals. You have big colonies of nesting birds. Most importantly, you have the calving ground of the Porcupine caribou herd. Any animal would be able to sense industry at a much greater distance on the coast than in the forest.

The most sensitive time in the migration would be the aggregation, a two-week period in the summer when the caribou come together in a single magnificent herd.

> These herds are under stress at the time, mosquitoes, warble flies and botflies attack them relentlessly. The energy demands for antler growth, moulting and nursing are at the maximum.... Calves are dying from exhaustion, accidents, predation...."

He said 40 percent of the calves die from these factors in July and concluded that any disturbance, such as a pipeline, would increase the stress level for the calves at a sensitive time.

Calef also expressed sharp views on the field experiments that the pipeline companies had funded, questioning whether the experiment could accurately mimic the disturbance caused by a pipeline. He pointed out that a compressor station consists of a large gravel pad, several buildings, and noise so loud it rattles the ground. Crews of men come and go in vehicles and helicopters.

He addressed his question to the judge directly: "Now I ask, Mr. Commissioner, is a small loudspeaker system producing compressor station noise in any way a simulation of the total impact of a compressor station on caribou?"

Calef concluded:

> I do not think we are in a position to say that the proposed CAGPL pipeline will not produce or contribute to similar declines in the Porcupine herd. When we're dealing with 115,000 animals, with one of the last wildlife spectacles on the face of the earth, with a very important part of the culture, the history and the current well-being of the Indigenous peoples who have inhabited this continent for the last 25,000 years, with the representatives of a group of animals whose lives have been a part of the world of human beings for tens of thousands of years, both here and in Eurasia, I feel that we have an awesome responsibility to proceed slowly and cautiously with projects which may ultimately destroy them.

So the inquiry heard the testimony of two experienced biologists. Both had immersed themselves in the field studies, both had presented reasoned arguments, but their conclusions were diametrically opposed. The fate of the Porcupine caribou herd hung in the balance.

Socio-economic hearings

The Calgary-based pipeline company competing for the Arctic pipeline, Alberta Gas Trunk Lines, recognized that the industry would benefit from a study illustrating the socio-economic benefits that a pipeline would bring. Gemini North was chosen to do the research. The company was owned by Pat Carney who had left her job as a business reporter at the *Vancouver Sun* to open a Yellowknife firm specializing in economic analysis. Alberta Gas Trunk Lines' CEO, Bob Blair, asked Gemini North to assess the impacts, both positive and negative, of a pipeline on both Indigenous and non-Indigenous people in the north.

The most important issue to tackle was an assessment of the number of jobs that might be created by pipeline construction. In an interim report prepared for the territorial government in 1972, Gemini North determined that 17,500 jobs would be created. The majority of these, 14,100 jobs, would be in preparing the right-of-way and in the construction of roads and airstrips. In an addendum, they noted that many of the jobs would be "of a seasonal or temporary nature."

Gemini North also collected data to determine how the pipeline construction might affect the existing economy of the Indigenous communities. To gather this data, Pat Carney and her team set off on a tour of the villages along the river. They visited the Hudson's Bay managers to collect information about the furs that were trapped and the income this produced. They asked the RCMP for information about social problems, such as alcohol and family violence, that might be affected by pipeline construction.

In each village, they held a meeting where residents sat in a circle around Pat Carney as she described the pipeline. Maps were placed on the floor and residents were encouraged to examine potential pipeline routes and describe the impacts construction might have on their traditional hunting, fishing and trapping. The Gemini researchers asked hunters to describe how many days each month were spent on the land. They used this measurement to divide hunters into groups: those who hunted full-time, part-time and those who were 'recreational hunters'.

This division, adopted from analyses of wage work in the south, led the Gemini team to conclude that very few Northerners were living from land-based activities. Pat Carney made a dour prediction about the future.

> It was a myth that the Indigenous people could live off the land. They could live part-time on the land, and some of them did, but because of the loss of hunting and trapping skills, because they were losing the Elders who taught the skills, the future was in wage employment.

At the community meetings, the Gemini North team encountered a problem. As Pat Carney recalled: "One of our difficulties was to explain natural gas. You couldn't see it, you couldn't smell it and you couldn't feel it." So she asked the pipeline engineers to build a working model that the Gemini team could transport in the tail of the Twin Otter that took them from community to community. The model showed the process of transporting natural gas from a miniature wellhead, through a pipeline to a tiny building that represented a cleaning facility. Then the gas went to a hot plate. With a flourish, Pat Carney would put a match to the gas and bring a kettle to a boil. Audiences in the remote communities would breathe an astonished: "Ahhh".

The strategy seemed to be working until the Gemini North team headed to the Gwich'in community of Old Crow, which sat in the path of the proposed Interior pipeline route. This village had maintained its traditional reliance on food from the land, living from fish in the rivers and the annual migration of the Porcupine caribou herd. But Old Crow families relied on wood stoves, and the supply of timber in the immediate area was slowly depleting. The Gemini team believed that the idea of a natural gas pipeline, running past the community, would be well received. But the Old Crow presentation did not go as planned. Pat Carney recalled:

> Unfortunately, by the time we reached [Old Crow] the model had bounced around the Twin Otter through many rocky landings on icy airstrips. So when I lit the match, the whole model burst into flame. The people cried: 'Ayiii!' And I knew we'd lost Old Crow.

The final report from Gemini North was released in six volumes, a total of 2,200 pages. But during the four years it had taken to write the report, Gemini North's client had changed. Alberta Gas Trunk Lines had joined forces with American pipeline companies to form the consortium, Canadian Arctic Gas Pipeline Limited. In its submission to the Berger Inquiry, CAGPL promoted only the positive conclusions of the study. Pat Carney recalled:

> The big companies discounted the social impacts and were pushing the economic benefits. Our client was loathe to portray the costs. They presented only the parts of the report that favoured the pipeline.

Meanwhile, a few blocks from the Gemini North offices, researchers at the Indian Brotherhood of the Northwest Territories were ramping up their own study. After the Calder case concluded, the federal government had changed its stance on land claims and announced that it would fund Indigenous organizations to lay the groundwork for comprehensive claims. There was one caveat. The claims would have to be accompanied by a Land Use and Occupancy Study, showing both how the First Nation had traditionally used the land and how it continued to do so.

The Dene Land Use and Occupancy Study was a dramatic contrast to the research that had been conducted by Gemini North. It did not add up the days that a Dene hunter spent on the land. Instead, the researchers conducted in-depth interviews with Dene hunters and trappers about the activities they had engaged in over a lifetime spent in the bush.

Phoebe Nahanni, who played a leading role in the study, described the goal of the project.

> We wanted to gather information that could be represented on maps to show all the lands we have occupied as far back as anyone can remember, and also the situation at present: how we used and use the land and what the land means to us today.

The Dene recruited teams of fieldworkers in communities across the Northwest Territories. They consulted with the chiefs to select a representative sample of 30 percent of the hunters and trappers in the community to be interviewed for the study. In the end, more than three hundred interviews were conducted.

There appeared to be only one drawback to the approach: hunters and trappers spent much of their time on the land so the researchers often had to wait weeks or months for them to return to the communities. Phoebe Nahanni noted the irony.

> The greatest frustration we faced in data collection was the difficulty in locating the men we wished to interview. Much of the time they were in the bush trapping and were inaccessible to our researchers. This minor frustration was, of course, far outweighed by its positive aspect: the men's absence was additional empirical proof of the widespread, continued use of the land that we had set out to document.

In Fort McPherson, Neil Colin was asked to lead the

project because he had a strong grasp of the Gwich'in language and was familiar with the Peel River and its tributaries. He began by interviewing hunters and trappers, marking the routes they travelled on maps. One of the maps illustrated the journeys of his father, Christopher Colin, who had been born in the 1880s. The Elder described his travels west into the Richardson Mountains, north as far as the Tuktoyaktuk Peninsula and south along the Mackenzie River as far as Fort Good Hope. The final map of his journeys was covered with a net of lines tracing pathways across a vast territory: 400 kilometres north to south and 300 kilometres east to west.

The researchers used a code to identify the wildlife that could be found in specific places on the land. "M" was a spot where moose could be found, while "m" marked an area known for muskrats.

"You could see our land, right there in front of your eyes," said Neil Colin. Whereas maps produced by the pipeline companies showed large swaths of empty land, the Dene maps were criss-crossed with detail. Neil Colin believed that detailed mapping was important for young people. "Every creek, every hill. That way our Gwich'in names for these places won't die away."

The Indian Brotherhood office also recruited young Dene in their twenties to participate in the Land Use and Occupancy study. As children, they had been sent to residential school, so their experience on the land was not as deep as that of the older men. But many of them were returning from colleges and universities in the south and were anxious to immerse themselves in their communities again.

One of those young fieldworkers was Ruth Carroll:

The Dene asked me to go to a workshop. Lawyers showed us a map, where the pipeline would be laid, where the construction camps would be set up. Back at home, we went around to visit the Elders. Nobody had phones, so we would drop in. I would always speak Gwich'in, our language. I'd lay out a map and the Elders would stand around the table. They'd notice something and point to it. You could see the excitement.

Ruth was glad she had been forced to learn shorthand in high school because the skill helped her keep notes of the conversation going on around the table.

We would ask: Where is your trapping area? They would say: Way up the river, around Caribou River or Wind River. Or around Hungry Lake, that's a wonderful place where you can't go hungry. Every place name was marked down. Neil Colin would say: What did you do there? And the Elders would laugh and talk. Slowly we developed a map with those place names, thanks to the hard work of those people.

Each community forwarded maps to the office in Yellowknife where the trails and traplines were painstakingly transferred to on a master map some four metres wide. The traditional lands occupied by the Dene people grew darker as thousands of lines traced the fish rivers, the traplines and forest trails.

In April of 1976, the map was transported to the hearing room at the Explorer Hotel where it was hung above the table where the Dene fieldworkers were to sit. The panel that gave evidence about the Land Use and Occupancy study was led by Phoebe Nahanni from the Dene Nation office. Her conclusions were an emphatic rebuke of the Gemini North study. The data showed that there were 1,075 Dene families actively engaged on the land.

The Land Use and Occupancy panel included field workers from four different areas of the north. Neil Colin had planned to make the journey from Fort McPherson, but the hearing was scheduled for April when the lucrative muskrat hunting season was in full swing. As if to illustrate Phoebe Nahanni's point, he was not able to appear on a panel describing Dene life on the land … because he was out on the land.

In his stead, the Dene invited another of the McPherson fieldworkers, 40-year-old Charlie Snowshoe. Charlie framed his evidence by telling the story of his own life, pointing out on the huge map the long journeys he had made.

As a boy, Charlie had been sent to residential school in Aklavik. But at fifteen he was kicked out for telling a supervisor: "Go to hell." The following fall, Charlie's father took him out on the land to teach him traditional skills. They travelled along the Peel River and its tributary, the Snake. Then, they followed a creek to a lake where they made camp. Charlie's father described how to trap marten. Then he sent his son out on his own to practice the skill.

> My father told me to cross that lake in a straight line. I was a greenhorn in the bush at that time, so I crossed that lake like he told me, and I started walking. But instead of making a straight line, I made a circle. That was my first experience with trapping.

The lessons continued over the next year as father and son trapped over a vast area. After Christmas, they left the Snake River and travelled 200 kilometres back to McPherson. Then they travelled northwest, to the Rat River, where they trapped until Easter. Then in March, they walked deep into the Mackenzie Delta. These journeys were made on snowshoes in winter and by boat in summer. At the end of the first year, the pair began to travel by dogteam. They took a well-travelled route from McPherson to Old Crow through the Richardson Mountains into Yukon. "We travelled all winter, barely feeding the dogs, and we never gave up," Charlie recalled.

Step by step, Charlie learned the skills practiced by his father's generation.

In the old days, they weren't only great hunters, they were great fishermen because they had to feed the dogteams. In springtime, they hunted muskrats. Then they dried the muskrat carcasses and made enough dog feed to last into July.

Charlie mastered the skills of a trapper and in time married Mary Effie Pascal. They settled into life in Fort McPherson and had six children.

Charlie established a trap line near the Pascal family's fish camp at Scraper Hill, on the bank of the Peel River. Years later, he remembered the day when that quiet life changed dramatically.

Between Christmas and New Years I had to go up and check my traps and my wife went with me. When we got up below the camp there was smoke on the bank. That was a surprise because everyone was in town for Christmas. I went up the bank and there was a big wide road, ploughed. I said: 'What the heck is going on?'

When Charlie got closer, he spotted a truck, with smoke from the exhaust trailing up into the air. He approached a workman to ask what they were doing. The man replied simply: 'Seismic line.' Charlie didn't know what that meant. No one in Fort McPherson had been informed about a major pipeline project proposed for their land.

Charlie remembered that as a sea of change, not only for his own family but for the Gwich'in people. When the Dene Nation came looking for fieldworkers who could contribute to the Land Use and Occupancy study, he was quick to join the team. He wanted to play a role in creating the maps that would illustrate that the Dene were the true owners of these Northern lands: "Those maps were like a tool—or a weapon."

The evidence given by the Dene fieldworkers was a sharp contrast to the study by Gemini North. The cross-examination by Alan Hollingworth, the lawyer for Foothills Pipelines, uncovered deep divisions in the way life on the land was viewed. Pat Carney had concluded that land-based activities were dying out, but the Dene study found 1,075 Dene who were actively engaged in the land. Hollingworth asked Phoebe Nahanni what she meant by 'actively engaged'.

> To us, hunting and trapping is a way of life.... It's done depending on the seasons, depending on the animals... and whether a person stops hunting and trapping for a while, does not necessarily make him inactive, because he still has the rivers and lakes to fish from.

Hollingworth suggested that Dene families were not completely dependent on the land for their livelihood or their food. Phoebe Nahanni explained that in contrast to the way southern Canadians live, where each family was responsible for its own survival, in Dene communities there is a community commitment to sharing. A family might eat food from the land, even when they were living in town, because relatives would go out and hunt for a moose or a caribou and bring it back to share with neighbours.

Hollingworth asked again about the term 'actively engaged'. "Do you mean anybody who has gone out and hunted and trapped or does so at any time is considered actively engaged?" Phoebe Nahanni, losing patience, snapped, "I'm trying to explain it." She repeated that hunters and trappers were unlike people with 9-to-5 jobs; they used the cycle of nature to guide their schedule.

> A person can go trapping in the winter, say from October to Christmas time, and not go out again until springtime; then go to his fish camp in the summertime right until fall to prepare for the winter, come back into town for a while and then go back to the bush again.

Phoebe was explaining a life that depended on the annual cycles of wildlife, with additions of store-bought food. It was not an either/or situation.

The Gemini North study had designated men who divided their time between a job and hunting as 'recreational hunters' but Phoebe Nahanni saw it in reverse: "When we work we consider it part-time only, so we can go back and live on the land, the way we understand, the way we feel comfortable."

The research studies by Gemini North and the Dene Nation sent opposite messages. The pipeline companies were using their research to promote an economic argument based on a southern model: full-time work with the weekends off. Using those assumptions, the Gemini North study suggested that life on the land was dying out. The income from trapping was small in comparison with the wages that might come from employment on a pipeline.

The Dene Land Use and Occupancy study made a broader argument about the importance of traditional land-based pursuits. They were not simply a way of making an income, they represented a profound and continuing commitment to the land and the traditional way of life. The Land Use and Occupancy hearing placed two vastly different ways of seeing life side-by-side, giving the Dene an opportunity to explain why they were so profoundly committed to controlling their land and their future.

The Formal hearings of the Mackenzie Valley Pipeline Inquiry presented a dramatically different model for evaluating major resource projects. By negotiating the 'loan' of a team of government researchers, the lawyers had a richer well of information to draw on than would have been possible with industry sources alone. By funding intervenors from the environmental and Indigenous organizations, the Inquiry expanded the debate. It was no longer a squabble between two industry proponents; it became a negotiation over the way decisions over Canada's industrial future would be made.

Moreover, Judge Berger's insistence that the examination and cross-examination of witnesses be carried out in a clear and comprehensible way invited all Canadians into the debate.

~

A CONVERSATION WITH RUSSELL ANTHONY, COUNSEL FOR ENVIRONMENTAL ORGANIZATIONS

"Early in the 1970s, getting environmental evidence into hearings was very difficult. The hearings were between industry and the government, and the public was not invited to participate. Gradually, some of the younger lawyers began trying to impose ourselves into regulatory hearings.

We got beaten up quite a bit. There was a proposal in the Yukon to dam the Ashiak River, which would destroy Ashiak Falls and a historic aboriginal burial ground. I went up there and slept on the floor of a local resident's home.

We attended a hearing but were not allowed to speak. Months later, they relented. It was the first time that happened.

Judge Berger was the first to find funding so environmental groups could be heard. But there were so many interests that wanted to be present: how do you accommodate that? Berger got the environmentalists from the north and south together and said: 'I will fund one environmental voice. So you're going to have to form a coalition and support it, all of you.'

The Berger Inquiry was looking at a gas pipeline. But we were concerned that later, when an oil pipeline was suggested, the companies would say: 'Let's not disrupt another area. Let's put the oil pipeline next to the gas pipeline. And then we might as well put in a road.' So we saw the pipeline as a transportation corridor.

The route proposed by Arctic Gas would cross the North Slope of the Yukon where the Porcupine caribou herd was an international treasure. What does a pipeline do to caribou migration routes? It would cross a critical calving area. So we argued that at certain times of the year, even a minor disruption would have catastrophic impacts.

The Mackenzie Delta is a sensitive area because of the interchange of waters and the inter-relationships between the species. Every impact has a ripple effect.

As the counsel for the environmental organizations, I had to make sure our evidence was credible. Sometimes I sat down with a scientist and he said: 'This will never happen.' I had to question him: 'Never? Or it just hasn't happened yet?'

Secondly I had to look for inconsistencies. So imagine a representative for the pipeline companies said: 'Don't worry, we can repair the pipeline within 24 hours.' Then we would comb through the evidence to find where another representative said: 'We are going to decommission the roads.' We had to ask: which of these things is true?

Finally, we had to admit to ourselves: this pipeline might go forward. If so, we had to recommend the controls, systems and procedures that should be in place to protect the environment. Our team pulled out all the important information so it didn't get lost.

As a counsel, that was my job: to structure the argument to have impact and credibility. "

A CONVERSATION WITH GLEN BELL, COUNSEL FOR THE DENE NATION AND THE MÉTIS ASSOCIATION OF THE NWT

"I was a young lawyer for the Canadian Civil Liberties Association in Toronto. A friend told me that the Indian Brotherhood of the Northwest Territories, later the Dene Nation, was teaming up with the Metis Association to make a joint presentation to the Berger Inquiry. I was hired as the lawyer representing both organizations.

The leaders of the Dene Nation and the Metis Association were all young, the first generation to receive post-secondary education. They were thrust into positions of leadership at a young age but they were very motivated. They didn't talk about anything but politics!

It was easy to identify our legal strategy at the Berger Inquiry: to get a recommendation that no pipeline be permitted until land claims had been settled. But proving our case was more complicated. We had to show that the Dene had an arguable case for Aboriginal rights and title to a large area in the Northwest Territories.

That meant proving that the Dene had used and occupied the land "since time immemorial", as the legal phrase goes. How would we do that? Through an ambitious mapping project run by a young Dene woman named Phoebe Nahanni. She devoted her waking hours to the work. This was not some outside expert flying in, taking a look, and flying back out.

Phoebe oversaw a group of Dene researchers who went out into the communities and conducted interviews with hunters and trappers. The office was a busy place as the maps emerged, with all the lines on them, showing hunting and trapping areas. They were irrefutable proof that Dene had used the land for hundreds of generations.

The maps demonstrated that the Dene way of life was still alive, that aboriginal people had a special connection to the land. When Judge Berger held hearings in the communities, this message was brought home by the people who spoke. It was a way of showing that the Dene claim of self-determination was realistic.

We were showing that the traditional economy of hunting and trapping was a real economy, an industry worth preserving because it provided food and income for Indigenous people. It was a viable way of life. Although a cash economy had come in, it was supplementary. It wouldn't necessarily take over. ""

CHAPTER EIGHT

THE SUMMER OF '75

Drew Ann Wake and Michael Jackson KC

As THE BERGER INQUIRY prepared to begin its hearings, Peter Gorrie arrived in Yellowknife to take up a new job with the local newspaper, *News of the North*. He had been working for *The Ottawa Citizen* for a few years, first as a copyboy doing odd jobs and fetching coffee. Later the newspaper gave him the occasional assignment to write an article in overtime.

One day the business editor at *The Ottawa Citizen* mentioned *News of the North*. "It was like a lightbulb turning on," Peter said later. He put in a call to the publisher, Colin Alexander. "His only stipulation was that I needed to be a photographer. I said: Sure! As soon as I hung up the phone I went out and bought a camera and started to learn how to use it."

Peter arrived in Yellowknife just after New Years Day. "It was a balmy minus fifteen degrees. But overnight the temperature went down to minus forty." The next morning when he walked to the *News of the North* office, the streets were dark, with a drifting ice fog. He wondered whether he had made the right decision.

The ramshackle offices of *News of the North* did not improve his spirits. The old wooden building had a room with a low ceiling on the second floor, where four desks were jammed together. A tiny darkroom for developing photographs sat behind a black curtain. There was no ventilation so the fumes from the chemicals filled the space.

Peter soon discovered that his new boss, Colin Alexander, was not enthusiastic about covering the Berger Inquiry. "Like many businessmen in Yellowknife, he felt it was a waste of time and money, a stopgap measure to make the government look like it cared about the environment and land claims."

Peter, in contrast, had a history of environmental activism. He was anxious for the hearings to begin. Peter said:

> Those were the early days of the environmental movement. Companies that were starting a new industrial project didn't have to have an environmental impact statement. That wasn't even considered. In those days people thought that a land mass as big and as seemingly empty as the North could not be destroyed. You could do what you wanted on the land and not much harm would come to it. The North was too big to be ruined by human activity.

Aklavik

Three months after he arrived in the North, Peter was given the task of going to Aklavik to cover the first community hearing of the Berger Inquiry. On his flight to Inuvik, Peter was amazed to look out the window and see a thousand tiny lakes stretching across the Mackenzie Delta.

When the plane touched down, Peter was gripped with a concern. The people of Aklavik had never been asked to give their opinion on any government proposal before, certainly not on a project of this size. What if no one showed up for the hearing?

But in Aklavik, Annie and Danny C. Gordon were anxious to testify at the Inquiry. They had one primary concern. One of the proposed routes called for a pipeline to pass along the Arctic coast, from the North Slope of Alaska to the Mackenzie Delta.

Both Annie and Danny had deep connections to that coastline. It was a hunting corridor that the Inuvialuit had used for centuries, a place where, in a few short weeks over the summer, families gained enough food to last them through the fall and winter. "I consider it our highway," Danny says.

Danny had first walked that coast as a boy of ten, when his family in Alaska had made the decision to move to Canada. They left Barrow in the winter of 1944.

We travelled with one sled, six dogs and eight of us: Mom, Dad, and six kids. Most of us walked. Mom and the youngest rode in the sled some of the time, but they walked too when the conditions were bad. The travel was very hard. There were times we could look back at the end of the day and see where we had started from.

Along the coast, the Gordon family encountered the Porcupine caribou herd as it travelled from the mountains down to the calving ground on the coast. Danny believed that the construction of a pipeline posed a threat to the herd. During construction, the trucks and crews would keep the caribou from the coastline where their calves fed in their first weeks of life. After construction was complete, the noise from the compressor stations along the pipeline might drive the caribou away permanently.

Annie Gordon's concern was for the whales. Every summer since she was a girl her family would leave the Delta and travel west along the coast until they reached the Blow River. There, they would erect their tents around a gathering place where food was cooked. They would wait, picking berries and wild rhubarb, until a man perched at the lookout shouted that he had spotted whales. Then, the men would grab their harpoons and rifles, jump into schooners and set off on the hunt. Often they returned with a single whale, sometimes with two or three.

Back at the camp, young women like Annie were helpers, cutting up the meat, making the traditional food, muktuk, and storing it in barrels. "They don't just give you one little piece," she recalls. "Every person who's camping there gets their share to put away for the winter."

As the migrating whales disappeared to the east, some families would fish for herring and char. Men went out to sea and threw a huge net across the water. Then, returning to land, the families formed two groups, one on each side, and pulled the net bulging with fish toward the shore. The women scaled the fish, hung them to drain the water, and then put them in 45-gallon drums.

At the end of the summer, families would load all the barrels into a scow, along with a tent, a stove and the dogs. Often the scow would be so heavily loaded that the deck sat barely above the waterline. Then they would head back to Aklavik with enough food to last until spring. Annie says:

> We never felt lonely, we never felt sad. We had lots of chores to do. We had to keep the house in order, lots of ice, lots of wood, fish for the dogs and people. We never went hungry, because the family worked together,

But the possibility of a natural gas pipeline along the coast put the traditional Inuvialuit life in jeopardy. Annie and Danny Gordon prepared to speak about the impact the North Slope route would have on their lives and livelihood. "I was asked to testify at the Berger Inquiry because I knew the land," Annie recalls. "I was nervous at first. My heart beat faster. But after that I just tell it."

Annie's first concern was the trapline the family had in the bush outside Aklavik. Annie had heard an oil company representative claiming that the seismic did not have an impact on the local trappers. She brought the judge a photograph she had taken of a muskrat den that had been crushed. "They say they don't run over rat houses but this is how I found the push-up (den) after the truck went by there."

Danny Gordon described the changes he had seen along the coast in the years since the oil industry had started planning the pipeline.

> You see the caribou in the hills, they want to come down, but the planes going by always chase them back inland.... Just a little thing can hold the caribou back from coming down into the flats. I am just wondering what more it will be when they begin to build this pipeline right through that area, when the caribou are migrating.

He concluded by saying:

> We don't have anything that burns natural gas in Aklavik. It will not benefit us to let that pipeline route come through these mountains. I believe we will only suffer the consequences if things go wrong. I think people in the Delta, Aklavik, the Yukon, will have to consider these things. Once the damage is done, it is hard to restore. It may be impossible to restore.

Peter Gorrie sat listening to the testimony, astonished. He had worried that people might not attend the hearing, but the hall was filled: Elders, young hunters and trappers, women and youth with an intimate knowledge of the land were sharing their experiences.

An additional surprise was to come. George Edwards, a hunter from Aklavik, entered the hearing with a set of caribou antlers entangled with seismic wire. He explained that during his travels on the land, he frequently picked up antlers to sell at a dollar a pound. On a recent trip, he had encountered a caribou trying to shake off the seismic wire wound around its head and antlers. Edwards told Judge Berger: "When the seismic crew comes and blasts holes, they leave wire. They say they clean it up, but that isn't true." Peter Gorrie was shocked.

> This evidence brought home the fact that no matter what reassurances the oil companies gave, there were going to be consequences that couldn't be predicted. The oil company people thought that if they had a permit to work on the land, even if they didn't have formal ownership of it, they could restrict what other people could do on it. That was a completely foreign concept for the people in communities like Aklavik. They lived on the land, they used it, it was a part of them.

"The Berger Inquiry was a clash of cultures," he concluded. "Caribou antlers wrapped in seismic wire was a stark example of that."

Fort McPherson

For Judge Berger to understand the impacts of previous developments and the cumulative impacts of the proposed pipeline, it was necessary for him to hear not just the voices of Elders but also those of the younger generation whose lives and future were at stake.

From this understanding emerged another important feature of the Inquiry's community hearings that differentiated them from previous commissions of inquiry: the intergenerational participation of community members. Elders shared their histories, experiences with development, and relationships with their homelands. Younger members of the community shared their hopes and vision for a future in which their rights and values as Indigenous Peoples would be recognized in determining developments, including the pipeline.

The speeches at the community hearing in Fort McPherson are a testament to Indigenous Peoples' determination to maintain their identity and the integrity of their culture. But they also asked probing questions on the values of non-Indigenous people. Philip Blake, who had worked as a social worker in Fort McPherson for more than five years, in his far-ranging speech, eloquently made the case that self-determination for the Dene was in the long-term interest of all Canadians, not just Indigenous peoples. In the speech, Blake said:

> The school is just a symbol of white domination and control. It is part of a system set up to destroy Indian culture and to destroy our pride in our Indian heritage. It is only part of that system. Look at some of the other parts. Do you think people chose to live in rental houses owned by the government instead of the houses they built for themselves and owned by themselves? Do you think they chose to have a system of justice which often they cannot understand and which does not allow them to help their own people and deal with their own problems? A system which punishes the Indians for stealing from the Bay, but does not punish the Bay for stealing from the Indians?
>
> Can you really believe the we have chosen to have high rates of alcoholism, murder, suicide and social breakdown? Do you think we have chosen to become beggars in our own homeland?..."
>
> Do you really expect us to give up our life, our lands, so that those few people who are the richest and most powerful in the world can maintain and defend their immoral position of privilege? That is not our way. I strongly believe that we do have something to offer your nation, something other than our minerals. I believe it is in the self-interest of your own nation to allow the Indian nation to survive and develop in our own way, on our own land. For thousands of years, we have lived with our land; we have taken care of the land, and the land has taken care of us. We did not believe that our society had to grow and to expand and

conquer new areas in order that we could fulfill our destiny as Indian people... I believe that your nation might wish to see us, not as a relic from the past, but as a way of life, a system of values by which you might survive.

As Philip Blake concluded his speech, Fort McPherson residents looked at Judge Berger with curiosity. How would he respond to such strongly worded views? The Judge thanked Philip Blake, and the audience realized that Northerners would be free to express their views before this judge, before this Inquiry.

Old Crow

The community of Old Crow was situated in the path of the alternative route that Canadian Gas Arctic Pipelines had selected for transporting natural gas from Alaska to the United States. The pipeline would run across the Old Crow Flats, a rich hunting, fishing, and trapping area of vital importance to the Gwich'in people living in the remote Yukon community.

In those days, families lived in the bush for most of the year; only the Elders and the RCMP stayed in town. Families would trap muskrat, marten, and beaver to gain a cash income. In summer, they would set nets for the fish that migrate up the river. In fall, the Porcupine caribou herd would return from its summer sojourn on the coast. Families would hunt, then hang the meat on racks to dry it for food for the winter. Women scraped and tanned moose hides and made beautifully beaded mitts and moccasins for winter. Considering this reliance on the land, it was understandable that the proposal for a pipeline across the Flats would worry the people of Old Crow.

When Judge Berger arrived for the hearing, three generations of Old Crow residents crowded into the schoolhouse. Myra Kaye, a woman in her eighties, described how Gwich'in had traditionally hunted caribou, by building fences in the path of the porcupine herd and driving the herd into the enclosure. Elder Peter Charlie invited the judge to walk in the hills above the village to see the land glinting white with fragments of bone and antler, left after centuries of hunting.

Robert Bruce Jr. spoke from the perspective of the younger generation. He had recently returned from training as a heavy equipment operator. When he arrived back in Old Crow he was hired by the oil industry, one of the first paying jobs ever offered in the community. But after a few weeks on the job, he became concerned that the industry was damaging the land.

> At that time, the oil companies were working at the head of the Porcupine River. The people of Old Crow didn't know what [the oil companies] were doing. Later on, the people found out [the oil companies] were damaging the land, so they tried to put a stop to it. The government had to make the oil companies put rollers six inches under the blade so that it cannot damage the land. But still, in some cases, it spoils the land. The head of the Porcupine River looks like a jigsaw puzzle.

As the community members spoke, sixteen-year-old Lorraine Netro sat and listened. She had been born in a tent on her family's traditional territory on the Crow Flats. Lorraine's mother, Mary, raised six daughters on her own, taking on the responsibilities that men and women usually shared in the bush. She hunted moose and caribou, and then cut and smoked the meat. She also ran a trapline to earn the cash to buy other supplies. Lorraine describes the life as "simple but very challenging."

Ever since the beginning of the Inquiry, the Netro family had gathered around the radio to hear the CBC reports from the hearings in the Northwest Territories. It was hard for a high school student to grasp the changes that a pipeline might bring to Old Crow. "I had never been out of my community, so the idea was overwhelming," Lorraine recalled.

Lorraine found the hearing intimidating.

> I listened to what our Elders had to say; everyone spoke in our Gwich'in language to get their point across. I felt strongly as a young person that I had to speak up. But I was afraid. I had never spoken in front of people before. I had never seen that many people before! There was a break that last day, and I took a walk to my mother's house and sat outside on a hot day, and I thought: If I speak up, at least I have given voice for myself.

Her speech embodied all her fear for the future of her land.

> I do not agree with this pipeline route at all. There will be many problems in this project and many good people will be ruined, not only good people but good land on which they make their living.

Over three days, Lorraine and fifty of her Old Crow neighbours voiced their concerns. The village was united against a pipeline route that would imperil the Old Crow Flats, which had sustained their lives for centuries. Their passionate rebuke threatened the plans of the pipeline consortium: both of their routes for a natural gas pipeline from Prudhoe Bay had been thrown into question.

The Dene Declaration

In the summer of 1975, the community hearings of the Berger Inquiry paused for the second annual Joint General Assembly of the Indian Brotherhood of the NWT and the Métis and Non-Status Association of the NWT. It was a critical meeting, an opportunity for the Dene and Métis to plan the foundations of their land claim.

At the opening session of the General Assembly, the Indian Brotherhood circulated a mimeographed document. The Dene Declaration began with a bold statement:

The document went on to place Dene rights in the framework of history: the unkept promises of Treaty 11 and the imposition of the federal and territorial governments on the Indigenous Peoples of the North.

> We the Dene of the Northwest Territories insist on our right to be regarded by ourselves and the world as a nation. Nowhere in the New World have the native peoples won the right to self-determination and the right to recognition by the world as a distinct people and as nations. While the native people of Canada are a minority in their homeland, the native people of the NWT, the Dene and the Inuit, are a majority of the population of the in NWT.... And while there are realities we are forced to submit to, such as the existence of a country called Canada, we insist on the right to self-determination as a distinct people and the recognition of the Dene Nation.

> We the Dene are part of the Fourth World. And as the peoples and nations of the world have come to recognize the existence of rights of those people who make up the Third World. The day must come and will come when the nations of the Fourth World will come to be recognized and respected. The challenge to the Dene and the world is to find a way for the recognition of the Dene Nation.

> Our plea to the world is to help us in our struggle to find a place in the world community where we can exercise our right to self-determination as a distinct People and as a Nation.

The Declaration ended with a clear statement of the direction that future negotiations should take. "What we seek, then, is independence and self-determination within the country of Canada. This is what we mean when we call for a just land settlement for the Dene Nation."

In contrast to the familiar documents drafted by lawyers, the Dene Declaration was overtly political and both aspirational and inspirational. It was to have a profound effect in changing the nature of the discourse between Indigenous peoples and other Canadians—and not just in the North. It introduced a new language, drawn from an emerging international movement amongst Indigenous Peoples, and indelibly proclaimed the presence of the Dene Nation. The principles of self-determination underlying the Declaration are now reflected in the UN Declaration on the Rights of Indigenous Peoples. Criticized at the time by federal and territorial politicians as rhetoric, the language of the Dene Declaration is now enshrined in foundational principles of international law.

At the Assembly, the three hundred Dene and Métis delegates broke into small groups to explore the document. Animated discussions took place. For young leaders, like Raymond Yakeleya of Norman Wells, the document provided a clear framing of the position that the Dene had held, but never articulated.

> The Assembly was the first time we heard those words, and saw them on paper, so we could decide whether we agreed with it. Once we said these thoughts openly, there was no going back. We were going to assert ourselves on our own land. The government had a tiger on its tail.

A vote was called. Photographs of the occasion show the Dene delegates around the tables, their arms raised in support of the document. But for some the Métis delegates, the strident wording of the Declaration was a concern. It was the first fracture in the united front that the two organizations had presented up to that point.

Fort Good Hope

Fort Good Hope sits on the banks of the Mackenzie River just below the Arctic Circle. A few miles downstream, the Dehcho, the Dene name for the Mackenzie River, narrows through 60-metre high limestone bluffs known as the Ramparts, perhaps the most dramatic feature along the 4,000 kilometres of the river.

Early in August, when Judge Berger arrived for the community hearings in Fort Good Hope, the excitement generated by the Dene Declaration was still in the air.

Almost all of the residents of the community gathered in the school gymnasium. Addy Tobac, who had been the interpreter for Chief George Kodakin at the Preliminary Hearings in Ottawa, sat with her sister, Lucy Jackson and her mother, Georgina Tobac. Georgina had prepared a speech describing the hurtful and disrespectful manner in which non-Dene had treated her people and their land. That speech would leave everyone in the community hall with a collective sense of shame. The imagery of the hurt and disrespect was visceral.

> Every time the white people come to the North or come to our land and start tearing up the land, I feel as if they are cutting our own flesh because that is the way we feel about our land, it is our flesh.

The young chief, Frank T'Seleie, opened the hearing with a stern speech.

> Mr. Berger, there will be no pipeline because we have plans for our land. There will be no pipeline because we no longer intend for our land and our future to be taken away from us, so that we are destroyed to make someone else rich.

In attendance at the hearing was Bob Blair, by then the President of Foothills Pipelines. Frank T'Seleie did not hesitate to direct some of his remarks to Blair. He suggested that, in his greed for money, Blair had lost his humanity: "Somehow in your carpeted boardrooms, in your panelled office, you are plotting to take away from me the very centre of my existence." Then T'Seleie labelled Blair "a twentieth-century General Custer."

Bob Blair asked to speak. He was clearly shaken by the suggestion that his behaviour could be compared to General Custer. He described congenial relations his company had with the 5,000 farmers in the south, whose land was crossed by his company's pipelines. He said that he hoped a similar arrangement could be reached with the Dene.

But other young Dene leaders rose to reiterate the demand that the pipeline project be halted. Stephen Kakfwi outlined the new, bolder approach.

> Our reality is that this is our land, that we are a nation of People and we want to live our own ways. Our reality is that the pipeline is just a poorly masked attempt to overwhelm our land and our People with a way of life that will destroy us. Our reality is that all the 'help' your Nation has sent us has merely made our People poor, humiliated, and confused. Our reality is that we are in danger of being destroyed. Our reality is that there is a very simple choice: Dene survival with no pipeline or a pipeline with no Dene survival.

With the tensions between the townspeople and the corporate representatives rising, John T'Seleie was asked to give a presentation on what could be learned from the Dene Land Use maps on the wall. He described what he had learned from the Elders who had been able to describe in detail the shores of Great Bear Lake, not from a map but from memory.

From time to time, Judge Berger raised questions, asking John to describe the areas that were most important for the

Dene. Where did they fish? Where did they hunt for moose? Through this thoughtful exchange, the pipeline company executives began to understand the attachment of the Dene people to their land was not the same as a southern farmer's feeling for his fields of grain. There was a profound connection that had given rise to the demand for a just land claim.

Bob Blair grasped the message. On the final day of the hearing, in what may have been a first for the petroleum industry in Canada, he stated that he hoped that land claims would be settled before pipeline construction began.

As the hearing closed, John T'Seleie offered Judge Berger some words of advice:

> When you receive strong words, when people tell you what is deep in their hearts, I think that ought to be listened to. I think our people understand survival because most of their lives they have had to struggle for survival... so the message I think is that the people of the North will approach the pipeline question with the same kind of determination that it takes to live off the land. And living off the land—well, it's a life and death struggle.

Confrontation in Norman Wells

Three weeks after the General Assembly ended, the Yellowknife newspaper, *News of the North*, published the draft of the Dene Declaration that had been discussed. It came with a stinging critique by the newspaper's publisher, Colin Alexander, who called it "... a draft plan of action for a war of liberation."

The article was picked up by the newspaper in Inuvik, *The Drum*. There the publisher, Tom Butters, aired his opinion that the Dene Declaration had been written by a 'white' theoretical revolutionary. "The objectives are general and vague and the prose loosely structured from the Maoist, Communist lexicon, ie. creating democratic and egalitarian organizations..."

The news about the Dene Declaration upset many non-Dene citizens who feared that the growing unrest might weaken the dominant role of industry and government in the communities.

Days after the newspapers published their opinions, Judge Berger arrived in Norman Wells. The community had a decades-long history with the petroleum industry. Raymond Yakeleya recalls that his grandfather had seen oil seeping onto his land.

> If you picked up a rock from one of the houses and threw it, the rock would land where the oil was seeping up. The Elders wanted to see what properties oil had so they'd take a little cup of oil and pour it on the fire and the fire would come up. So for many generations, our people knew about this oil.

In the early 1900s, the family took a pail of the oil to the Bishop and authorized him to send it south to be analyzed. It went to Pittsburgh, where they discovered that the oil was of very high quality. But the report was never sent back to the family.

> All of a sudden we saw geologists staking claims around our grandparents' houses. They sent a drill rig down in 1919. My grandparents came back home one day and these white men were occupying their homes. They drilled and went down 700 feet and hit the main pool of oil.

Very quickly, Norman Wells developed into a white man's town. Imperial Oil built huge oil storage tanks along the bank of the river. A pipeline followed. During World War II one of the large tanks burst, and oil flooded into the river. Thousands of ducks died. By mid-century, Norman Wells was divided between Dene families and newcomers from the south.

So, when Judge Berger opened his hearing in Norman Wells on August 9, Northerners braced for a confrontation.

Raymond Yakeleya believed that the Inquiry offered a forum where the Dene could express the opinions they had kept to themselves for so long. When he spoke, he did not temper his anger:

Mr. Berger, this is Dene land. The land shall serve the needs of Canada only when the rightful owners have been compensated. Give this message to Ottawa: the day that a pope in Rome can draw a line dividing the new world between the imperialistic nations of Portugal and Spain has passed. The day when a government in Ottawa can divide the resources of this land between Arctic Gas and Foothills Pipelines shall not even dawn."

And he concluded with a dark prediction: "This pipeline will be built only with our consent, or it will flow red to the south."

That precipitated a sharp retort from Clare Barnabe, a former nun. She accused the Dene of exaggerating their loss of the land.

It hasn't been a one-way street. It hasn't been all bad for the native people of the North... They dream they want to live in the past, live off the land, but when they wake up in their thermostatically controlled three-bedroom houses, they change their minds pretty fast.

At that moment, Whit Fraser, sitting at the table with his fellow CBC reporters, threw down his pen in disgust. "It was a hard hearing, so much bitterness in the air. So many people made so many put downs of the Dene. I felt I just had to say something, so I asked to be sworn in."

Judge Berger wisely called a recess. He asked Commission Counsel Ian Scott to take Whit Fraser into the hallway and talk to him. Scott asked: "Do you know what you're doing?" Fraser replied: "I can't *not* do it." In his view, the other CBC reporters had testified in their home communities. Surely he had the right to give his opinion too?

His speech rocked the room.

> In this country, the majority of the people make the rules. If we want to live and work in this country, and [Indigenous people] are the majority, then we are going to have to let them take over. And don't anyone tell me that there isn't the talent in this country to do it.

The speech was carried across the country on the evening news and by the next day there were calls for Fraser to be fired from the Canadian Broadcasting Corporation. Whit says he fell back on a boxing strategy he learned from boxer Mohammed Ali: rope a dope. "Put your guard up and let them punch themselves out." He refused to comment further and waited for the furor to die down. Eventually, it did.

Fort Simpson

The Inquiry had moved into a new phase. There was a vocal segment of white Northerners who were heading into combat with Indigenous organizations, looking for ways to weaken their fight for their rights.

That struggle became even more intense as the Inquiry moved into Fort Simpson. When Michael Jackson went there to schedule the community hearing in August, he found a village deeply divided. Over the previous few years, some large industrial projects had been proposed, including the pipeline. A large influx of outsiders had assumed positions of authority. There was a pervasive sense among the Dene people that the newcomers had taken control over their future.

Continued on page 165

NORTHERN ALBUM

PHOTOS BY MICHAEL JACKSON AND LINDA MacCANNELL

BELLA T'SELEIE
Special Counsel Michael Jackson captured photos of the people he met and
worked with in the North, including Bella T'Seleie.

Two moments from the Inquiry: Judge Berger (above) greets people at a hearing and Michael Jackson and others (below) observe testimony in Fort Simpson.

In 2010, Michael Jackson returned to the North. Linda MacCannell took portraits of Michael and those who worked with him during the Inquiry.

CHIEF GEORGE KODAKIN
Chief George Kodakin invited Michael Jackson to live in Fort Franklin
for a year so he could better understand the Dene way of life.

Above: Suzie Tutcho described his walk from Great Bear Lake to the Arctic coast, alone.
Below: Chief George Kodakin and others testifying to Tom Berger in Fort Franklin.

Above: Tom Berger and Chief Johnny Charlie in Fort McPherson
Below: Chief Johnny Charlie and Jane Charlie.
In the early days of the Inquiry, Chief Johnny Charlie and his wife, Jane
introduced Judge Berger and Michael Jackson to their way of life.

CHARLIE SNOWSHOE
Charlie Snowshoe described how he quit residential school and
developed the hunting skills needed to live on the land.

In Aklavik at the first community hearing, Rosie Albert
was the Inuvialuktun language translator.
Chief Jim Koe was the Gwich'in translator.

In Inuvik, Rosie Albert worked for the Committee for Original Peoples Entitlement, preparing Inuvialuit communities for the inquiry.

Above: Addy Tobac helped members of the community to prepare their presentations.
Below: John T'Seleie (left) and Chief Frank T'Seleie made strong presentations.

John T'Seleie interviewed hunters and trappers in the Sahtu for the Dene Land Use study. He presented his maps at the hearing.

Above: Jim Antoine sat with Elder Mary Margaret Moses at the hearing in Wrigley.
Below: Chief Francois Paulette spoke in Fort Simpson.

Jim Thom and Michael Jackson travelled to bush camps, and villages like
Kakisa Lake, to encourage Dene families to testify in Fort Providence.

Above: In Ulukhaktok, Elder Agnes Aleekok described
surviving a shipwreck in icy waters.
Below: Hunters raised concerns about a blowout in the sea.

David Nasogaluak's trapline ran 300 kilometres across Banks Island.
He was shocked at the damage done to the land by oil companies.

Above: In Paulatuk Rosemary Kirby challenged the wisdom of offshore drilling.
Below: Judge Berger described the evidence from scientists who testified in Inuvik.

Continued from page 148

So, the inquiry team decided to hold two hearings.

We decided to have two hearings, one for the non-Ab-
original community, one for the Dene community. But
neither would be a closed meeting. The two hearings
would give us a sense of the different perspectives.

The hearing with the business community was dominated
by Gordon Erion of the Fort Simpson Chamber of Commerce.

We feel Fort Simpson needs the pipeline to move
into a permanent healthy economy. The Chamber
of Commerce has been promoting the concept of
Simpson becoming a major transportation centre for
several years. With the construction of the Mackenzie
and Liard highways, and the development of port
facilities, logistically Fort Simpson would be the most
economical staging point for any type of development
along the Mackenzie corridor.... We urge both appli-
cants to consider the possibility of making Simpson a
major staging point for pipeline construction.

A few days later, the second hearing drew Fort Simpson's
Dene citizens. They were not keen on seeing their quiet river-
bank become an industrial hub. Jim Antoine had been asked
to take the position of chief. He had recently returned from
university. The Elders felt that his grasp of English made him
the ideal person to respond to the business community's proposals. In sharp contrast to the speeches of the newcomers,
Chief Antoine's speech traced the history of the Dene people
making their living off the land. He described how Treaty 11
was, in the eyes of the Dene, a peace treaty and not a cession
of Dene rights to their land:

Before 1921 people used to live off the land along
the rivers and if you go along the river you'll still see

cabins, and people are still using these cabins today and this is where the people used to live. Life was hard but it was healthy and it was good and clean. There were many hardships that my forefathers encountered at that time. The people were honest, respectful of one another, and they treated each other with respect.

My people at that time were a Nation. They had their own leaders, they had Elders who gave direction, they had learned men who knew how to cure people, and give good directions to the people, so that they could continue living off the land. There was game and fish, plants and berries as food to make the people grow,. Life was good, and only the strong and the smart survived. I feel that my people were a nation at that time and today we're still saying that we're a Nation. We're the Dene Nation. We are the Slavey people here and we're part of this Nation."

I think we were a Nation at the time because the country of Canada in 1921 signed a peace treaty with us, Treaty 11, and there are still old members of my Band today who were alive at that time and who are still alive today, who tell me that first treaty was a peace treaty, and now the government is saying that the land was ceded over to the Crown as the result of the signing of the treaty.

But I say that the government is lying and the government has cheated the people, and now they're stealing the land. We all feel as Dene people that this land is still our land, and since 1921 as Chief and Band Council we speak for the people, the treaty people, and a lot of the non-status and Métis, because they are our relatives, they are our brothers and our sisters. So it doesn't matter if there are 1,500 in this town, the majority of the people who I think I speak for are the permanent residents of this community, not somebody who has just been here two years, three years, looking to make a fast buck and then going home."

Sharing

The theme contrasting the greed of southern entrepreneurs with the Dene commitment to sharing came up repeatedly through the hearings. The ethic of sharing is seen as an essential part of Indigenous cultural inheritance. At Fort Liard, Joachim Bonnetrouge told the Inquiry: "We do not conquer, we are not like that. We are sharers, we are welcomers."

Joe Naedzo at Deline told Judge Berger:

> We native people, we help each other. Our ancestors have taught us a lot of things. They have taught us how to make life continue. They teach you that for your neighbours, when they are in need and when you are in need, the neighbours will feed you. Take care of each other and share with each other.

Dene Elders recalled not only how sharing and generosity characterize relations among themselves, but also how they have characterized their relations with fur traders. They told the Inquiry how, during the days of the fur trade, they shared with the traders their knowledge and their food, both of which were indispensable to the traders' survival in the North.

This is how Philip Simba of Kakisa Lake remembered those days:

> When the first snow comes, they come into camp and the Hudson's Bay [manager] has at least 12 men working for him. Each man had a team of six dogs. These people went and got the moose. This was provided to the Hudson's Bay for his food. In the winter time they provided him with rabbits and all that. This is how they helped the Hudson's Bay. That's how he grew rich on the misery of the people, I guess. That's how come he's got a beautiful store today.

Both Dene and Inuvialuit people reflected on the lack of

reciprocity which characterized federal and territorial governments' dealings with the mineral resources of the North. Cecile Modeste at Deline expressed the collective experience of many Indigenous people in the North:

> In Port Radium, radium was discovered. In Norman Wells oil was discovered. In Yellowknife gold was discovered. All of these discoveries were [made] by Indian people. But all of the people who have discovered those minerals and stuff like that, the ways of making money, have died poor. They have died really poor. And those, the white people who have come in—we just go ahead and let them have all of these things, we never say anything about getting money back.... But now it has come to a point where they are deciding to take the whole land. Then we have to say something about it.

It was to address and redress these historical injustices that the movement for Indigenous self-determination expressed in the Dene Declaration was directed.

Bella T'Seleie's speech was delivered in the hamlet of Colville Lake, still one of the most traditional communities in the Northwest Territories, where sharing and reliance on the land were an integral part of peoples' daily lives. Bella had been born in Colville Lake and after her mother contracted tuberculosis and was hospitalized in the south, Bella was taken in by the people of Fort Good Hope. She returned to Colville Lake after she was adopted by a family there and spent the rest of her childhood in the community. In the tiny community hall, with the community gathered shoulder to shoulder, she told Judge Berger in soft, measured tones about her past and her dreams for the future:

> In the summer we lived in fish camps, always working together, making dry fish, cutting wood, and I

look back on those days as really happy... I look at Colville Lake today... [The people] still have their own lives: they still have their pride. I don't want my people to have nothing but memories of what their life used to be.

There's a lot of young people, like myself, that want to have something other than memories. That is why we want control of what is going to happen to us and our lives in the future. I think about all that and I know that we are one of the last people to have our own land and still have our own kind of life in the world. I think the government and oil companies should consider that, after all they have done to the native people in the south.... They are not happy people, they are not proud people. All they have is memories."

Fort Rae (Behchoko)

There were other historical and continuing injustices that were raised before the Inquiry. The Community hearings provided Judge Berger with the opportunity to learn about the history of Treaties 8 and 11. The Dene told the Inquiry about some of their leaders of the past. The Tlicho people of Fort Rae spoke of their great Chiefs Edzo and Monfwi, respected leaders when Treaty 11 was signed in 1921.

At Rae Edzo, now Behchoko, Alexis Arrowmaker former Chief of the Tlicho people, after recounting the promises made at the time of Treaty 11, made it clear that the government's agenda of assimilation of the Dene and other Indigenous peoples was one rejected by his people.

It seems that the government's intention is ... to persuade native people to become like or act like white people. And there is no way that we native people want to lose our culture. There is no way they are going to change native people or have them like white man.

His point was reiterated by the younger generation. Georges Erasmus, President of the Dene Nation, told Judge Berger how the Dene had always understood their place within the Canadian Confederation.

> The decision that is before the Dene people today, as it has been now since Confederation, since the beginning of Canada as a nation, for the original people, for the native people, is: do we assimilate? Do we remain distinct people? For us in the valley here, it's a decision: do we want to continue on as Dene people? Or do we want to forget that and become like everybody else? The decision before us, I think, has been made already, and people are acting on it. Clearly we want to remain as Dene people. We do not want to assimilate.

Arctic Red River (Tsiigehtchic)

In early 1976, the Berger Inquiry moved north to hold hearings in the communities of the Mackenzie Delta. A few weeks before the hearings began, the federal government sent two civil servants from Ottawa to discuss the pipeline route south to Alberta. They brought an offer: if the Indigenous communities would agree to give up their rights to a strip of land for a pipeline along the east side of the Mackenzie, the government promised to negotiate a land claims settlement in the future.

It seemed odd that these meetings would coincide with the formal hearings of the Inquiry. Why establish a commission of inquiry and then send two civil servants to hold parallel talks? The CBC asked Drew Ann Wake to cover their discussions in the Gwich'in communities of Arctic Red River and Fort McPherson.

On the way, the two civil servants chatted in the front seat of the car. One explained a problem he was having in Manotick, a suburb of Ottawa. The town had proposed to widen his street, cutting a meter off the front of his property. If he were at home, he said, he would be attending a meeting to protest the loss of his land. He appreciated the irony: he had been sent to the north to persuade Indigenous people to give up a vastly greater swathe of their territory.

On arrival in Arctic Red River, now Tsiigehtchic, the community manager, Robert Andre was at the hall. He explained that the men of the village were all away on their traplines. Only the older women of the community would be attending the meeting. As the room filled, Robert studied the maps the two men had brought with them. The land that the government wanted for a pipeline passed near Travaillant Lake, where the people of Arctic Red spent much of the year. Three generations of his family hunted, trapped, and fished on that land. Robert shook his head and silently took a seat among the elderly ladies.

The men from Ottawa introduced themselves and pointed to the area on the map that they hoped to secure for a pipeline. Within minutes, the women began to murmur. Then, as a group, they rose from their seats and began moving toward the men, shaking their fingers as if they were small boys caught stealing apples. Although they were speaking in the Gwich'in language, the message was clear: they were not giving up their land. The men from Ottawa grabbed their maps and hurried from the room.

It is rare that a reporter is handed such a story. Government representatives driven from their meeting by a group of elderly women? Drew Ann filed her story with the CBC, just in time for the evening news.

Minutes later, she joined the two civil servants in their car. They were shaken by the encounter. It was a silent journey to the next meeting in Fort McPherson. There, Chief Johnny Charlie was standing in front of the darkened community hall, arms crossed. As the government representatives disembarked from the vehicle, he shook his head. The people of Fort McPherson had decided there would be no meeting with the government representatives. The people had communicated their thoughts to Ottawa through their testimony at the Berger Inquiry.

Weeks later, Judge Berger arrived in Arctic Red River (Tsiigehtchic) for the community hearing. It took place in the same hall where the government representatives had held their meeting weeks before, but this time all the chairs in the room were taken. The men of the village had travelled back from their traplines to speak to the judge.

One of the first speakers was Robert Andre's grandmother, Julienne Andre, who addressed Judge Berger in the Gwich'in language. She searched for a way to describe the deep connection she felt for the land that had provided food through all of her eighty years.

> I was born between Thunder River and Tree River and I want to die there of old age. But Travaillant Lake, that's my lake. Even you try to chase me away from there I wouldn't go. This land is ours. I was born in it. God gave it to us. We didn't buy it. Why they want to buy it from us? We don't need your money. All my life I lived on the land. I don't know anything about garden stuffs. Every time something killed fresh, that tastes good. If we give our land away, what our children's children will do?

The following speaker was Robert Andre's uncle, Gabe Andre. To speak at the hearing, he had driven 100 kilometres from his trapline on a snowmobile. His words created a strong visual image of the impact the oil industry had on Gwich'in traditional territory.

> I trapped in this country, I don't remember the time that I got stuck. That's because I know how to hunt in my country. But since the oil companies start in this country, lots of places I go, there's nothing. I remember one time in June, I come from Travaillant Lake

by dogs by myself. I come to one creek with a seismic line going across the creek. They blow that creek up so good that.... I drove my dogs across that creek. And all the bush they put in there is still there.

As Gabe Andre spoke, his voice became more agitated.

Today, coming down that river, I just feel mad you know. What's happening to us? Nobody know what's happening to us. My great grandfather had a good time, my grandfather had a good time. My father had a good time. And we're the ones who are going to get it. Not too bad now, but think of our children, our children's children!

The speeches at the community hearings were not only rich in personal and collective descriptions, and condemnation of the legacy of colonialism, but also were enriched by an articulation of how the Indigenous people of the North saw the process of decolonization and self-determination evolving. Perhaps the most complete statement of that process was given by Robert Andre as part of the intergenerational presentation by the Andre family.

We are saying we are a distinct people, a Nation of people, and we must have a special right within Canada. We are distinct in that it will not be an easy matter for us to be brought into your system because we are different. We have our own system, our own way of life, our own cultures and traditions. We have our own languages, our own laws, and a system of justice...

Land claims... [mean] our survival as a distinct people. We are a people with a long history and a whole culture, a culture which has survived... We want to survive as a people, [hence] our stand for maximum independence within your society. We want to develop our own economy. We want to acquire political independence for our people, within the Canadian constitution. We want to govern our own lives and our own lands and its resources. We want to have our own system of government, by which we can control and develop our land for our benefit. We want to have the exclusive right to hunt, to fish, and to trap. We are saying that on the basis of our [Aboriginal] land rights, we have an ownership and the right to participate directly in resource development.

We want, as the original owners of this land, to receive royalties from [past] developments and for future, developments, which we are prepared to allow. These royalties will be used to fund local economic development, which we are sure will last long after the companies have exhausted the non-renewable resources of our land. The present system attempts to put us into a wage economy as employees of companies and governments over which we have no control. We want to strengthen the economy at the community level, under the collective control of our people. In this way many of our young people will be able to participate directly in the community and not have to move elsewhere to find employment.

We want to become involved in the education of our children in the communities where we are in the majority. We want to be able to control the local schools. We want to start our own schools in the larger centres in the North where we are in the minority ...

Where the governments have a continuing role after the land settlement, we want to have a clear recognition as a distinct people, especially at the community level. Also at the community level, powers and control should lie with the chief and band council. To achieve all this is not easy. Much work lies ahead of us...

We must again become a people making our own history. To be able to make our own history is to be able to mould our own future, to build our society that preserves the best of our past and our traditions, while enabling us to grow and develop as a whole people.

We want a society where all are equal, where people do not exploit others. We are not against change, but it must be under our terms and under our control. We ask that our rights as a people for self-determination be respected.

Six months after the delegates from across the Northwest Territories had approved the Dene Declaration in Fort Simpson, a firmer idea about the future was emerging. The theoretical concept of a Dene Nation had evolved into a series of concrete steps to ensure that the decisions about the future rested in the hands of the Dene themselves.

Yellowknife

The Dene land claims debate at the Berger Inquiry stimulated debates across the North. In cities like Yellowknife and Inuvik, tensions grew. Even a normally quiet event might erupt into controversy. In the summer, the member of the Territorial Council for Yellowknife, David Searle, was invited to speak at a community meeting. About thirty people attended.

Searle used the opportunity to attack Justice Berger. He also criticized the staff of the Dene Nation, which included Mel Watkins, a professor from the University of Toronto who had spent his sabbatical year as an advisor to the Dene Nation. Finally, he attacked George Barnaby, who had been elected to the Territorial Council to represent the Sahtu. Barnaby had resigned from the Territorial Council stating that the Dene land claim was not an issue of racism but of fairness.

David Searle's speech illustrated the deep chasm that had

grown between those who supported and those who opposed the movement for Indigenous rights. He said:

> We have become the outdoor laboratory for the do-gooders of Canada. The North is crawling with the lice of southern Canada: biologists, anthropologists, economists, sociologists, and political scientists, to name only a few. They have secured grants from government or industry and pry and prod on our every act, whether that act be natural or unnatural, every thought and every pore of our bodies. Ranking high in the numbers of the foregoing groups are the left-wingers, doing their unproductive, selfish thing, planting and cultivating their sluggish sickness among our innocent and idealistic native peoples.
>
> What I am saying is that we are a sick, sick society. We cannot afford more social services. We must cast out the socialists. We must call out their names, loud and clear—Mr. Berger, Mr. Watkins, to mention only two—and tell them they are not liked, they are unwanted—and tell them to leave.
>
> Now I have an example of the sort of thing that's happening. George Barnaby, a ex-member of the Territorial Council who resigned. He then appeared before the Berger Inquiry and made comments about the Territorial Council and I'm going to quote. 'Some people might think of the land claims as a racial issue but it really issue an issue between the rules and the rulers, the oppressed and the oppressors. Under Dene law there is freedom and equality. The system in the south is oppression and exploitation, where a few have a lot and a lot of people have very little'.
>
> Ladies and gentlemen, I know George Barnaby and those are not his words. Listen to it: the rulers and the ruled. George wouldn't know how to use those words.

At that point, angry shouts rose from the audience and the meeting descended into mayhem.

⌒

A CONVERSATION WITH RICK HARDY, MÉTIS ASSOCIATION OF THE NORTHWEST TERRITORIES

When the Berger Inquiry opened, the Dene Nation and the Métis and Non-Status Association of the Northwest Territories were represented by one lawyer, Glen Bell. But after the vote on the Dene Declaration in the summer of 1975, the two organizations began to take different approaches to key issues. This conversation illustrates the growing fissure.

"I was born and raised in what was then called Fort Norman, now called Tulita. My mother's family were the Gaudets, a big Métis family.

My great-grandfather was the chief trader. Every winter he would make his rounds by dog team from his headquarters in Fort Good Hope. He would travel to Colville Lake and Great Bear Lake. There were no communities there then, but families populated the whole area. Then, he would travel to Fort Norman, where there was a trading post, and then back to Good Hope. All by dog team. They were amazing people.

In 1921, the Treaty Commissioner came to the north, accompanied by the Half Breed Commission. As they made treaty with the Dene people, those Métis people who didn't want to take treaty were able to apply for scrip. My grandfather took scrip for himself, his wife and his eleven children and received $2,600. In the 1920s, that was a fortune. That solidified our identity as Métis people.

In the early 1970s, the newly formed Métis and Non-Status Native Association sent fieldworkers into the communities. Wally Firth had his own airplane and Ed Lafferty from Fort Simpson was also a pilot. They flew into each community and asked, "Are you interested in being part of this?"

We felt there was one major issue that had to be dealt with: the Aboriginal rights of the Métis people of the NWT. In the early days the interests of the Dene and the Métis seemed to be aligned. James Wahshee was leading the Indian Brotherhood in a direction that the Métis were comfortable with, so we decided to present a common front at the Berger Inquiry. Together we hired lawyer Glen Bell to jointly represent the two organizations.

In July of 1975, I was the co-chair of the Assembly in Fort Simpson where the Dene Declaration was put on the table. There was no warning. A sizeable number of people were excited about it and they pushed pretty hard.

But there was a larger group that said: 'Let's slow down here. This is pretty radical stuff. We want to think it through.' The Métis vision was a society that supported the rights of individuals to have their own businesses and to try to be successful that way. Of course, not every Métis subscribed to that theory, but by and large the majority of the members thought this was the way our future was going to be. This was how our children were going to make their way in the world.

The Dene, on the other hand, took a different view. They wanted to continue living from the land. So there was a parting of ways. It was terribly disappointing but we had a clear understanding of our view and we intended to stand by it.

I presented the final argument for the Métis Association. I said the Métis had come to depend on wage employment so 'we look to the construction of the pipeline as one of the major economic projects that we wish to take part in.'»

CHAPTER NINE

A WINTER WARNING

Drew Ann Wake

~

THE BOOM IN ALASKA inspired a frenzied search for oil a thousand kilometres away, in the delta where the Mackenzie River reaches the Beaufort Sea. It is a land of low-lying lakes, each narrowly protected from the sea by thin strips of land.

In the 1960s, crews began to cut seismic lines through the delta across the lands where Inuvialuit families have their traditional camps. Three branches of the Allen family had cabins side by side. Colin Allen remembered the yearly cycle on the land. "In wintertime they'd go hunting or snaring ptarmigan or rabbits. In March, muskrat season would open. Everyone was happy in April, May, June. Muskrat is good grub."

Muskrats also offered a cash income. As a young man, Colin Allen got a government job, but the income was not sufficient. Store-bought food in Inuvik was expensive, so he continued to trap muskrats. At three dollars a skin, his income from trapping provided more money than his government job.

The sudden appearance of seismic trucks concerned the Inuvialuit. The giant vehicles ground their way across the delicate tundra, destroying the threads of land that wove between the lakes. They churned up muskrat dens nestled along the shores, crushing the tiny rodents that kept Inuvialuit families in food. Colin Allen remembered the first time he encountered a seismic crew.

I was making coffee in my tent on my trapline and I
saw trees falling. The oil companies had put a seismic
line through the bush. They put dynamite in the lake
and when they pushed a button, they blew up muskrat
push-ups (dens). Afterward, we'd open the push-ups:
all dead muskrats.

The seismic blasting took a toll on fish as well. "Boom,
boom, boom.... Sometimes the jackfish would fly up out of the
water. Other times they'd float up slowly," Colin remembers.

Many Delta trappers traded their fur at Slim Semmler's
store in Inuvik. While waiting for their fur count to be tallied,
they would describe the damage that seismic was doing to the
land. Agnes Semmler, a Gwich'in lady from Old Crow who ran
the store with her husband, listened to the stories and began
looking for a way to bring the destruction of the land to wider
attention.

One of the first people she reached out to was Nellie
Cournoyea, the young Inuvialuit manager of the CBC in
Inuvik. Nellie felt that the Inuvialuit had to move quickly to
secure a claim to their traditional lands.

We knew that once the companies proved up the
resources, the Inuvialuit would be alienated from the
lands we wanted for ourselves. So we became determined to create an organization that would ensure that
the Inuvialuit would be protected.

In 1970, the activists founded an organization called the
Committee for Original Peoples Entitlement (COPE). Said
Nellie:

Here in the Western Arctic we had to get the job done
or change would roll right over us. We went out to the
communities and spoke to people, individual to individual. We did the grunt work, door to door. Then

we followed up with community meetings. That way, even though people were isolated, we could speak collectively.

COPE's president was Sam Raddi, a genial man with a talent for pursuading people to work together. He had lost his eyesight, but he held to many traditional Inuvialuit pursuits. For example, he continued to run a trapline. A friend would drive the snowmobile and, at intervals along the trail, Sam would jump off and check a trap.

When the Berger Inquiry began, the COPE office received a big package with all the engineering, environmental and social research that Canadian Arctic Gas Pipelines had conducted on the proposed pipeline. "We tried to read it but we didn't understand it," Sam Raddi recalled. "We had to get experts who could interpret it into simpler English. Then we hired Inuvialuit to translate it into our language." Finally, COPE sent its own team of experts and translators into the communities to explain what Arctic Gas was planning to do.

One of the translators was Rosie Albert. She travelled to the meetings that were held in each of the Delta communities. Then, when she returned to Inuvik she would go to her job at the CBC radio station and describe the ideas discussed in each community. "I told what had happened in the Inuvialuktun language. People were excited. They were saying: 'Finally the government is going to recognize us. Finally, we can run things ourselves.'"

As the influence of the Inuvialuit grew, so did the challenges they faced. By the end of the 1972 drilling season, 66 wells had been drilled in the Mackenzie Delta. The large multinational oil companies had all made discoveries, but they had not found the hoped-for bonanza: four wells hit oil, 11 hit gas, and the remaining 51 were dry holes. Many of the wells were in the shallow waters of the Beaufort Sea, not far from the harbour at Tuktoyaktuk. Exploring for oil there required the construction of artificial islands made by dumping huge quantities of gravel into the ocean. Ships laden with heavy machinery filled the harbour during the few ice-free weeks of the summer.

A young trapper, Randy Pokiak, recalled coming home to Tuk after months on his trapline and discovering that his community was utterly changed. "We had rigs all over the place. Winter roads were destroying the traplines. By that time the Mackenzie Delta was up for leases. Imperial Oil tied up the basin." That summer the people of Tuktoyaktuk were shocked to discover the toll that the industrial activity was taking on the traditional whale hunt. Randy noted: "We used to get 75 to 90 whales a year. That year we got one."

Tuktoyaktuk residents were surprised that the Canadian government had allowed, indeed encouraged, such a rapid escalation of the industry in Arctic waters. They were also surprised at the lack of regulation. The industry was moving forward without the environmental or social impact studies that would have been required in the south. Randy Pokiak put the question bluntly: "So who was protecting us? Who was protecting our interests as hunters and trappers?"

When the Committee for Original Peoples Entitlement was established, the Inuvialuit finally had an organization through which to express their frustration. An inner circle of Elders and leaders began to meet quietly, developing a plan for pursuing legal title to their traditional lands. But Randy Pokiak recalls that the group had a rule: none of the planning was to be discussed with non-Indigenous people outside COPE. "They said: 'No, we can't show our cards until the time comes.' They knew what was at stake."

Offshore Drilling

The greatest threat to the Inuvialuit was a proposal from a Calgary-based oil company called Dome Petroleum. The company was run by Jack Gallagher, who earned the nickname

'Smilin' Jack' because of his upbeat attitude in an industry that presented great risks.

Unlike many of the oil companies operating in the Delta, Dome Petroleum had its roots in Canada. The company received its first boost in the early 1950s, shortly after the major discovery of oil at Leduc, Alberta. Jack Gallagher, who was both the CEO and the sole employee of the company at the time, had wanted to get into the Alberta oil play, but didn't have the money to compete for oil leases against the major international firms. So he went to Saskatchewan, where the government was opening leases south of Regina.

Gallagher was aware that many Saskatchewan farmers possessed both the surface and the mineral rights to their farmland, so he sent an envoy to visit the farmers, one by one, offering to buy their mineral rights. He explained the mineral rights were of no value to them, so most of the farmers signed the agreements. Their attitude changed when Dome drilled in the Weyburn area and made a significant discovery. The farmers protested vigorously that they had been duped. The Saskatchewan government of Tommy Douglas appointed a commission to review the mineral rights fiasco but its recommendations were weak. The farmers stood by and watched as Dome Petroleum built its first successful oil field, literally in their back yards.

A quarter of a century later, Dome Petroleum eyed the potential of the Beaufort Sea with great interest. But once again the firm did not have the financial resources to bid against big international oil companies, so Dome secured drilling leases in the deep waters of the Beaufort Sea.

This posed an even greater concern for the Inuvialuit than the artificial islands. For most of the year the Beaufort Sea was covered with a deep layer of ice. The ice usually cleared for two months in mid-summer, but that wasn't always the case; in 1974, the Beaufort remained locked in ice all summer long.

Dome Petroleum had purchased two World War II-era ships that had been lying abandoned in Galveston, Texas. The ships were cut in half so that a drill rig could be placed midship. The plan was that the drill ships would make their way up the West Coast, through the Bering Strait around Alaska, and into the Beaufort Sea. There they would drill two exploratory wells in the brief summer months when the sea was free of ice.

The plan horrified the Inuvialuit. If there was an oil blowout, ships might not be able to reach the site to drill a relief well for months, perhaps not until the following summer. Oil might pour into the frozen ocean for a year or more. In that time, the Arctic gyre, a current that circles the North Pole, would carry the oil across the Beaufort Sea to Alaska and beyond. COPE's president, Sam Raddi, described the concern of his people: "If there were a blowout, it would kill whales, seals, fishes and polar bears. How could the people in the Inuvialuit communities survive without their traditional food?"

When asked about that prospect, Jack Gallagher was his usual upbeat self. "Remember," he told me in an interview at his Calgary headquarters. "Oil is natural in the sea. Oil is formed from marine organisms decomposing. People get all upset about a little oil in the sea, but it's really not all that serious."

Inuvik: The Formal Hearing

In February of 1976, Judge Berger arrived in Inuvik to hold both formal and community hearings on the proposal for a pipeline through the Mackenzie Delta. His mandate was not to decide whether offshore drilling could begin—the federal cabinet had retained the right to make that decision—but he was permitted to hear evidence of the impact of deep water drilling on the land, wildlife and people of the delta. The Cabinet would make its decision to approve the drilling in March of 1976, just as Berger's hearings in the Delta were drawing to a close.

The intervenors, the environmental organizations and the Committee for Original Peoples Entitlement, knew that the southern media would be attending the Berger Inquiry hearings in the Mackenzie Delta. That would give them the opportunity to explain the challenges of offshore drilling to a national audience. Lawyer Russell Anthony, representing environmental organizations, collaborated with John Bayly of the Inuvialuit to bring some of Canada's leading scientists to Inuvik. Their purpose was to provide testimony on the potential impact of an oil blowout in the ice-infested waters of the Beaufort Sea.

The testimony of the Beaufort Sea Project, a group of government scientists based in Victoria, BC, was led by Dr. Allen Milne. They explored the impacts of an oil blowout depending on the season when it took place. They first projected the impact of a blowout in early October, 1976, in the last days before drilling ended, when it would be too late to drill a relief well. Key wildlife species, such as the whales and geese, would have departed from the Beaufort Sea by then. However, the spill would result in significant contamination of 400 kilometres of shoreline around the Tuktoyaktuk Peninsula. This would endanger five species of whitefish that migrate to the area for the winter, a critical source of food both for Inuvialuit families and their dog teams. If large quantities of oil were buried in the sediments on the sea floor, they might have a toxic effect on bottom-dwelling organisms. "The recuperation of fish stocks could be delayed for at least a decade," the scientists concluded.

But what if the blowout took place in winter? The scientists had determined that 15,000 ringed seals and 2,500 bearded seals lived in the ice leads off the coast. Their report stated that there was a high probability that oil contamination would destroy the cod on which the seals depended. Moreover, the danger travelled up the food chain. The scientists could not hazard a guess as to the damage that would be caused to a polar bear's insulating fur if it came into contact with an oil-soaked seal.

The study moved on to consider the impact of a blowout in the spring, when the oil captured by the winter ice would be released into the ocean. This is the time when huge populations of seabirds arrive from the south. The scientists reached a disturbing conclusion: "Since very small quantities of oil, often a few drops, can contaminate the birds' thermal protection, and waterproofing, the kill of seabirds would be great." They estimated that 15 per cent of the total migration, as many as 175,000 birds, might perish.

A second concern was the migration of whales—5,000 belugas and a smaller number of bowheads that travel along the Beaufort coast each summer to reach their calving grounds in Shallow Bay and Kugmallit Bay, on either side of the Tuktoyaktuk Peninsula. The scientists estimated that a summer blowout would send an estimated 3,800 cubic metres of oil into the sea over the summer. They were not able to reach a conclusion on the impact this would have on the whales or their calves, but they did note that the machines, ships and aircraft heading to the two drill sites might cause an intolerable level of noise for the whales while they rested at their calving ground nearby.

The scientists were similarly unable to state with any certainty what impact the spill would have on the Porcupine caribou herd along the north coast of Yukon. The caribou were known to fend off clouds of mosquitoes by soaking themselves in the sea. What would happen to the herd if the water were covered with a thin film of oil?

On the final pages of the study, the Beaufort Sea Project evaluated the effect of the offshore drilling program on the Inuvialuit living in nearby communities. They noted that the community of Tuktoyaktuk consumed 50 to 75 tonnes of fish each year, so an oil spill "could destroy a sizeable proportion of the domestic fishery." The study estimated that the cost of substitute foods from the store would be ten to one hundred times greater than the cost of food from the land. To this, they added the potential losses that the Inuvialuit would suffer if the tourism and commercial hunting economies were disrupted by a spill.

The testimony at the Inquiry was buttressed by the release of a book, *Oil Under the Ice*, by Dr. Douglas Pimlott, a leading voice from the Canadian Arctic Resources Committee. In an interview after his testimony, he said:

> If we have the ice conditions of 1974, we may have to wait more than a year before a relief well can be drilled. In that time, the well could put a couple of hundred thousand barrels of oil into the sea. It would wipe out many of the seabirds and have a disastrous effect on the seals and polar bears. It would be catastrophic.

Kit Vincent, the executive secretary of CARC, summarized the book's thesis: "The government has its head in the sand if it thinks the capability exists to clean up an Arctic oil spill." He explained that the book held information that the government had kept from the public. CARC had gained the information through secret sources because "it was being hidden at every level of government." He added: "The minister is denying the risk in order to give the public the impression that everything is under control." With the Inuvik hearings of the Inquiry completed, the secrets were out.

Inuvik: The Community Hearing

The first community hearing in the Delta opened in Inuvik, a town of 3,000 that had been built by the federal government twenty years before as the administrative centre for the Western Arctic. The community hearings there attracted a diverse audience of Inuvialuit and government employees, most of whom had relocated from the south. The mix promised that the Inuvik hearings would be tense.

The first people to speak were four members of the Inuvik Hunters and Trappers Association. The president, Ishmael Alunik, began by addressing an issue that was frequently under debate in a government town: jobs. "We hear all the time, from the oil companies and the government, that trapping and living off the land is dying out, that the people all want jobs. This is not true."

188 AGAINST THE ODDS

As proof he brought out a list of 77 full-time hunters and trappers who lived wholly from the land. He pointed out that many others had been driven off their land by seismic activity, so they moved to Inuvik and took jobs until they could get back on the land again. He had a list of those names as well. Families that had moved to Inuvik also hunted on weekends so they could continue to eat traditional food. Those who were not able to hunt could order wild food from COPE. A phone call would bring delivery of a box of Arctic char or the hind quarter of a caribou.

Alunik himself had held a government job for many years, frequently telling his wife that soon they would go back to their traditional way of life. Finally, she scoffed: they would never return to the land. He quit his job the next day and used his savings to buy the gear he needed to hunt and trap again.

In his speech, Ishmael Alunik pointed out that those who left their camps ran a risk: sometimes strangers burned their cabins or stole their traps, stretchers and gear. They needed their jobs to get money to go back on the land again. He concluded: "We do not think of our jobs as a substitute for living off the land. Jobs are another way to help us live."

Suddenly the meeting was disrupted by an irate woman, Lynn Stewart, who objected that "the foreman of this meeting" was allowing the Inuvialuit to speak for too long. "I think this should be stopped. You should allot a time of three to five minutes. People should make their point in that length of time and allow people to speak." The interruption was followed by a moment of shocked silence, then a smattering of applause by a few non-Indigenous people in the room.

Judge Berger began to answer, but she cut him off to complain that the translation into the Inuvialuktun language was taking too much time. "We came to listen to citizens off the street," she concluded.

In words that were calm and measured, Judge Berger promised the gathering that he would sit and listen as late into the night as people wished. Moreover, there would be more community hearings in the weeks to come. But he was firm:

> I want to hear from the people of Inuvik, white and native, and it may take a little while .... These gentlemen took advantage of the hearings this evening to come and speak and I intend to hear them, as I intend to hear you. And I intend to make sure the proceedings are conducted in both languages. I am afraid you and I are at odds about that, but I am running the hearing, so I'm afraid we'll do it that way.

As he concluded, a loud round of applause erupted from the Inuvialuit and a few non-Indigenous people in attendance.

But the outburst had made the representatives of the Hunters and Trappers Association uncomfortable. The other two speakers offered a few sentences and the association's participation in the hearing concluded.

The combative back-and-forth continued through the evening. A helicopter pilot raised an objection to Ishmael Alunik's assertion that industrial activity was interfering with traditional hunting practices. The Inuvialuit translator, Rosie Albert, disagreed. She described a goose hunt the previous fall, when Inuvialuit hunters travelled to Shallow Bay in sixteen canoes. They knew the route the geese would take in the morning, so they camped overnight in a spot that the geese would fly over in the morning. "But while we were there a helicopter flew early in the morning and chased them all away. We had to travel three or four hours to find where they stopped."

At the next hearing, Dr. Peter Usher rose to speak. A geographer, born and raised in Montreal, he had travelled to the North a decade before to lead a study of the trapping economy on Banks Island. He embedded himself in the community, travelling with the trappers as they collected the island's rich bounty of white fox fur. His three-volume report, *Bankslanders*, was studied by university classes across Canada. In the years after the study was published, Peter Usher returned to the North to help COPE prepare its evidence for the Berger Inquiry. Most of the time he provided advice in the background, but the verbal bullying by the white residents of Inuvik compelled him to speak.

> I think the biggest change I've noticed over the years is that southerners can now come North and live in a place like Inuvik, and maybe even Tuk and Aklavik, and insulate themselves from the real North. They don't ever have to travel on the land. They don't have to eat local food. They need never be without running water and electric power, and they need never even meet local people except in a very formal way, you know, by their business or their work. That's not the way Northern community life used to be. But it seems that the society and the economy that southern Canadians have by and large chosen to build here is for their own peculiar purposes, deliberately insulated from the land and pre-existing life of the North, with little reference to native people of this land, and less knowledge of them. I do not think that southern Canadians have any God-given right to do that."

With that, the division was clear. There was a gulf between the Inuvialuit who continued to pursue many of their traditional ways and the newcomers who felt that Northern existence must soon replicate life in the south. In Inuvik, people stood on one side of that argument or the other.

Holman Island (Ulukhaktok)

The Inquiry chartered a plane to take the judge, his entourage and a handful of reporters to the Inuvialuit communities scattered through across the Beaufort Sea. The first was held in the village of Holman Island, now Ulukhaktok, on Victoria Island.

The hearing began with remarkable testimony by Elders who had grown up living a nomadic life. They travelled great distances with dog teams in winter. In summer they travelled in homemade schooners, as far as the trading post at Hershel Island, 800 kilometres away. They knew the challenges of the Beaufort Sea better than anyone.

Elder Agnes Aleekok described an experience she had as a young mother fifty years before. Agnes and her husband were travelling by schooner when the engine failed. "The ship was sinking, big waves. At that time too, they started getting cold from the snow." The passengers fought their way through the waves to the beach. "While they were staying on the shore, that boat started breaking up and drifting ashore so they started picking up all these things. They found some logs on the shore, they started making some kind of a house."

It was late summer, so ice began to pile up on the shore. The stranded families realized they might be marooned on the beach for months before they could be rescued, so the men struggled back to the spot where the boat had sunk. "It was clear water so they started to hook whatever they need from the bottom of the sea. They get a few rifles like that." The rifles came in handy the next day, when a polar bear crept along the beach and confronted a woman who was retrieving wood to build the shelter.

For days the survivors of the shipwreck found barely enough food to survive.

> They got nothing to eat, they got no tea, no flour, no sugar. But there happened to be five bags of muktuk (whale blubber) in seal bags, that drift ashore. That's how they lived, with these five bags of muktuk."

At the Inquiry hearing, the residents of Holman used their sea-faring experience to raise questions about Dome Petroleum's plans to drill offshore. Roy Inuktalik described how the ocean currents became stronger in the spring, flooding the islands and the bays. Oil from a blowout would be spread across vast distances. Simon Kataoyak reminded the judge that even a small oil spill could be harmful. He described fishing in summer, looking into the calm ocean and seeing the reddish tinge created by masses of krill. "If an oil spill occurs, if it's drifting around, that is the first thing that's going to be killed." Krill are a vital part of the diet of seals and whales, so the impact would travel up the food chain. The effects would not be immediate, but they would be dire.

Sachs Harbour

As Judge Berger travelled through the Beaufort Sea communities, the concerns over the coming drilling season expanded. Initially worry was directed largely at the oil industry's plan to drill offshore in the Beaufort Sea. But it became clear that the Inuvialuit were also worried that the government was so anxious for a major oil discovery that it would not uphold its responsibility to protect the environment. Proof of this was offered when David Nasogaluak spoke.

Months before, on his first visit to Sachs Harbour, Michael Jackson had met Nasogaluak.

> "[David Nasogaluak] was a famous trapper who had one of the lengthiest traplines in the country, over 300 kilometres long, 600 kilometres round trip. He was one of the most successful trappers in Canada and had been featured in *Time* magazine. He took me out of the village on a snowmobile and showed me a whip he had. Usually when hunters finished a season they closed their traps and brought them back to town so no one got caught in a trap over the summer. But with such a long trapline, it was a pain for David to bring them all in. So he closed his traps by taking this long caribou hide whip and snapping them shut."

When they chatted about the upcoming hearings, Michael suggested to David that he didn't have to make a speech. He could explain to the judge what he had done during he previous week: what he had seen on his journey, what he had gathered from the land to feed the community.

David told the judge about a recent journey where he had seen proof that the oil industry's activities were threatening both the land and the sea around Banks Island. Years later, I asked him about his testimony.

> At the time Judge Berger came to Sachs Harbour there was a lot of pressure from the oil companies. I knew the pressure would be more and more, not less. They don't give up, eh? They changed the Delta region. It was not good. On dry land it's okay to drill, but not near the water. The geese used to be plentiful in the fall, but they don't stop anymore. The soil got contaminated from those substances and then it froze over. Clean up not good enough. In the springtime, west wind comes and thaws it out, just enough for the water to flow. The contamination flows from there.

If the government was not able to control standard drilling activities, how would it oversee offshore drilling that depended on new and untested technologies? The trappers from Sachs Harbour explained to Judge Berger that they didn't need the oil industry. Their people had lived on those Arctic islands for centuries. They had the freedom to travel where and when they wanted. Many of the trappers had incomes that rivalled that of wealthy southerners. Why should the oil industry be permitted to put all of that at risk?

Paulatuk

In Paulatuk, the hearings took place in a classroom at the school. The judge sat at the teacher's desk, while the townspeople, the Inquiry staff and the press crowded together in the student seats. Speakers sat at a table at the front of the room, with the maps of the Inuvialuit Land Use and Occupancy study spread across the wall behind them.

When Judge Berger invited comments, one of the first speakers was a teacher, Rosemary Kirby, who had grown up in Paulatuk. She told the judge that her family's food came from the land. They only went to the store for flour, salt and sugar. "We depended on the land for meat, fish, berries and seal. I can remember, when I was a kid, fighting for seal flippers. They were so delicious."

But each year in September a plane landed and the children of Paulatuk were herded on board. They spent ten months of the year in residential school in Aklavik, 500 kilometres from home. Rosemary recalled that over time the children were taught to be ashamed of their families, their traditions. But she fought back. "I finally figured out that even though I was ashamed of being Eskimo, there was a spark of something inside of me...." Rosemary trained as a teacher and returned to her home community to teach in the school.

In describing her experience, she made an analogy that was meaningful to the hunters and trappers of Paulatuk.

> When a wolverine is cornered, there is only one thing he does, and that is to fight, to live, to survive. And I feel that the Eskimo and the Indian people of the North... are like trapped wolverines. The only way they can give anything to the future of our generation is to fight back for what they want, what they think the future children need.

She impressed on the judge the gravity of the hearing for the people of Paulatuk. "I think this is probably the first occasion that we have had to have someone fight for us. And Mr. Berger, I think you are that person and I will leave that on your conscience."

Rosemary asked to address some questions to John Hnatiuk, the spokesperson for the two oil companies, Dome Petroleum and Gulf Oil, that had applied to drill in the Beaufort Sea that summer. She peppered the oilman with questions. Would permission for drilling in future years be granted automatically? How would the drilling impact negotiations for an Inuvialuit land claim? Could the companies not pause the drilling until land claims were settled?

Hnatiuk replied that the company would drill just as safely before or after land claims were settled. He repeated the oil industry's assessment of the likelihood of a blowout: only one in 20,000 wells had suffered a serious blowout.

After twenty minutes, Rosemary was frustrated. She turned to the judge and asked: "Do you think I have received an answer?" In an unusual response, Judge Berger went to the front of the room and, using the map on the wall, described past evidence he had heard from the oil industry, government scientists and the environmental organizations. He explained issues where the evidence disagreed: the oil industry claimed that there was a one in 20,000 chance of a blowout, but Dr. Pimlott, a witness for the environmental organizations, testified that the likelihood was one in 500. The people of Paulatuk leaned forward, listening intently as the judge walked them through the scientific debate that had taken place in Inuvik a few weeks before.

Then the judge invited John Hnatiuk to respond. This time the oilman gave a much fuller answer, painting a vivid picture of the damage that would be done by an oil spill.

I do not claim that we could clean up all of the oil if there was a blowout, but all of the companies that work together with the government, all of the equipment available would be put to use. There would be long rubber booms that would contain as much of the oil as possible so that it could be picked up by boat. If the waves got high this would not work. If the ice moved in during the summer, this would not work. Then after it froze over you might be able to burn some of the oil right at the well because it is coming up mixed with natural gas. Some of it could be burned there until the ice gets too thick to be broken. Then the oil would collect under the ice and would be locked in the ice like a sandwich.

The judge's intervention gave Rosemary the courage to return to her questions. An oilspill on ice would become a floating iceberg in spring, would it not? Would the company follow the floating ice? What if the ice moved in early?

An hour into the discussion, John Hnatiuk was being more judicious with his answers. He agreed that there were a host of issues where the answers were still unknown. Rosemary Kirby, encouraged by the judge, had the answer she had been looking for: offshore drilling in the ice-infested waters of the Beaufort Sea was a dangerous experiment.

Tuktoyaktuk

It was not surprising that the community hall in Tuktoyaktuk was packed for the community hearing there. The two wells that would be drilled in the deeper waters of the Beaufort Sea were located less than a hundred kilometres from Tuktoyaktuk. That community would be most severely hit if a well were to blow out the following summer.

On the opening day, a community leader, Vince Steen, gave Judge Berger a summary of a century of disappointments that the Inuvialuit had suffered in their encounters with new-comers from the south. It was a litany of greed.

From my point of view it goes way back, back to when the Eskimo first seen the white man. Most of them were whalers and the whaler wasn't very nice to the Eskimo. He just took all the whales they could get and never mind the results. Who is paying for that now? The Eskimo. There's a quota on the number of whales he can kill now. Then next, the white traders and white trappers. The white traders took them for every cent they could get. You know the stories in every history book where they had to pile fur as high as your gun. Those things were not fair. The native lived with it, damn well had to, to get that gun, to make life easier for himself. Then there was the white trapper. He came along and showed the Eskimo how to use the traps, steel-jawed traps, leg-hold traps. They used them, well they're still using them today, but for the first seventy years there were no complaints from down south about how cruel those traps are, as long as white trappers were using them.... After them we have all the government people coming in and making settlements all over, telling the people what to do, what is best for them, live here, live there, that place is no more good for you. So they did, they all moved into the settlements and for the '50s and '60s they damn near starved, most of them were on rations because they weren't going out in the country any more. Then came the oil companies. First the seismographic outfits... and he watched them plough up his land in summertime, plough up their traps in wintertime. What are you going to do about it? That cat is bigger than your snowmobile or your dog team.

Vince Steen ended with a pessimistic prediction of the impact of drilling in the deep waters of the Beaufort Sea.

If they drill out there, if they kill what little whales are left, what little seals are left, what little polar bears are left, with one oil spill of any size to hurt those animals, we're finished. The Eskimo population and culture is finished, because you have to live as a white man and you have nothing left.

Four months before the drill ships reached the Beaufort Sea, Vince Steen had given a dour assessment of the future.

March Madness

The news reports from the Inquiry hearings in the Delta had drawn attention, much of it negative, to Dome's plans in the Beaufort Sea. The combined testimony of the Beaufort Sea scientists and the Inuvialuit communities had been sent south by the media outlets covering the Inquiry. Suddenly, a drilling proposal that had gone largely unnoticed in the south had become front-page news.

In response, Dome Petroleum mounted a media campaign to calm fears about an offshore oil spill. Senior executives made statements describing the expected bonanza in the Beaufort, predicting gas reserves in the Mackenzie Delta of 250 to 320 trillion cubic feet of gas, a number five to six times higher than the estimate made by the company's drilling partner, Gulf Oil of Canada.

Then Dome invited a reporter from the *Globe and Mail* to travel to Texas, to observe the refitting of the two drill ships so they would be strong enough to cope with Arctic sea conditions. The reporter described how a double hull, with steel up to an inch thick, had been placed around the ship.

> Openings, similar to torpedo tubes, have been put in the sides from which water jets with a thrust of 17,000 pounds can be used to deflect troublesome floes. Each ship has a safety valve capable of withstanding blowout pressure of up to 15,000 lb per square inch.

Eight anchors would hold each ship over the drill hole. The optimistic report ended by noting that the ships would be tested off the Texas coast before heading north in April. That would ensure their passage through the Bering Strait which had only been ice free for two weeks the previous summer.

Days later, *The Globe and Mail* printed a follow up story that dismissed the idea of testing an Arctic drillship in Texas waters. The article, headlined "Cold Comfort" began with a joke. "The incidence of ships being crushed by ice in the waters off Houston,

Texas, is not very high. They are in fact more likely to be pecked to a watery grave by angry seagulls." The article concluded that Dome's test for seaworthiness was "really no assurance at all."

In Ottawa, the federal Cabinet was preparing to make its decision on issuing Dome Petroleum a final permit to drill. The Cabinet ministers were not of one mind. Jean Marchand, the Minister of the Environment had stated openly: "The risks are just too high." The Minister of External Affairs, Allan MacEachen, was under pressure from the US government, which was concerned that a blowout in the Beaufort Sea would pollute the Alaska coastline. But statements from other cabinet ministers suggested that approval had already been granted; all that remained was to decide conditions that would be placed on the company.

The Cabinet meeting was lengthy, the debate was described as "vigorous." When it concluded, reporters descended on the ministers as they headed out the door. Environment Minister Jean Marchand was tight-lipped but Judd Buchanan, the Minister of Indian Affairs and Northern Development, was optimistic. He announced that Dome Petroleum and Gulf Oil would be permitted to drill two wells in the summer of 1976. The *Globe and Mail* covered the press conference:

> The government concluded that the risks are low enough to be acceptable and, balanced with the need to confirm Canada's energy resources, justify proceeding with drilling this year. A review will be done on September 15 and if conditions are favourable, drilling will be allowed for a further ten days.

The government would also require a bond of $50 million to cover the costs of clean-up in the event of an oil spill. Jack Gallagher complained that the bond was $20 million higher than bonds elsewhere in the world. But John Amagoalik of the Inuit Tapirisat of Canada disagreed: "You can't put a price on the Beaufort Sea."

Days after the announcement, at an oil rig off the coast of Norway, a plume of oil shot 180 feet into the air and an estimated 49,000 gallons of oil an hour spilled into the North Sea. Fifteen-foot waves and gale force winds sent the oil slick across the ocean.

In the *Globe and Mail*, Geoffrey Stevens opened an editorial by quoting Vince Steen's powerful speech in Tuktoyaktuk the month before. The headline read: "If they drill out there..." The journalist opined:

> One wishes that before making up its mind on the Beaufort drilling, the Cabinet had sat in on the Berger hearings in Tuktoyaktuk and Paulatuk last month. The ministers might have been disturbed by some of the unanswered environmental questions. They might have been swayed by the opposition of the native people or the concern voiced by Justice Berger.

September Surprise

The federal cabinet had given Dome permission to drill in the Beaufort Sea until September 14. Then, depending on a review of the drilling, the company might be given permission to continue drilling for an additional ten days. In early September the company began a relentless drumbeat of positive news reports. The drilling had progressed smoothly. There were of signs of hydrocarbons in the deep waters of the Beaufort Sea. The drilling permit was extended.

In late September, I travelled to Tuktoyaktuk to get an assessment of the drilling season from people in the community. Had Dome's program brought any benefits? What had come of the industry's promise of jobs?

Most of the Inuvialuit families I spoke to were on the fence: the oil activity had brought a few jobs, but it had also disrupted community life. No one was comfortable talking about their concerns.

The next morning, I saw a Dome supervisor who was picking up workers for their shift. At one cabin, a young worker was still in bed. The Dome boss pounded on the door, then kicked his way in and delivered an expletive-laced tongue-lashing. Then I understood why Tuk people had been afraid to describe the impact of oil company jobs on the community.

Late in the day, I joined a crowd of men who were waiting to head out to the drillship for their shift. There was a lengthy delay. One man, with a strong Texas accent, cursed the company, saying the managers were fools. When asked why a Texan was so far from home, he said he had been brought north to help handle an emergency. There had been a blowout.

Back in Inuvik, our story hit the evening news in the North. But the next morning, the national newscast held a surprise. Dome Petroleum had announced that its Beaufort Sea well showed a flow of gas. Jack Gallagher boasted: "We know we have gas down there. We are in full-control of the well."

At the COPE office, Sam Raddi said that the federal government should suspend Dome's licence to continue drilling in light of the blowout threat. "We now see that the claims of infallibility made by Dome and Canmar for their equipment have been refuted by events."

A small three-paragraph article appeared in back of second section of the *Globe and Mail*. It announced that one man had been killed and another taken to hospital as a result of an explosion aboard the drill ship, *Explorer 1*.

It was another six months before the Canadian Arctic Resources Committee released a government report: the drilling company had lost 3,000 feet of drill pipe in the Tingmiark well before it was abandoned.

The encouraging signs of a major gas accumulation that a subsidiary of Dome Petroleum had thought it had tapped in the Beaufort Sea last fall now seem at least inconclusive and possibly a false alarm. According to a federal government report on the 1975 Dome drilling experience in the Beaufort area high pressure zone in the Tingmiark well close to the 10,000 foot level 'is thought to have been from a gas zone which quickly depleted into a water flow.'

Randy Pokiak summed up the concern in the Inuvialuit communities:

It scared the heck out of us because there was no one there to protect our interests. We were looked at as hindering progress. They wanted to develop the North through its resources, but they were leaving out the people who relied on the land.

A CONVERSATION WITH SAM RADDI

By 1977, Dome Petroleum was looking forward to its second summer of drilling in the Beaufort Sea. Despite the loss the year before—both of the Tingmiark well and the life of a rig worker—the company was pressing the federal government to grant approval for a five year drilling plan. This was despite the fact that a government report had revised its estimate of the likelihood of a blowout. The estimate in 1976 had been one well in 20,000. The new estimate was one well in 300. In Inuvik, I went to interview Sam Raddi about COPE's relationship with Dome and the federal government. Were the lines of communication more open than they had been in the first difficult year? The answer was no. The Inuvialuit organization had been by-passed.

"All the way back to the 1930s and 40s, the Inuit were telling the experts what they knew about what could damage the environment. The government always says: we have to get experts to look into it before we take your word for it. But our people always know what is best for the fish and wildlife. The government never likes to acknowledge that. They always get scientists to prove it. But in the end it always seems to be right, what the Inuvialuit said in the first place.

When the Berger Inquiry came, the community hearings were like a court case with the Judge sitting there. It was hard for some people to speak at first, but when people relaxed, they gave very good evidence.

I was quite disappointed when the government gave Dome permission to drill last summer because communities like Sachs Harbour, Paulatuk, Tuk, Holman Island, they had always objected to any drilling in the Beaufort Sea. The Committee for Original Peoples Entitlement and the Beaufort Sea communities knew—and Dome Petroleum knew—that Dome didn't have an adequate contingency plan in case of a blowout. That's the reason we were opposed to the government issuing Dome a permit to drill.

When Thomas Berger went to the settlements, people told him that they didn't want to see any drilling that year. When the government group, the Arctic Waters Oil and Gas Advisory Committee, went round to the settlements, the Inuvialuit told them the same thing. I was there.

The government assessment said if there's an oil spill or a blowout in the summer, it could flow for a year, through the winter until the next summer, because they won't have time to drill a relief well before the sea freezes up again. The government assessment said that if the oil spills, it will kill a lot of whales and seabirds, fishes and seals and polar bears. That was a fact and we were concerned about it.

The people of the Beaufort Sea were concerned that Dome should try to improve their clean up facilities. The company didn't want to hear that. They said they had the best clean up facilities in the world. They might have had the best facilities, but they weren't good enough for the Arctic. All they had was four-foot booms and they won't work. Gordon Harrison, the president of Canmar Drilling, told the people in Tuk himself: four-foot booms couldn't handle the ice in an oil spill. They'd just break.

After the Berger Inquiry hearings ended, Dome Petroleum came north. They bypassed COPE and went to the settlement councils. We tried to sit down with them to tell them how things could work better for them and our people, but they didn't seem to want to co-operate. They ignored COPE.

In May, Dome Petroleum wrote letters to the settlement councils, saying that they would like to get one or two people from each settlement to go down to Victoria to see those drill ships that they had. They didn't send a letter to COPE. I found out about it when I went to Ottawa. Mr. Arthur Kruger, the deputy minister of DIAND, told me that himself. The government thought it was a great idea.

Mary Collins, who was a consultant to Dome, said that it was her idea to form an advisory committee with the town councils. But if she wanted to get better information, she could have dealt directly with COPE or the Hunters and Trappers Associations. So I got the feeling that she and Dome had set up this advisory committee with a lot of money - $90,000 - to fool around. Dome was just using this advisory committee."

A CONVERSATION WITH PETER GREEN

When the plane with the Berger Inquiry team landed in Paulatuk, young Peter Green was there to meet the Judge on behalf of the community. He took the Judge to meet some of the families in the community, then dropped him off at the school where the hearing would take place. Over the years, Peter Green became a respected Inuvialuit leader. In 2015, I asked him about his memories of the day the judge visited his community.

"Development was active in the 1970s. Oil and gas people were up here. They were causing a disruption, a disturbance in the way of life of the Inuvialuit people.

We heard complaints from hunters in Sachs Harbour. They told us that seismic lines, the wires that were used on shot holes, were tangled up in the horns of caribou. That was the beginning of our awareness.

Hey, development is good to a certain point but it was not doing any good to the wildlife on the land. There was a disturbance to fish, implosions in the water. Something had to be done.

In 1970, the Committee for Original People's Entitlement (COPE) was organized as a society. It was for all Aboriginal people to begin with: the Inuit in the east, the Dene in the south, and the Inuvialuit in this area. In the years that followed, the groups that formed COPE decided to go on their own because of the operating costs. One of them was travel.

So from then on COPE worked hard to get a moratorium on development activities because of the mess that was happening to the wildlife, to the land, to the people. And COPE hasn't stopped. It kept going right up to the day the Inuvialuit Final Agreement was signed with the federal government.

Those were the days of Dome Petroleum. They were drilling in our Beaufort Sea. The company was supported through a federal government programme set up for offshore drilling. And an incident happened with a blow out preventer on the bottom of the Beaufort Sea.

So that's what we focused on. COPE has maintained: If you're going to drill out there, do it properly. Get the resources you need. If you don't have them, don't come.

When Judge Berger came to Paulatuk, I testified. I said: 'I'm tired of hearing government and the oil company people and the resource people as well saying 'We are the experts. You tell us what and how your life is and we'll judge it from our standpoint.' I say that's all hogwash because it's no longer the government people or the oil companies or any other type of research type people that are the experts.

This is no longer so. Who are the experts on this very land you people are sitting on now? I'm saying that we, the Inuit people, consider ourselves to be experts... we are the experts because we know how animal behavior is, how weather changes might affect the patterns. We are the people to consult with because we are the ones that have been, and are, living on this land. We are for development but development has to be according to our terms. If certain guidelines are set up by the people that live here in this country, then maybe types of development can go on. If no, if no consultation is done with the Inuit people that live here, then forget about it because it will, for one thing, be a failure.

I was a young man then. I went to meet Judge Berger when his air-craft landed. I was asked by COPE to take him to meet people. Right in the first few minutes you could tell Berger had stature, he had charisma. He was calm about the proceedings, the work that needed to be done, and he understood people. I still respect and admire the work he did."

CHAPTER TEN

INQUIRY: THE RECOMMENDATIONS

Thomas R. Berger

~

T HE PIPELINE ISSUE confronted us in Canada with the necessity of weighing fundamental values: industrial, environmental and social, in a way that we had not had to face before.

The Northern native people, along with many witnesses at the Inquiry, insisted that the land they had long depended upon would be injured by the construction of a pipeline and the establishment of an energy corridor. Environmentalists pointed out that the North, the last great wilderness area of Canada, is slow to recover from environmental degradation; its protection is, therefore, of vital importance to all Canadians.

It is not easy to measure that concern against the more precisely calculated interests of industry. You cannot measure environmental values in dollars and cents. But still we had to try to face the questions that are posed in the North of today: Should we open up the North as we opened up the West? Should the values that conditioned our attitudes towards the environment in the past prevail in the North today and tomorrow?

The Northern Yukon is an Arctic and subarctic wilderness of incredible beauty, a rich and varied eco-system: nine million acres of lands in its natural state, inhabited by thriving populations of plants and animals. This wilderness has come down through the ages, and it is a heritage that future generations, living in an industrial world even more complex than ours, will surely cherish.

If you were to build a pipeline from Alaska along the Arctic coast of the Yukon, you would be opening up the calving grounds of the Porcupine caribou herd. This is one of the last great herds of caribou—110,000 animals—in North America. Every spring they journey from the mountains in the interior of the Yukon, to the calving grounds on the Arctic coast. There they are able to leave the wolves behind; they can forage on cotton grass, and bear their young before the onset of summer mosquitoes and bot flies.

In late August, as many as 500,000 snow geese gather on the Arctic Coastal Plain to feed on the tundra grasses, sedges and berries, before embarking on the flight to their wintering grounds. They must build up an energy surplus to sustain them for their long southward migration to California, the Gulf Coast, or Central and South America.

The peregrine falcon, golden eagle, and other birds of prey nest in Northern Yukon. These species are dwindling in numbers because of the loss of their former ranges on the North American continent and because of toxic materials in the environment. Here in these remote mountains they still nest and rear their young, undisturbed by man.

The proposal by Arctic Gas to build a pipeline across the Northern Yukon confronted us with a fundamental choice. It was a choice that depended not simply upon the impact of a pipeline across the Northern Yukon, but upon the impact of the establishment of an energy corridor across it. This eco-system, with its magnificent wilderness and scenic beauty, has always been protected by its inaccessibility. With pipeline construction, the development of supply and service roads, the intensification of the search for oil and gas, the establishment of an energy corridor, and the increasing occupation of the region, it would no longer be inaccessible to man and his machines.

The wilderness does not stop, of course, at the boundary between Alaska and the Yukon. The Arctic National Wildlife Refuge in northeastern Alaska, contiguous to the Northern

Yukon, is a part of the same wilderness. In fact, the calving grounds of the Porcupine caribou herd extend well into Alaska, along the coastal plain as far as Camden Bay, 100 miles to the west of the international boundary; the area of concentrated use by staging snow geese, by nesting and moulting waterfowl and by seabirds, also extends far into Alaska.

So the future of the caribou, of the birds—of the whole of this unique wilderness region—was a matter of concern to both Canada and the United States. The proposal by Arctic Gas to build a pipeline across the North Slope of Alaska and across Northern Yukon confronted us with a fundamental choice. For if a pipeline were built and an energy corridor established along that route it would result in the Porcupine herd being driven from its calving grounds, reducing it over time to a remnant. The occupation of the lands used by staging snow geese would constitute a threat to the survival of very large numbers of these birds.

No one had sought to weigh the evidence of biologists in this way. No one had foreseen that the weight of the evidence would have fallen so heavily on the side of those who argued there should be no pipeline built across the North Slope of Alaska and across Northern Yukon.

I therefore recommended against the Arctic Gas route. I urged that an International Wilderness Area should be established comprising, on the Canadian side, nine million acres in Northern Yukon and, on the American side, the nine-million-acre Arctic National Wildlife Refuge in Alaska. Together these two areas, nine million acres on each side of the International Boundary, would constitute a magnificent area large enough to provide for the long-term wellbeing of its wildlife, and especially of the Porcupine caribou heard and the snow geese. It would be one of the largest wilderness areas in the world.

Preservation of the wilderness and of the caribou herd would plainly be in keeping with the interest of the native people on both sides of the border. But certain essential conditions would have to be observed: the people would have to be guaranteed the right to live, hunt, trap and fish within the park. I also suggested that they should play an important part in the management of the park and, in particular, of the caribou herd.

I had to consider the welfare of another international resource—the white whales of the Beaufort Sea. I recommended that a whale sanctuary be established in Mackenzie Bay. In summer the white whales of the Beaufort Sea converge on the Mackenzie Delta to calve. Why? Because the Mackenzie River rises in Alberta and British Columbia, and carries warm water to the Arctic. Some 5,000 animals remain in the vicinity of the Delta throughout the summer, then leave for the open sea. For these animals the warm waters around the Mackenzie Delta, especially Mackenzie Bay, are critical habitat. In these warm waters, the whales stay until the calves acquire enough blubber to survive the cold oceanic water. Nowhere else, so far as we know, can they go for this essential part of their life cycle. The evidence—and it was not contested—was that oil and gas exploration and production activity could so disturb the whale herd that they would be unable to reproduce successfully. In time, the herd would die out.

I concluded that we must preserve these waters from any disturbance that would drive the whales from them. I recommended that a whale sanctuary be established in Mackenzie Bay, in waters where the greatest concentration of whales is found in summer.

Is a whale sanctuary in west Mackenzie Bay a practical proposition? What will its effect be on future oil and gas exploration? Will it impose an unacceptable check on oil and gas exploration and development in the Mackenzie Delta and the Beaufort Sea? We are fortunate in that the areas of intense petroleum exploration, to date, lie east of the proposed whale sanctuary, both offshore and onshore. A whale sanctuary can be set aside and oil and gas activity can be forbidden there without impairing industry's ability to tap the principal sources of petroleum beneath the Beaufort Sea.

I sought to reconcile these goals: industrial, environmental and social. I proposed an international wilderness area in Northern Yukon and Northeastern Alaska and urged that no pipeline cross it. But at the same time, I indicated that the Alaska Highway route, as a corridor for the transportation of Alaskan gas to the Lower 48, was preferable from an environmental point of view. This route lies hundreds of miles to the south and to the west of the critical habitat for caribou, whales and wildlife which I sought to preserve. Construction of a pipeline along the Alaska Highway route would not threaten major populations of any species. If a pipeline is to be built then it ought to be along this route.

What I have said will give you some idea of the magnitude of our task. The Inquiry had to weigh a whole series of matters, some tangible, some intangible. But in the end, no matter how many experts there may be, no matter how many pages of computer printouts may have been assembled, there is the ineluctable necessity of bringing human judgment to bear on the main issues. Indeed, when the main issue cuts across a range of questions, spanning the physical and social sciences, the only way to come to grips with it and to resolve it is by the exercise of human judgment.

I advised the Government of Canada that a pipeline corridor is feasible, from an environmental point of view, to transport gas and oil from the Mackenzie Delta along the Mackenzie Valley to the Alberta border. At the same time, however, I recommended that we should postpone the construction of such a pipeline for ten years, in order to strengthen native society and economy—indeed, the renewable resource section—and to enable land claims to be settled.

This recommendation was based on the evidence of the native people. Virtually all of the native people who spoke to the Inquiry said that their claims had to be settled before any pipeline could be built. It should not be thought that native people had an irrational fear of pipelines. They realized, however, that construction of the pipeline and establishment of the energy corridor would mean an influx of tens of thousands of white people from all over Canada seeking jobs and opportunities. They believed that they would be overwhelmed, that their villages would become white towns, and they would be relegated to the fringes of Northern life.

They realized that the pipeline and all that it would bring in its wake would blend to an irreversible shift in social, economic, and political power in the North. They took the position that no pipeline should be built until their claims had been settled.

Settlement of their claims ought to offer the native people a whole range of opportunities: the strengthening of the hunting, fishing, and trapping economy where that is appropriate; the development of the local logging and lumbering industry; development of the fishing industry and of recreation and conservation. I urged in my *Report* that in the North priority be given to local renewable resource activities—not because I feel that such activities are universally desirable, but because they are on a scale appropriate to many native communities. They are activities that local people can undertake, that are amenable to local management and control, and that are related to traditional values. But that need not exclude access to larger companies—where large-scale technology predominates.

We in Canada have looked upon the North as our last frontier. It is natural for us to think of developing the North, of subduing the land, populating it with people from the metropolitan centres, and extracting its resources to fuel our industry and heat our homes. Our whole inclination is to think in terms of expanding our industrial machine to the limit of our country's frontiers. We have never had to consider the uses of restraint, to determine what is the most intelligent use to make of our resources.

The question that we and many other countries face is: are we serious people, willing and able to make up our own minds, or are we simply driven by technology and egregious patterns of consumption to deplete our resources wherever and whenever we find them?

I do not want to be misunderstood about this. I did not propose that we shut up the North, as a kind of living folk museum and zoological gardens.

I proceeded on the assumption that, in due course, we may require the gas and oil of the Western Arctic, and that they may have to be transported along the Mackenzie Valley to markets in the metropolitan centres of North America. I also proceeded on the assumption that we intend to protect and preserve Canada's Northern environment, and that, above all else, we intend to honour the legitimate claims and aspirations of the native people. All of these assumptions were embedded in the Government of Canada's expressed Northern policy for the 1970s.

Indigenous Northerners believed that the building of the pipeline would bring with it complete dependence on the industrial system, and that would entail a future which would have no place for the values they cherish. For native people insist that their culture is still a vital force in their lives.

The culture of native people amounts to more than crafts and carvings. Their tradition of decision-making by consensus, their respect for the wisdom for their Elders, their concept of the extended family, their belief in a special relationship with the land, their regard for the environment, their willingness to share—all of these values persist in one form or another within their own cultures, even though they have been under unremitting pressure to abandon them. Their claims are the means by which they seek to preserve their culture, their values and their identity.

The emergence of native claims should not surprise us. After years of living on the fringes of an economy that has no place from them as workers or consumers, and without the political power to change these things, the native people have now decided that they want to substitute self-determination for enforced dependency.

It will take time to limn these claims, especially as regards their implications for native people entering urban life. Nevertheless, some elements are clear enough; for instance, native people say they want schools where children can learn Indigenous languages, history, lore, and rights. At the same time, they want their children to learn to speak English or French, as the case may be, and to study mathematics, science, and all the subjects that they need to know in order to function in the dominant society. These proposals are not limited to a frontier or rural context.

It is not only we in Canada who must face the challenge that Indigenous Peoples with their own languages and their own cultures present. There are all the countries of the Western Hemisphere, with their Indigenous minorities—Peoples whose fierce wish to retain their own common identity is intensifying as industry, technology, and communications forge a larger and larger mass culture, extruding diversity.

The judgments that we had to make about these questions were not merely scientific and technical. They were, at the end of the day, value judgments. It is impossible—indeed it is undesirable—to try to lift scientific and technological decisions out of their social and environmental context, to disentangle them from the web of moral and ethical considerations which provide the means of truly understanding the impact they will have.

A CONVERSATION WITH JACK MARSHALL,
COUNSEL FOR CANADIAN ARCTIC GAS PIPELINES

"I was working for the legal team for Canadian Arctic Gas Pipelines (CAGPL), a consortium of 26 energy and pipeline companies in Canada and the United States. Parallel cases were being presented in each country, so we had a trans-border team of lawyers in Vancouver, Calgary, Toronto, Ottawa, Montreal, Chicago, New York, Washington, and Louisiana.

At that time, there was a big concern about whether North America was going to be short of energy. The expectation was that, without this gas supply, we risked running short. Natural gas was an environmentally desirable fuel because it has lower emissions and greenhouse gases.

It was essentially an engineering project, a construction project. Our focus was on the technical issues related to building a high capacity, high pressure pipeline in an area of discontinuous permafrost. The emphasis was on proving that the pipeline could be built and operated safely, that construction presented no inordinate challenges.

The major drivers that the consortium was trying to get across were: the need for clean energy and the desirability of a large investment project that would provide opportunities for employment in exploration and maintenance. And all of this could be accomplished in a socially responsible way.

Canadian Arctic Gas favoured the Y-route. The only way that we could make the project economically viable was to hook up at the earliest possible point with the much larger supplies of gas from Prudhoe Bay. But Bob Blair of Foothills Pipelines proposed a competing route. He was an ardent nationalist and he wrapped himself in the flag.

Berger broke new ground by holding community hearings in all the villages that might be remotely considered to be affected. I remember going to Holman Island which had no connection with the pipeline at all. It may have been a diversionary trip that the Commissioner wanted to have.

What is the impact of a pipeline? In Alberta, there are pipelines running everywhere and, barring the odd incident, no one is even aware they exist. But at the Berger Inquiry, this great bogeyman was created, an army of construction workers coming through and devastating the land.

Arctic Gas was slow to realize that politics was becoming the main driver. They didn't appreciate that the Mackenzie Gas pipeline would become a political, rather than an economic, issue. The decision would be made principally on political grounds. Maybe with the best intentions, but with no basis for it in reality."

~

A CONVERSATION WITH ALAN HOLLINGWORTH, COUNSEL FOR FOOTHILLS PIPELINES

"The Arctic Gas consortium was made up of Canadian and American companies. It was sort of like an ocean liner, it was hard to get it to change course. Arctic Gas wanted to construct a 'bullet' pipeline that would go right into the United States. That motivated Alberta Gas Trunk Lines and Westcoast Transmission to split off and form Foothills Pipelines.

The Canadian companies saw that their systems in Alberta and BC were being by-passed, they were left out in the cold. Also, Bob Blair of Foothills was a nationalist and he felt there was a better way to build this pipeline.

So Foothills had to find new counsel. One day Reg Gibbs called me into the office and said: "They are having this Inquiry in the north..."

It was a nationalist time and Foothills had a Canadian proposal, the Maple Leaf Line. They felt there were sufficient reserves to take gas from the Mackenzie Delta down the Valley to the southern provinces. The Foothills case was built around three issues: the pipeline route, the environmental consequences, and the nationalist card.

In those days, everyone sincerely thought that Alberta was running out of gas. There was a perception that the northern reserves would be needed soon. But Alberta was only running out at a given price.

I do remember that John Masters and Jim Grey were saying to anyone who would listen that Canadian Hunter had uncovered this absolute bonanza of gas, trillions and trillions of cubic feet. But there was a lot of skepticism in the industry about whether it was really as much as they said.

In any regulatory hearing, you first decide on your long-term goal. What do you want the decision maker to say? Then you present evidence and cross-examine other expert witnesses. You have to fashion your argument based on that. You can't just pull a fact out of the air, something that wasn't discussed in the evidentiary portion.

The regulatory process can certainly be adversarial, it can be testy at times, and during the Berger Inquiry there were times like that. I remember when Reg Gibbs came up to cross-examine Vern Horte, president of Arctic Gas. They were very skilled lawyers going after very skilled witnesses.

The process is a contest of wills. It has worked for centuries. "

PART III

THE LATER YEARS

"These are questions of fundamental fairness
to the constituent peoples of Canada.
They are the foundations of Canada's claim
that it is a plural democracy."

CHAPTER ELEVEN

CAUGHT IN A CONTROVERSY

Drew Ann Wake

∿

F OR MOST OF US, there comes a moment when we have to
sit down, take stock and make a decision that will dras-
tically alter the years to come. Tom Berger's father, Thore
Berger, faced one of those moments when he had to make an
important ethical decision while serving as an officer in the
Royal Canadian Mounted Police. Years later, Tom described
his father's experience:

> My father was a Mountie in northern British Columbia
> and my mother was a homesteader's daughter from
> Telkwa. They met, they got married and by the time I
> came along my parents had moved to Victoria where
> my father was assigned to criminal investigation.
>
> We always thought that the Mounties were spe-
> cial people. My dad had trophies for marksmanship.
> Stories had been written about him in men's maga-
> zines about the pursuit of some well-known criminals
> in the North.
>
> In Victoria, he arrested a very high-ranking and
> well-connected officer in the Canadian Navy. He was
> told that he should not proceed with the charges,
> that he had to drop the charges. He went ahead, nev-
> ertheless, because he believed that the law had to be
> enforced against everyone, including those who were
> well-connected.

That seemed to represent a roadblock in Thore's career. It was made clear to him that he'd best resign. So he left the force.

He was only 50 or 51 years of age. He had four kids and he had to find work. He had trouble getting a good job—or any job—but he never complained. He never told me this story, my mother told it to me later. But I've always thought it was admirable.

Tom Berger would face his own crucible in 1980, as the Canadian government began its debate on whether to insert a clause protecting Indigenous rights into the Canadian constitution.

The Brown Envelope

In September of 1980, Grand Chief George Manuel sat in the Vancouver office of the Union of British Columbia Indian Chiefs (UBCIC), and worried. He was an experienced leader, who had spent six years at the helm of the National Indian Brotherhood in Ottawa before returning to his home province. But despite all his experience, he was facing a dilemma he wasn't sure he could solve.

The Grand Chief called the two lawyers for the Union, Louise Mandell and Leslie Pinder, into his office and showed them a brown envelope marked 'confidential'. Inside was a document that should not have been in his possession. It was a confidential memo, detailing the federal government's strategy to not engage Indigenous Peoples before patriation of the Constitution, but to leave engagement with them until after patriation.

The writer of the document warned that First Nations might try to gain wide support by drawing the world's attention to the distressing statistics on the lives of the nation's Indigenous citizens: a life expectancy 10 years less than the national average; a 32 percent employment rate; and 50 percent of houses without adequate services. Canada's international reputation would be tarnished if these sobering statistics were broadcast abroad.

But Indigenous leaders wanted to have their rights addressed during the process of constitutional renewal, and not after the constitution returned to Canada. If they were to wait until after repatriation, they feared that Canada would have the power to override Indigenous rights, abrogate their treaties which were made with the British Crown, and under the protection of Great Britain which, under the Canadian constitution, held the power of amendment.

Lawyer Louise Mandell remembered that "Grand Chief George sounded the alarm." George Manuel asked the two lawyers to travel through the province to apprise First Nations leaders of the situation. A consensus emerged. Later that fall, when more than one hundred leaders met at the Union of British Columbia Indian Chiefs Assembly, they released a statement vowing to take action:

> ... exclusion of Indian participation from a broad constitutional review (is) the first mistake that the federal authorities have to correct. Until this is done, Indian Nations reject the intended federal resolution in total as a hostile and aggressive measure and are prepared to employ all means to resist its implementation.

UBCIC followed up its manifesto with an idea that was both bold and creative. A train would go across Canada to deliver their message to the people of Canada, to England, to the world. Two UBCIC staff members took on the task of organizing the Constitution Express. The train departed from Vancouver shortly before Christmas, bound for Ottawa. At every stop along the way, Indigenous people from British Columbia were joined by supporters from other provinces, keen to make their voices heard.

Inside Ottawa

In late January 1981, the federal government and nine pro-
vincial premiers reached an agreement on the wording of the
Charter of Rights and Freedoms. A key clause in the land-
mark document protected the rights of Indigenous people.
Politicians from all parties gathered in a room in the West
Block of Parliament to celebrate. Indian Affairs minister
Jean Chrétien invited Indigenous leaders representing the
National Indian Brotherhood, the Inuit Tapirisat and the
Native Council of Canada to sit next to him and announced
with pride: "Now they are my advisors."

Nine months later, Prime Minister Pierre Trudeau and
nine provincial premiers made a backroom bargain that con-
firmed the wording of the *Canadian Charter of Rights and
Freedoms*—minus the protection of Indigenous rights that
they had greeted with such fanfare a few months before. The
new wording also removed Quebec's traditional veto over
proposed constitutional changes.

That week, Tom Berger was touring Canada to launch
his new book, *Fragile Freedoms*, which recounts moments in
Canadian history when the country failed to protect minority
rights. As part of his book tour, he had been invited to give a
speech at the University of Guelph. He used that opportunity
to criticize the governments' action in direct and unequivo-
cal terms.

Days later, on November 12, 1981 excerpts of the speech
appeared in two newspapers, the *Ottawa Citizen* and the
Globe and Mail:

> The agreement reached in February this year by
> all parties in the House of Commons, to entrench
> Aboriginal rights and treaty rights in the new
> Constitution, has been repudiated by the Prime
> Minister and the premiers.
>
> In fact, they were unanimous on this question.

The Prime Minister and all the premiers were in agreement—not only the nine premiers of the English-speaking provinces, but Premier René Lévesque, too, for the reasons he gave for his refusal to sign the constitutional agreement did not include any reference to native rights. There was, at the end, not one of our Canadian statesmen willing to take a stand for the rights of the Indians, the Inuit and the Métis.

No one would expect that a Constitution drawn up by the provinces would affirm aboriginal rights and treaty rights... Now the federal Government has, in order to obtain a constitutional agreement, surrendered on the issue of native rights. I confess that I never did believe they would...

Why were native rights affirmed in February and rejected in November? I think it is because the native peoples lie beyond the narrow political world of the Prime Minister and the premiers, a world bounded by advisers, memoranda, *non obstante* clauses and photostat machines. It is, in fact, in our relations with the peoples from whom we took this land that we can discover the truth about ourselves and the society we have built. Do our brave words about the Third World carry conviction when we will not take a stand for the peoples of our own domestic Third World? How can anyone believe us when we say that we wish to see poverty eradicated in native communities, an end to enforced dependence and a fair settlement of native claims?

The constitutional agreement is a defeat for the native peoples but it is also a defeat for all Canadians. The agreement reveals the true limits of the Canadian conscience and the Canadian imagination. For the statesmen who signed the agreement of November 5, 1981, represent us. They know us well, and they believed they could, with impunity, delete native rights from the Constitution.

It is true that the Prime Minister and the premiers have promised to hold another conference to discuss native rights. But, of course, then the urgency will be gone, and in any event the opting-out formula in the new Constitution —the right of the provinces to opt out and the threat to opt out—will make it impossible to reach a meaningful amendment defining native rights and applying throughout Canada. Native rights will be defined according to the constitutional checkerboard that Canadian statesmen have given us.

In the end, no matter what ideology they profess, our leaders share one firm conviction: that native rights should not be inviolable; the power of the state must encompass them. Their treatment of native peoples reveals how essential it is to entrench minority rights, without qualification.

No words can disguise what has happened. The first Canadians—a million people and more—have had their answer from Canada's statesmen: they cannot look to any of our governments to defend the idea that they are entitled to a distinct and contemporary place in Canadian life. Under the new Constitution the first Canadians shall be last.

This is not the end of the story. The native peoples have not come this far to turn back now. But it is an abject and mean-spirited chapter. No one can rejoice that it was written in Canada.

Controversy in the Capital

The article provoked a firestorm of controversy in Ottawa. Justice George Addy of the Federal Court submitted two complaints to the Judicial Council in quick succession, accusing Judge Berger of misconduct for speaking out. In his letter, Judge Addy stated his belief that, after many years of "political posturing, wrangling and gamesmanship," Canada had finally reached a consensus on the framework for a constitutional accord. In his view, Judge Berger could not have chosen a more politically divisive subject on which to register an opinion. In his missive to the Judicial Council he wrote:

> The harm that pronouncements of this kind in such circumstances is capable of creating to the independence of the judiciary, the administration of justice and the maintenance of the principle of separation of powers is, in my view, incalculable.

Then his attack turned personal. Judge Addy stated that this was not the first time that Judge Berger had stepped beyond the bounds of proper judicial restraint in political matters. He ended his communication with an insult, suggesting that Berger's "pronouncements were not worthy of a neighbourhood newspaper." For Thomas Berger, who had authored the Mackenzie Valley Pipeline report which sold 90,000 copies, that comment must have been the proverbial 'unkindest cut of all'.

For the Liberal government, the key problem was the public humiliation stemming from Berger's criticism. To blunt the outcry, the Prime Minister appeared on a Vancouver radio show hosted by Jack Webster, a cranky Scotsman who regularly grilled political figures. Webster asked for Trudeau's frank opinion on the controversy. Trudeau replied that he took strong exception to a judge speaking out on a political matter. "I hope the judiciary will do something about it."

The Judicial Council, made up of Canada's senior judges, responded. They appointed a three-man committee to investigate the issue, in private, and to write a report.

If Trudeau hoped to keep the debate off the front pages of the newspapers, he was to be disappointed. Allan Fotheringham opened an article in the *Vancouver Province* newspaper with a quip: "For a man with such a famed steel-trap mind, the prime minister of Canada has large pockets of illogic rattling inside his headbone." Fotheringham pointed out that a minister in Trudeau's own government had been caught pressuring members of the judiciary on behalf of a colleague. Trudeau had let that issue slide. Now, Fotheringham quipped, "they are about to spank Berger."

Reporter Michael Valpy took a full page of the *Globe and Mail* to chronicle how politicians had betrayed Indigenous Canadians. In an article entitled "The Sellout of native rights," he pointed out that none of the three party leaders in the House of Commons had objected when the critical Indigenous rights clause had been removed. Moreover, only two Members of Parliament—Svend Robinson from British Columbia and Warren Allmand, a former Minister of Indian Affairs—had refused to support the agreement because of the deletion. Valpy noted that a great stride forward had been taken eight years before, with the success of Nisga'a case in the Supreme Court. "That stride has now been un-taken," he concluded.

Berger declined to appear before the committee, but he wrote a memorandum to his colleagues on the bench, defending his actions. He chose to create a parallel with a painful episode in Canada's history, one that he had explored in the book he had published a short time before, *Fragile Freedoms*.

> This is a miserable business, but its ramifications may be important. If a member of this court had spoken out against the internment of the Japanese Canadians in 1942, or against their deportation in 1946, would that have been regarded as misconduct?... The public knows that judges hold strong views, but they do their best to ensure that they do not determine the content of their judgments. Occasionally, judges feel that, as a matter of conscience, they must give expression to those views.

A War of Words

In May of 1982, the investigative committee appointed by the Judicial Council issued a report criticizing Berger's behaviour, concluding that he should be removed from the bench. The full Judicial Council met and decided that although it was an indiscretion for Berger to express his views as to matters of a political nature, this was the first time the issue had been explored in depth in Canada. The standards for behaviour were not cast in stone. Berger would be permitted to remain on the bench.

In conversations with friends, Tom Berger admitted that this was a difficult time. But his spirits were buoyed up by the occasional letter that came from those who admired his stance. One was written by Joyce Green, a young Indigenous woman from Alberta, who explained that she had spent a "hideous" year in law school. "It seems impossible for any kind of thinking to survive in a legal system so hidebound by precedent... Therefore it is heartening to see that a few brave souls do survive in law." Project North, an organization that had promoted the political stance of the Dene Nation during the Mackenzie Valley Pipeline Inquiry, wrote that their activists often felt that was impossible to make their voices heard. "It is therefore gratifying and encouraging when a person of your stature in the public eye is willing to take the risk of speaking out."

Tom Berger might have thought that the fuss would die down once the Judicial Council made its decision, but that was not to be. Three months later, Chief Justice of the Supreme Court, Bora Laskin, was invited to give a speech to a meeting of the Canadian Bar Association in Toronto. He took the opportunity to reprimand Berger for his outspokenness, suggesting that Berger was merely trying to keep himself in the public eye. "To a large degree, Judge Berger was reactivating his Mackenzie Valley Pipeline Inquiry, a matter which is years behind him and should properly be left dormant."

The Chief Justice spoke for more than an hour, and Judge Berger was not the sole target of his ire. He also criticized the news media for broadcasting Berger's views.

> Unbelievably, some members of the press and some in government office in this country seemed to think that freedom of speech for judges gave them the full scope of participation and comment on current political controversies, on current social and political issues. Was there ever such ignorance of history and of principle?

The speech reignited the issue, and Tom Berger found himself under scrutiny again. In *Maclean's* magazine, Allan Fotheringham had lost none of his barbed wit. He pointed out that the Liberal government was failing in the polls, possibly headed for defeat in the next election. Pierre Trudeau had already announced his departure from politics. Jean Chrétien was champing at the bit to lead his party. Said Fotheringham:

> The losers have turned out to be Mr. Chretien and Mr. Trudeau—once thought of as stout champions of individuality and intellectual courage. They now come out as surly, testy... and most of all as men who cannot abide criticism.

An Issue of Conscience

Thomas Berger, like his father before him, was fifty years old and facing an issue of conscience. He believed profoundly that Indigenous rights were fundamental to Canadian law. He had spent much of his career crafting arguments on the issue. But if he spoke out in the future, he would face the implacable opposition of the Chief Justice of the Supreme Court of Canada.

Tom Berger elected to resign and return to the practice of law. There he would be free to speak out on human rights and fundamental freedoms. In his resignation letter, he wrote:

> It used to be thought that an appointment to the bench

was for a lifetime. But the judiciary, like all of our institutions, is changing. When I went on the bench I was 38. I am 50 now—a good time of life to consider a change.

But this rancorous debate had brought the issue of Aboriginal rights to the fore. The government slipped the contentious clause confirming Indigenous rights, back into the *Canadian Charter of Rights and Freedoms.* After more than a year of discussion, triggered by Thomas Berger's protest, the Indigenous people of Canada had taken a vital step forward.

⁓

A CONVERSATION WITH LOUISE MANDELL, KC, LAWYER, UNION OF BRITISH COLUMBIA INDIAN CHIEFS

Louise Mandell was a founding partner of Mandell Pinder, a law firm specializing in Aboriginal and Treaty Rights law. She began her career working with the late Grand Chief George Manuel of the Union of B.C. Indian Chiefs, who played a pioneering role in the achievements of the Indigenous rights movement.

"The strategy of the federal government was to press ahead with patriation, without involving Indigenous Peoples. They planned on leaving Indigenous rights for discussion after patriation occurred. This erupted into what became a grassroots movement of Indigenous people seeking to protect their rights, putting their foot in the door to stop the patriation of the Constitution without their consent. First Nations were seeking respect – which meant honouring Treaties, respecting their inherent rights and aboriginal title to their unceded lands, honouring their laws and legal orders, as the oldest root in the living tree of Confederation. They saw themselves as a partner in Confederation, not a footnote.

The Constitution Express was a train that was hired in Vancouver. At Christmas of 1980 it went across the country, gaining support and supporters along the way. People funded the Constitution Express themselves. They sold cows, they picked mushrooms, they fundraised the old-fashioned way to hire the train and to take the trip. It was a very exhilarating time.

Nobody knew the road we were travelling. As we took a step, the road emerged. We had no precedent for what we were doing. We had no idea how to amplify indigenous voices so that they would make a difference in the constitutional process.

I met a brilliant Indigenous historian at a conference. She began by saying that when she was a little girl, she went with her grandpa to the train station when the Constitution Express was passing through her prairie town. She remembered waving to the people on the train. And then her grandpa said, "Go tell your mom I've gone to Ottawa." And without so much as a toothbrush, he jumped on board, inspired to give his support. He returned several weeks later, inspiring her life's work.

When the Express landed in Ottawa, in the early part of 1981, the Standing Committee was hearing submissions about the Canada Bill in Parliament. The government had previously said that they were going to exclude Indigenous participation. But as the train was arriving in the Ottawa station, Trudeau said, 'You can come and speak at the Standing Committee.'

But those on the train did not go to the Standing Committee. They went to the Governor General's House and presented a Petition and Bill of Particulars about formally being included in constitutional renewal and how decolonization under the present constitutional structure could take place to include them. Canada did not respond to this invitation. So the Constitution Express went to the United Nations in New York, and then to European cities. It ended up in London, England. There they hosted a potlatch, celebrating their ties with the British Crown, and making clear how Britain could help, by rejecting the Canada Bill until the constitutional process was done properly.

There were multiple strategies within the Indigenous movement about protecting their rights during the constitutional process. Some leaders and their supporters were working very hard in Ottawa to try to get a provision in the Constitution which recognized Aboriginal and Treaty rights. That was one strategy. Get our rights entrenched in the Constitution.

A strategy through the Constitution Express, was to stop the Canada Bill altogether. Go slowly, get Indigenous people at the table, get a process for decolonization, for constitutional renewal, which involved Indigenous people. Then we can move forward together with the Canada Bill.

This is where Tom Berger's courage, his integrity came into play. Speaking as a judge, he voiced his opposition to the removal of Section 34 from the Canada Bill. Tom stood up for what he believed and what he fought for in leading cases like Calder and White and Bob, where he pioneered the recognition of Aboriginal and treaty rights. His was not the only voice opposing the draconian deletion of Section 34; there were many people speaking out. This wasn't a single man, a single act. From across Canada, there was a lot of public discussion, editorials about the right way to include Indigenous people. So when this clause was pulled out, Tom stood up. He spoke out. It was unusual for a sitting judge to do that.

Bora Laskin, who was the Chief Justice of the Supreme Court of Canada at the time, spoke out against what Tom did. That was also unusual, that you have high members of the judiciary entering the political fray. That's how powerful the debate was. It pulled people away from their desks into the public realm.

Ultimately, Tom's voice contributed to the inclusion of a provision recognizing Aboriginal and Treaty rights in the Canada Bill which is now Section 35 of the *Constitution Act*, 1982. Section 35 has resulted in a body of jurisprudence recognizing colonial wrongs and requiring reconciliation. What has emerged from the Supreme Court of Canada is legal pluralism. This is what occurs when different cultural narratives, worldviews, titles, and jurisdictions co-exist. This partnership within Confederation creates space for the reemergence of Indigenous laws on a landscape where these laws were deliberately erased. These ancient laws containing wisdom and sacred connections, are helping and teaching us how to love the land and the sea and to treat it properly.

I honour Tom and thank him. He deeply believed in the rule of law and the rights of Indigenous people, the power and wisdom of Indigenous laws and the beauty of their cultures. We are better together. ”

CHAPTER TWELVE

ALASKA NATIVE CLAIMS REVIEW

Dalee Sambo Dorough PhD

~~

For three years, the Iñupiat of Alaska watched as the Mackenzie Valley Pipeline Inquiry unfolded in Canada's Northwest Territories. They were particularly interested in the hearings that were held in the Mackenzie Delta and Beaufort Sea communities, which bordered on their traditional territory in Alaska.

In 1976, Eben Hopson, the Mayor of the North Slope Borough, was invited to address the Inquiry. In his speech, he gave an overview of the issues confronting his people. He explained how, in 1923, the US government had taken 23,400,000 acres of their land, without compensation, to create Naval Petroleum Reserve No. 4. Later, natural gas was discovered at Point Barrow, but it took the Iñupiat twelve years to get permission to hook up their own homes to the gas mains that ran across their back yards. In the 1960s, without the permission of the Iñupiat people, the state of Alaska handed out leases so the oil industry could explore for oil on Iñupiat territory. The leases sent $900 million to the state treasury.

With the discovery of the largest oilfield in North America at Prudhoe Bay, industrial activity expanded. Indigenous groups across Alaska demanded that their land claims be acknowledged, and in 1971, the Alaska Native Claims Settlement Act was signed.

But in the years that followed, Indigenous Alaskans began to wonder if the claim had been a mistake. Shortly after Thomas

Berger returned to private practice, Eben Hopson inquired whether the former judge would be interested in leading the Alaska Native Claims Review.

As head of the Inuit Circumpolar Conference, Dr. Dalee Sambo Dorough, an Iñupiat advocate for Indigenous rights, played a key role in the Alaska Native Claims Review. She helped establish the framework for the commission, led the fundraising campaign and organized the round table discussions.

I BECAME AWARE of the *Alaska Native Claims Settlement Act* (ANCSA) when I was in middle school. I read the *Act* and as soon as I saw the words 'extinguishment of hunting and fishing rights' I knew something was wrong. When I read about the further extinguishment of Aboriginal title to all lands outside of the settlement I thought: This territory is massive and we are recipients of only ten percent. Our families depended on hunting and fishing and harvesting. How can somebody take something so fundamental to a people and extinguish it? How does that happen—in law? That moved me to understand our place in American law.

A lot of parents and grandparents were aware that young people born after December 18, 1971 could be disenfranchised, that our knowledge and life ways would be impacted because of this date. So the 'afterborn' issue was an element very early on. That was combined with the 'blood quantum' issue, the provision that you had to be one quarter or more native blood, born on or before December 18, 1971, to be included. So if you think of those two dynamics together, there was concern.

Also, there was concern about the provision that tax exempt status would be lifted on December 18, 1991. As Tom Berger later pointed out, if the tax on land were as low as $1 an acre, some of the village corporations and the regional corporations, which owned the rights, wouldn't be able to pay the tax. They could lose the land through taxation. So the potential for takeover was tied to that date in 1991.

I think many felt concern when ANCSA was adopted by the US Congress and signed into law by US President Richard Nixon. We thought that it was going to be a settlement for land, that Alaskan people would hold that land forever, in perpetuity. Then we looked at the *Act* and realized: that's not what this says.

I was fairly young and, like a lot of Alaskan native people, I was passionate about making sure that we were not going to lose our land. I was also aware of the very strong distinction between the tribal governments, the original traditional councils, in contrast to the corporations that were created through ANCSA. There was a clear division. Yet at the same time there was no state-wide organization of the tribes.

Everybody was aware that the deadline was central. The shareholders could be preyed upon by more powerful economic forces. That is the continuing problem of the corporate structure: rather than being members of a First Nation or a tribal government, shareholders could do what they chose to do. We had also heard that there were other, more powerful forces ready to do hostile takeovers of the corporations. The land was in the process of being transferred to the regional corporations and the village corporations who would hold title. Once they had 51 percent or more, the shareholders would not be concerned about our Aboriginal rights.

Eben Hopson, the mayor of the North Slope Borough in 1976, delivered testimony at the Mackenzie Valley Pipeline Inquiry. It was remarkable how Tom Berger conducted his work in the Northwest Territories. In the US during the 1970s and 80s, testifying before the US Senate or the House of Representatives was common, but national commissions of inquiry were not part of our tradition. Thus, preparing and delivering testimony to an independent commissioner was a significant and meaningful experience.

To my knowledge, this was the first opportunity for Inuit in Alaska to deliver testimony regarding ANCSA. It allowed us, as Inuit, to connect with our relatives across the imposed borders between Alaska and Canada. We have always closely followed legal and political developments in Canada, including the Mackenzie Valley Pipeline Inquiry, as they impact our rights as well.

The idea of creating an inquiry focused on the impacts of the *Alaska Native Claims Settlement Act* of 1971 emerged from the mind of Archie Gottschaulk, a man from southwest Alaska, the Bristol Bay region. He and many other individuals were acutely aware of the potential threats to our people maintaining control of the land and the corporations, created by ANCSA, because of the twenty-year time frame from 1971 to 1991. In the early to mid-1980s, this became a real threat, in Archie's mind. Knowing the work of Berger in Canada, the Mackenzie Valley Pipeline Inquiry in particular, Archie formulated the idea to establish an independent commission, not one led by government, but by Indigenous people themselves.

At the time, I was the director of the Inuit Circumpolar Conference's (ICC) Alaska office, which I established in 1982 as the organization's first office. Despite his region never becoming a member of the ICC, Archie was a frequent visitor. He often shared his ideas and managed to persuade the then-executive council members of the ICC to develop them further. Notably, James Stotts, an Iñupiat from the North Slope region, recognized the usefulness and constructiveness of Archie's ideas. He believed that the ICC, as an Indigenous peoples' organization with familiarity with developments in Canada and Greenland, was well-suited to lead this initiative.

So that is how I first came to meet Tom Berger, personally and professionally. Arrangements had been made for Tom to travel to Alaska to have a conversation, a dialogue, about what we had in mind. We had powwowed over the idea and had some thoughts for him to consider. I picked him up at the airport and got him settled in his hotel with the plan that he would rest up and we'd meet the following morning. We have earthquakes often here, about every fifteen minutes, and that evening we had a tremor. I woke up and thought: "The Judge! In the hotel! On the eleventh floor!" The following day I collected Archie and Jimmy Stotts. When we met Tom, Archie said: "Boy, you just got here and you're already starting to shake things up."

We went to the Alaska office of the ICC and held our first meeting about the idea. Tom had a lot of very detailed questions for us. We didn't have any experience with the amount of money it took to do something like this. We gained insights from Tom. We could tell that, unlike the Canadian government, we didn't have the significant resources we needed. He was pretty straight up about it. He said: "You're a small organization, with two employees in this office. You're talking about a fairly extensive inquiry into ANCSA, which has been going for ten or twelve years now." Clearly Tom was interested. I think from that moment on he knew he could have an impact if we used his approach.

He left after his short visit and we put our heads together about how we could make this a reality. We were convinced that we could—but who was going to get the money? At the outset, the North Slope Borough was one source of funding but we knew it would take additional resources so that Tom could hire staff to run the project from 1983 to 1985. The minimum budget we worked on was $1.5 million. In 1982, that was gobs of money. So Tom assisted with the fundraising to make sure that the project would happen.

The two of us travelled to New York no fewer than eight times to fundraise. Tom would meet with the directors of the Ford Foundation and explain how he intended to do the work. Then I explained the organization and the importance of the project. I spoke as a rights-holder, as a person who would be impacted by this. We ended up being a pretty compelling team.

We were fortunate to secure all the remaining necessary funding. I had never done a scrap of philanthropic fundraising in my life, and in hindsight it was remarkable that we managed to show up and convince the list of donors that this was an important project.

The round tables that come to mind focused on those individuals who had a firm grasp of federal Indian law, Indigenous leaders from the United States who were leaders in the area of tribal government. A person who made a great impact was the late Ada Deer, who led the campaign for the restoration of the rights of the Menominee Indians after their rights were terminated by the US government.

She was a charismatic individual. Hope came from her spirit. The way she told the story of the lobbying campaign to regain their status as a federally recognized Indian tribe, that was extraordinary. Ada Deer said:

> All the major policies on Indians have come from the top down. They have not come from the bottom up. They have not been based on the needs, the wishes and the aspirations of the informed people at the grassroots level. And if we look at all the examples that have been mentioned today… you can see that this is true. Now, in contrast, the *Menominee Restoration Act* came from the people, came from the bottom up, and I'm very proud to say that it's my tribe that worked to demonstrate what can be done by a small group of people who utilized the political process and who keep in mind their convictions and their dedication and their desires.

One of the things that raised the bar was her message: If you see a problem, look at the issue, take a step forward. The most important message that Alaskan people heard: "Take action."

Browning Pipestem's commentary focused on the fact that as soon as oil was discovered on the land of Osage Indians, the government terminated the status of the tribes and created a policy of individual allotments. In Alaska, ANCSA was promoted by the discovery of oil as well.

One of the key messages that Browning Pipestem offered was that the solution lies in tribal governments recognizing that we have inherent sovereignty as Indian people. He always wondered about the term Alaska Native and urged people in Alaska not to make the distinction between themselves and native Americans. Rather we should recognize ourselves as native Americans, like all other Indians across the United States. Sharing that was important. He said:

> It really boils down to this. If you don't see a tribe as being very significant, then it won't be. If you see it as being a government of significance, then you will build it to be that... If you accept the definitions that are cast by people about it—that it is nothing—then it will be nothing because you won't act.

The roundtables were a chance for extraordinary individuals to tell us about the experiences of Indigenous people elsewhere, primarily in the Commonwealth countries. Verna Kirkness, a Cree scholar from Canada, was teaching at the University of British Columbia. She described the day when she decided she had to stop teaching 'nonsense', her word, and to find new ways to encourage Indigenous students.

> I was teaching and I suddenly realized: you know, this is not right at all. This isn't the history of Canada. This isn't the history of our people. So I went completely the other way and started talking about real people, our people, our lives. I said to the Grade 7 students: 'Write me an essay about Canada in 1965, without the white man.'
> You know, a lot of times they say: Indians don't like to write, they hate writing because it is in English. These kids wrote pages and pages and pages. They really enjoyed the topic of Canada in

1965 without white people.... You know people say we romanticize the past, but the students saw it as their own development. They saw it as a way they would be productive and happy people today.

Community Hearings

For the communities that are on watersheds, the timing of the community hearings had to be organized to maximize the number of people who could show up and testify. This was a key strategy in organizing the hearings. Once a village site had been identified, word could go out to communities upriver and downriver, to come to this hearing. The message was: if you have anything to share, especially in your own Indigenous language, be here. Tom never ended such an important opportunity until everyone had been heard.

I remember that questions were raised because we held hearings in 62 villages out of 223 villages in Alaska. Did we reach a threshold? But we heard from nearly 1,500 people who were well-respected, including Elders who came forward. It was compelling, the imperative was so clear. What many were sharing were fundamental issues to all Alaskan natives. I don't think anything was missed.

The report is accessible and readable. Significantly, the voices of the rights-holders, the purported beneficiaries of this policy of Congressional legislation, are on every page.

Tom was skilled in substantiating his recommendations with the words of the people concerned. That was an important dynamic. He had the ability to genuinely listen and then distill the key elements in his recommendations. If it were done in a massive report, it wouldn't have had the impact.

This was all taking place against the backdrop of the corporations that quietly, behind closed doors, thought that the ICC had created a mechanism for a witch hunt. They thought that Tom was going to finger who was responsible for what many people thought was a crime against Alaskan native people.

It was this threat, and the possible demise of us as a distinct people, that was really at the heart of it. That was a constant political battle. The younger generation of Alaskan native people have no idea of the battle that ensued between the corporations and the tribes and traditional councils. Some might say it persists today.

Unfortunately, many of the recommendations that Tom put forward remain outstanding. However, he did establish the mechanisms for transferring land from village corporations to tribal governments and provisions to extend enrollment dates for those born after the original cutoff. Both corporate entities and tribes implemented changes and strategies based on his groundwork. In hindsight, the core of Tom's recommendations aligned with what people were genuinely testifying about: the importance of land, self-government, self-determination, and hunting, fishing, and harvesting rights. These are the foundations of village life.

So Tom was echoing—articulating—why these things matter, why justice matters. He listened and he got it. The fact is that those issues persist to this day. So the report had an impact, but it wasn't the major overhaul of the framework. He put in place key elements, but wholesale, there was not sufficient reform.

The other dynamic, a footnote to this, is that Alaska is a Republican state and the sole source of revenue is oil. When you complement that with provisions that ensure that every renewable and non-renewable resource that Alaskan native people hold will always be open for development because of the corporate, for-profit objectives, how do you stop that machine? It brings to mind the young man in front of the tank in Tiananmen Square. How do you stop it?

A CONVERSATION WITH JIM SYKES,
AUDIOVISUAL PRODUCER

Jim Sykes was in charge of recording the proceedings at the 57 village hearings of the Alaska Native Claims Review. After the hearings were complete, he produced fifteen radio documentaries, "Holding our Ground," which explored key themes raised by Alaskans.

"The Commission only went to places where we were invited. Outreach visits to villages and towns were made in advance of the hearings so people knew something about the commission and were encouraged to talk about their experiences with the *Alaska Native Claims Settlement Act:* what they remembered about it, how it affected them, subsistence, self-government or sovereignty, and anything else they thought was important.

We tried to visit several towns and villages within a region, and encouraged visits of people from nearby villages to attend hearings. When we arrived, there was generally something traditionally important happening, in addition to the hearing: a potluck, a potlatch, singing, dancing, sharing traditional food. We were warmly welcomed with important cultural traditions everywhere we went.

The first hearing was in Western Alaska, near the mouth of the Yukon River, Emmonak. None of us knew what to expect. When we got there, the meeting hall was prepared, chairs were ready. I think the meeting was scheduled for 5:00 pm. At 5:00, the Tom Berger and his team were the main people there.

But Tom seemed to recognize that the clock didn't rule everything. He sat patiently in his chair at the front of the room and talked to a few people informally. After an hour or so people began to filter in and before long the room was full. It was a heart-warming hearing. It spoke to Tom's patience. It was obvious he was there to listen as long as people wanted to talk. It was a wonderful start.

We heard powerful personal stories everywhere. At our second hearing, the weather was also powerful. When we arrived in the Bering Sea coast village of Tununak, it was 40 below with a 40 mile-an-hour wind. The plane came in 90 degrees to the runway. The pilot touched down on one wheel, pivoted onto the runway, and got the plane on the ground.

As we entered the village, an old lady walking in front of me got blown over and she started rolling on the ground. We helped get her up and stabilized. Once inside, someone noticed a little patch of frost bite on my cheek. It happened during the short walk from the plane.

The gym was full for the hearing. Practically the whole village turned out. The meeting was led by Mike Albert, the head of the tribal government. He translated for Elders, like Jens [Yenns] Flynn. Mike talked about what their land meant to them in terms that reflected traditions of occupation and use and settlement without consent. You could almost hear a pin drop.

> The early days Alaska was occupied by native people only, and no Kass'aqs [white men]. They used it freely and used their own rules only. Right now I'm asking Congress, 'Why have Congress worked on our land to settle it in the ways we do not agree without talking with us first?' Right now I am talking as if talking face to face with the people in Congress. Before you intended to work on the land settlement and if native people in Alaska were consulted, I don't think anybody would have agreed to settle it.

By the time we were holding the hearings, the cash economy had made things easier and subsistence was not totally necessary, but it was still an important part of life in most places, especially the small remote villages. We saw people smoking fish in the smokehouses in the summertime as well as frozen and smoked fish and meat stored in winter.

Jasper Joseph from Emmonak pointed out that living from the land required discipline: 'In our Eskimo way of life, getting food was a daaaay-ly effort. It had to be done every day, it could be bad weather, it could be a nice day, but it was an everyday effort that Eskimo had to go out and gather his own food so he could survive.'

We boated down the Yukon River from Stevens Village to Rampart and Tanana, visiting fish camps along the way. We sat in a circle and people talked with Tom. I held the microphone and recorded everyone who spoke. That was the most remote series of hearings.

When we flew to the small Yukon River village of Holy Cross, we were warned ahead of time that we might not be able to meet because everybody would be fishing if an emergency opening was called. That is exactly what happened. We landed and there were only four or five people left in the village.

Fifteen minutes after we arrived, another plane arrived. A couple of agents from the Bureau of Land Management (BLM) wanted to talk to people about the relatively unlikely possibility of an oil lease sale proposed in the general area, but a public meeting was required. We went to the community hall where there were more of us outsiders than people from the village. The BLM wrapped up their information session, nobody testified and then they said: 'Well, we've had the public hearing. Thanks a lot,' and they took off.

It was an example of the way state and federal governments affect people. They have meetings with all sorts of bureaucracies—the oil industry, the environmental agencies. They have regional corporations, both for-profit and non-profit, village corporations, each with its own board of directors. People are faced with a barrage of mail. I think it was in Holy Cross, most of the official positions were held by the same person. He said: 'The other day I realized I was writing a letter to myself.'

Caribou live in many parts of Alaska from the North Slope, Interior and Alaska Peninsula. In the Eastern Interior, just south of the Brooks Range mountains, one can see caribou antlers everywhere in Arctic Village. They use all the parts of the animal for their subsistence. Jonathan Solomon talked about their hunting practices and how their lives and future were intertwined with survival of the caribou.

> The caribou, as my people believe for many years, is part of the Gwitch'in people religion. We eat it, we use parts of their fur and stuff for our own clothing. But we also believe that the population of the Gwitch'in people in the Yukon Flat goes up and down with the numbers of these animals.... This is why it is very important to us when we talk about the Porcupine caribou herd, that it be protected for our generations to come, because this is our belief....

We are not a visitor upon these lands, we are in the same ecosystem as the animal on these land.

Even in villages where subsistence activities appear to have declined, people speak of subsistence with the same passion as they do in villages where it is flourishing.

In Point Hope we were invited to join the celebration of sharing a bowhead whale that had been caught by Whaling Captain Luke Kunuk. Most people from Point Hope and some other villages joined the whaling ceremony. The whale was brought ashore, cut and shared, and it was the most joyous and important event. The ceremony itself demonstrated the continuing life with deep seated traditions and sharing local resources.

We sat on the beach gravel with a whaling captain from another village who explained the food and the ceremony. And I also received a gift muktuk slice from Captain Kunuk's wife, which I took home to my family.

It was an unforgettable experience with the importance of tradition, subsistence resources and the importance of sharing local food. A few people attended the hearing in the evening, which was also interesting, but the whaling celebration spoke volumes. Alice Kulowiyi lives in Gambell on the northwest tip of St. Lawrence island. Much of her food comes from the Bering Sea. Said Alice:

> We St. Lawrence Islanders are just like those farmers on the outside. We eat from the plants of the sea just like farmers eat from their farm. We collect the plants that grow on the water and we collect them when they are washed up on the shore.

For centuries the people of the Arctic coast have depended on the whale for survival. They know its migration and behaviour patterns. Burton Rexford is a member of the Alaska Eskimo Whaling Commission. He says a whaling captain relies on the knowledge handed down from generations of experience. Said Burton:

> A whaling captain is faced with great responsibilities; his number one priority is of course the immediate concerns

of safety while out on the hazardous and icy Arctic waters. It is his knowledge and preparation that the people depend upon for their daily food. If a village did not catch a whale, then we knew, beyond the shadow of a doubt, that we would experience extreme hardship and fear the oncoming hunger that would strike us. We know that when we caught a whale we then would be able to sleep easily and eat well.

Life in the communities was precarious, so a successful hunt was greeted with joy, not only by the hunters but by the entire community.

The people are happy, they're smiling, they're excited and you think about it. Boy, they caught a whale. They get really excited and the happiness extends all the way from the deep inside. And when you go into the house that caught a whale, that happiness, that excitement, that crying for joy and because they are glad that they have been given that gift.

My work was straightforward: to record what people said onto audiotape for the record that would be transcribed and made publicly available. Once the recording was done I looked for funding to duplicate the recordings and archive the originals and copies. While Tom wrote his book for the Commission, called *Village Journey,* I looked for funding to turn portions of audio from the hearings into a series of 15 half-hour radio programs, "Holding Our Ground," which were broadcast across Alaska and in parts of the continental US.

We were using cassettes to record at the time. Copies of cassettes were also made available. I would check the tapes before sending them out and often I listened for several minutes to the powerful voices of the people, speaking from the heart.

Tom Berger and the Alaska Native Review Commission provided a genuine opportunity for people to be heard directly without any time limits. It also gave space for people to talk with others in the same room, in other villages, in other places across Alaska, and to outside policy makers. The hearings across the state were definitely the most interesting and important project I've been involved with."

CHAPTER THIRTEEN

ALASKA IN RETROSPECT

Thomas R. Berger

~

In 1985, Thomas Berger published the report of the Alaska Native Claims Review as a book, Village Journey. *Some of his conclusions sparked discussions across Alaska. Forty years after the original book was released, Berger revisited his conclusions in this essay.*

THE AUTHORS of the *Alaska Native Claims Settlement Act* (ANCSA) had a vision of economic development and assimilation for Alaska Natives. That vision was driven by the prospect of oil and gas, mining and other development. Under the settlement, their aboriginal title to the whole state of Alaska was extinguished, in exchange for 44 million acres they believed would be theirs in perpetuity. But in fact the land they received would belong not to them, nor their tribes, but to the corporations.

Alaska Natives, to a great extent, now as then, live off the land, relying upon hunting, fishing, and trapping—their traditional subsistence economy. To them, their land is the basis of their lives. Under the settlement, their aboriginal title to the whole state of Alaska was extinguished in exchange for 44 million acres they believed would be theirs in perpetuity.

It should not be altogether surprising that during my travels in Alaska in the mid-1980s I found that, except for a few,

the settlement had not worked out for the benefit of Alaska
Natives. The village corporations were, many of them, dormant or insolvent, and few Alaska Natives were employed by
them. The same was true of the regional corporations. The
$962.5 million that the regional and village corporations had
received had declined in value, and the land that was to be
theirs under the settlement, the 44 million acres vital to the
Alaska Natives' future, was in jeopardy.

How was the land in jeopardy? When ANCSA was passed
in 1971, it placed the ownership of all Native lands in Alaska
in the Native corporations. All Alaska Natives then alive
received a hundred shares in their village and regional corporations. The shares could not be sold for twenty years, not
until January 1, 1991.

The great fear as 1991 approached was that since the shares
in the Native corporations would become available for sale on
that date, and could be bought and sold like the shares in any
corporation, control of Native corporations would be lost as
shares in village corporations and regional corporations were
bought up by outside interest speculators, large corporations,
wealthy non-Natives. Once shares became freely negotiable,
an outsider could come into a Native village and conceiv-
ably buy up a majority of shares in a village corporation over
a weekend, thus acquiring control of the villagers' lands. For
outsiders, acquiring control of regional corporations might be
more difficult, but not at all unlikely.

The commitment to the corporate model established by
Congress in the *Alaska Native Claims Settlement Act* of 1971
had become embedded in Alaska politics. The Congressional
delegation, the state government, and many Native regional
corporations opposed any fundamental change in it.

Indeed, the federal and state governments were not willing even to recognize traditional tribal governments and
tribal powers. But even the Social Darwinists who conceived
of ANCSA were not prepared twenty years later, as 1991

approached, to have the 44 million acres of Alaska Native lands thrown on the market. Alaska's congressional delegation, though opposed to any fundamental change in ANCSA, realized that amendments to ANCSA had to be made.

In 1988 Congress passed amendments (known in Alaska as the "1991 amendments") which continued the ban on the sale of shares, unless the shareholders of a Native corporation vote to eliminate the ban. Under the 1991 amendments, in order for Native corporations to lift the prohibition on the sale of ANCSA shares, the corporation's board of directors or 25 percent of the shareholders must put the question to the shareholders' vote. If no vote is requested, the restrictions on the sale of shares remain.

Another great concern was that, after 1991, undeveloped Native land would become subject to taxation and pass out of Native ownership in the same way as two-thirds of Indian land in the Lower 48 had passed out of Indian ownership a century before, under the *General Allotment Act* of 1887, which exposed Indian land to sale and confiscatory taxation. Under the "1991 amendments," the undeveloped land of a village corporation is exempt from taxation; therefore, unless the corporation borrows money against such land or develops it, the land cannot be taxed.

I have referred only to the main features of the 1991 amendments. The amendments, however, are bewildering in their complexity, stemming from the attempt by Congress in 1971 to convert Alaska Native peoples into players in the corporate world. ANCSA was designed to ensure that tribal lands would eventually pass out of Native collective ownership, once they could be bought and sold like any other private land in the state. The 1991 amendments, however, are a patchwork job; they alleviate some of the worst features of ANCSA, but do not address the principal issues which concern Alaska Natives. Hence the confusion.

The 1991 amendments do not deal with the flaw at the heart of ANCSA. Under the settlement, shares remain individual property. If shares can in the future be freely sold, ownership will tend inevitably to be concentrated in the hands of non-Native interests. If the restrictions on the sale of shares are maintained, they will tend to reduce the value of the shares as an economic asset. The 1991 amendments do nothing more than postpone the 1991 deadline for the sale of shares.

The ANCSA scheme cannot be made to work; yet many still resist any fundamental changes. My main recommendation in 1985, which reflected the hopes and aspirations of the hundreds of Alaska Natives I had met with, was to permit the "retribalization" of Alaska Native lands; that is, to restore tribal ownership of Alaska Native lands is the only certain way to ensure that such lands remain in the control of Alaska Natives in perpetuity.

Moreover, the Native tribal governments are the appropriate vehicles to ensure that the traditional subsistence culture flourishes for Alaska Natives—and there are many— who still depend on the land. Congress did not adopt my recommendations. But what I have found most striking in my visits to Alaska in recent years is that there is truly a consensus that the settlement of 1971 has failed. However, it cannot be officially acknowledged. Nevertheless, although Congress did not act on my recommendations, they were listening. The movement among Alaska Natives to fully restore the authority of their tribal governments has flourished in the last decade.

Tribal governments had established the Alaska Inter-Tribal Council to formulate statewide policy on Native affairs.

In 1990, in response to the tribal movement, President George Bush and Governor Walter Hickel set up a federal-state Alaska Natives Commission (Joint Federal State Commission on Policies and Programs Affecting Alaska

Natives), which recommended, in 1994, a renewed and enlarged role for Alaska tribal governments. Alaska Natives, they found, believed that "Native communities should be able to freely allocate ownership of and control over Native lands between Native corporations, tribal governments, individuals, and other Native institutions."

Moreover, Alaska Natives had urged the Commission that "Native communities should be able to guide land use decisions where competing uses threaten tribal and subsistence interests." In October 1993, President Bill Clinton's new Assistant Secretary of the Interior for Indian Affairs, Ada Deer, issued a list of federally recognized tribes in the United States, including 226 Alaska tribes which were to be treated on the same footing as other tribes in the Lower 48. For the first time, federal recognition of tribal government in Alaska was achieved.

On April 29, 1994, President Clinton invited tribal leaders from every state in the Union to the White House. In his address, the President affirmed the federal government's government-to-government relationship with Indian tribes from Alaska. Only tribal leaders, no corporate leaders, were invited from Alaska. President Clinton said on that occasion:

> In every relationship between our people, our first principle must be to respect your right to remain who you are, and to live the way you wish to live. And I believe the best way to do that is to acknowledge the unique government-to-government relationship we have enjoyed over time.

Today I reaffirm our commitment to self-determination for tribal governments. All along, there has been a consensus that the ANCSA settlement has failed. Now a consensus is emerging that Native lands must be held by tribal governments, that Native corporations may be useful as vehicles for economic development where it is feasible, but that they ought not to be the custodians of Native land for all time.

Alaska Natives are—and in the end will be—true to their own idea of themselves, their own institutions, and what they see as the necessity of holding onto their land and maintaining their subsistence economy. Of course, they believe in economic development, but not at the expense of their way of life. Theirs is not a faded vision; it is a modern vision, one that they have found more in keeping with the realities of today's world than ANCSA has been.

I believe that the concerns expressed in *Village Journey* are as alive as ever, their relevance undiminished.

A CONVERSATION WITH DAVID S. CASE, COUNSEL, ALASKA NATIVE CLAIMS REVIEW

"I was the lawyer for the Commission. It surprised me that I was offered that position because I didn't know Tom Berger. But I had just finished a book called *Alaskan Natives and American Laws*. It was the only book around that purported to encapsulate the laws applicable to the Alaska Natives.

Tom took me to lunch. When I asked him why he wanted to hire me, he said, 'You wrote the book.' So, I think that must have been my job application, even though I didn't know it.

Tom was focused on the tasks at hand: to take testimony from a variety of sources in some 57 villages over a two-year period. In between the village hearings, he convened subject matter roundtables of experts to frame the questions from legal, political, sociological, and philosophical perspectives so he could get a framework for the analysis of the situation in Alaska. Finally, he was to write a report on the implementation of the *Alaska Native Claims Settlement Act,* "ANCSA" as it is commonly called.

It was remarkable to work with Tom because he was so calm. Nothing would fluster him. He never seemed concerned about conflicting testimony or potential political fallout.

Tom would listen. That was especially true in the villages where people were upset because ANCSA hadn't done many things they thought were necessary, like protect subsistence and the ability to engage in hunting and gathering in their usual places. They were also concerned that the children who were born after December 18, 1971, (the date ANCSA was enacted) were not part of the *Claims Act*. Tom sorted that out.

Tom had an inquiring mind, but he wanted to know the truth—without fear or favour, as they say. He identified the problems with the *Claims Act*: the fact that the land held in corporations was in jeopardy; those children born after December 18,1971, were not enrolled in the corporations; that in 1991 the stock ownership would expire and could be bought up by strangers, so that Alaskan Natives would be strangers on their own land. That would be the worst of all possible outcomes.

Tom's solution was you ought to reconnect the people, the land, and the tribal governments. Corporate land should be conveyed to the village tribal governments. He had identified the real problem, the *Settlement Act* separated the people from their patrimony, not just from their land but from their community existence, their Tribes, or First Nations. They were not able to be shareholders through the generations. In his report, I think Tom identified these problems and the essential solution to them, which was to reunite Indigenous People and Indigenous lands with their tribal governments.

The recommendation was not well-received by the Alaska Native Regional Corporations, which were by then ten to fifteen years into the *Claims Act*. They were corporations, they had stockholders, they were making or losing money.

But the Native people understood that these problems existed. They went to Congress before 1991 and got Congress to change the law so that the stock would never be sold unless the corporations agreed to it. The land was also restricted from any risk unless the corporations put it at risk and signed documents that allowed the land to be alienated. The land was protected from involuntarily disposition.

The Claims Act was amended in 1987 to work these changes and also to enable the corporations to admit new shareholders without requiring them to buy stock. That is an Indigenous way of doing things. Property is not valued because it has monetary value. Its value is in the relationship of the people to the land and to each other.

We non-Indigenous people think that all land can be owned. I think that what Indigenous people believe is that they inhabit the land and use the resources as part of the mix: the sky, the land, the animals are part of the same world view. When those are torn apart, as settlements have often done in the Americas, the United States in particular, then you lose that relationship. ANCSA did that: it took the patrimony of the Indigenous Peoples of Alaska and created individual property called stock.

The changes reflected the ideas behind Tom's recommendations: you have to get the people and their patrimony back together. Now there are corporations that are opening their shareholders rolls so that people born after 1971 become a part of corporations. There is tension there because the corporation is then compelled to make more money to give dividends to more people. But all of that is less important, in the Indigenous sense, than having your family, your clan, recognized as part of the whole.

Tom said: This is the problem, and this is my solution. I don't think it was wrong, but it was fraught with difficulty. ANCSA had scrambled the omelet. There were village corporations, regional corporations, and non-profit corporations that provide services—and a mix of Alaska politics.

So, Tom's solution was in some ways the solution to the problems posed by the way ANCSA divided the Indigenous Peoples from their patrimony.

How Indigenous people go about linking to their patrimony is unfolding now. When you go to some corporations, the Northwest Arctic, for example, they have a philosophy called Iñupiat Ilitqusiat. It includes 16 ideas of what it means to be Iñupiat, such as Humour, Cooperation and Family Roles—all things that speak to the positive relationships that people have with each other. There is also an Alaska Native Heritage Centre that is funded by the corporations to perpetuate the heritage of the Alaska Natives. So, I don't think Alaska Native corporations have rejected their underlying values. You find that everywhere.

The vision that Tom had, of the Alaska Native organizations being the focal point of Indigenous society, is not lost. This is a capitalist democracy, and you can't participate in the democracy unless you have capital. That's my view.

The Alaska Native people have capital, in their corporations, and they have influence in Alaska politics. An example: when U.S. Senator, Lisa Murkowski, was beaten in her primary for reelection, the Alaska Native corporations got together, funded her campaign, and got her elected as a write-in candidate. That wouldn't happen if they didn't have the capital.

The Alaska Natives, who represent 18 to 20 percent of the population, can control the outcome of a state-wide election if they all vote together.

Some of the corporations were going bankrupt when Tom was writing his report, but today they generate about 25 to 30 percent of the gross domestic product of the state of Alaska. Of the fifty largest corporations in Alaska, twenty-five are Alaska Native corporations. They vary in size from $8 billion dollars to $175 million for one of the village corporations. That's my way of suggesting that the Alaska Natives have capital and influence.

Tom's conclusion was that ultimately the land had to be transferred to the Tribes, to bring the people back together with their patrimony. I think he was right. I think it will happen.

It may not happen the way he envisioned it, it may not happen in the short term, but I think, given the chance, the Alaska Natives will resolve their own issues. It may take generations of Native lawyers, doctors, teachers, corporate, and tribal leaders, but they will put it together, generally in a way that Tom foresaw. Not because he said so, but because it is the inevitable requirement of the Indigenous world view. Tom took the time to listen to and report on that world view, and his recommendations, without fear or favour, reflect its inevitability. "

CHAPTER FOURTEEN

THE MANITOBA MÉTIS CASE

Jean Teillet

~

Jean Teillet is the great-grandniece of the Métis leader, Louis Riel. Her legal career spanned thirty years. She is the author of an award-winning book, The North-West is our Mother: The Story of Louis Riel's People, the Métis Nation. *She shared this oral history about the roots of the Métis 150-year struggle for justice.*

MUCH OF THE DISCUSSION in the Manitoba Métis Federation case speaks about "Red River." For the Métis, Red River was a region that went south into North Dakota, west as far as Qu'appelle in Saskatchewan, and east to where the prairie ends. That's the territory the Métis referred to when they use the term "Red River." That's the land our ancestors fought and died for.

They marked it out in July of 1869. This is before the time people usually say the Red River Resistance began. That's why I call July the beginning of the Red River Resistance. I think it started in July, because I think resistance starts when people stop talking and start taking action. And the Métis stopped talking in July and started setting up armed patrols, they marked out their territory. They said, this is our land. They set up patrols to protect it. They booted off people who were squatting on their Métis lands. They filled in wells, which is a serious action. Somebody spent weeks digging a well and they filled it in and kicked those people off their lands. This was the

Red River Métis taking action saying, this is our land. You can't live here unless we say so. They were prepared to take up arms to protect their land.

Riel sent a three-person commission to Ottawa to negotiate terms and conditions on which the Métis would bring Red River, and what is now two-thirds of Canada, into the country. It was the world's largest peaceful land transfer.

It is important also to know that the residents of Red River were very united about opposing what Sir John A. Macdonald was doing. They had their differences, there's no question about it. The English Métis had a more laissez-faire kind of response: "Let them come in and we'll work it all out later." The French vehemently disagreed. They said: "No, no, no, you have to negotiate before they arrive. You can't do it afterwards."

Nobody liked the fact that Canada thought it could take over without even talking to them, without even deigning to come, without having the basic courtesy to say: "By the way, you're now going to be part of another country."

The whole community was angry. They didn't agree with Riel's tactics. They did not like the fact that the francophone Métis took up arms to achieve their goals. But they agreed with Riel on the underlying principle. That's why they had these big conventions. Riel sent out notices to all of the leaders of the communities, to the Anglophone and the Francophone leaders of the parishes. They all met in big conventions for days and days, where they debated on what terms they would join Canada. It was an extraordinarily democratic process.

It stands in stark contrast to the tactics of John A. Macdonald, who didn't think he had to talk to anybody in Manitoba and was busy creating an army that he would send out to put them down. So the Métis established this democratic process. It was very inclusive. The Ojibwa Chief attended, the French were there, the English were there, the non-Indigenous people were there. Everybody was included in these big conventions.

The Francophone Métis were the ones who were very interested in this as a matter of their culture and their traditional territorial rights. They talked about it in those terms, as being "natives of the country." That was very different from the way the English talked about it. The convention drafted a list of rights, and then they picked the commissioners to go and negotiate for them in Ottawa and they gave them specific instructions.

In those instructions, it's interesting to note there is nothing about the acreage of land that the Métis are going to get. That's because that wasn't their idea at all. They wanted local control over the territory and their lands. That's what they sent their negotiators to negotiate. The Métis were the majority in Red River. There were about 12,000 people in Red River in 1870. Of the 12,000 people there, 10,000 were Métis. They wanted Métis control of government and they wanted their traditionally held lands recognized and preserved. They wanted to have their culture of governance respected.

All those things are in the Bill of Rights and they included a veto or override to ensure their local control.

But when the negotiators got to Ottawa none of that was on the table. John A. Macdonald wanted to set up what today we would call a 'carpet bag' government: his people from Eastern Canada would be in control. There was no possibility of local governance, certainly not one in Métis control.

But the one thing Canada did put on the table was land.

Macdonald was only there for the first meeting. He went off on one of his drinking binges and Cartier handled the rest of the negotiations. Cartier just put land on the table, threw down a pittance of land at first and Joseph-Noël Ritchot, the main Red River negotiator, negotiated him up to 1.4 million acres. This was not what he was mandated to negotiate. It was not what the Métis wanted. But it was what he could get.

When Ritchot came back to Red River with this acreage in his pocket, he went into private meetings with Riel's council.

He bluntly told them that this was basically a take it or leave it offer. The Métis then had to go back into the convention, with all the people of Red River, and sell the deal. This was a huge step down from the mandate that the negotiators had been given. Together, Ritchot and Riel had to work hard to sell the deal to their own people. Eventually everyone agreed.

After the bill passed ensuring that the "children of the half-breeds" of Red River would receive 1.4 million acres of land, the people immediately went into big meetings in their local areas. In all the parishes, they began to select land in enclaves. This was not the idea of an Indian reserve, although they used the word "reserve." It was ownership of adjoining land parcels. The Métis wanted to keep their family groupings together. They wanted to have family holdings to preserve their lands and their way of living. Ritchot pushed for the idea that they would not be able to sell their lots for many years. He hoped to ensure they hung onto the land by doing that.

And that is exactly how the selection of lands began. But then it all went to hell when they changed to a lottery system. The lottery system meant that a father could have land in one place and his son could have land 400 miles away. It was a way of breaking up the Métis family groupings—to devastating effect. That is one of the reasons that the Métis sold their lots. Because they didn't want to live on the land the lottery gave them. They wanted to be with their parents, their brothers and sisters and their cousins.

They also sold their land because of the reign of terror. The reign of terror is what happened when John A. Macdonald sent troops to Red River. They arrived in August of 1870 and from the first day they started a violent regime that lasted for two and a half years. The violence was a massive influence on people fleeing Red River. To understand the reign of terror, we must go back to the execution of Thomas Scott in the spring of 1870. Scott was a member of the Orange Lodge, a self-pro-claimed white Protestant supremacist organization with a plan they called "ascendency." It meant putting white Protestant British men in control in all institutions—chief of police, the mayor, the city council, the premier of the province, the judges. That was their "ascendency" plan.

It is estimated that in 1870 fully one-third of all Protestant men in Canada were members of the Orange Lodge. Toronto was known as the "Belfast of Canada," a reference to the Orange influences in municipal government. The "orangists" permeated all levels of Canadian government. The Orange Lodge did not shy away from using violence to attain its ends. The two-thirds of the army that Macdonald sent to Red River were Orange Lodge members. They blatantly stated that their goal was "extermination" and that they would "never be satisfied till we have driven the French half-breeds out of the country."

They arrived in August of 1870. *The Manitoba Act* had been passed and everything was peaceful in Manitoba. Riel had been asked by Macdonald to be the caretaker governor and Riel was doing just that. He even planned a big welcoming festival for the lieutenant governor.

But the army arrived first, and from day one they were hell bent on retribution for the death of Thomas Scott. From the minute they arrived, they started assaulting people, they burned houses, they raped women and they murdered people. They were completely out of control. This was supposed to be a military operation but it was a violent armed mob that arrived, with all the tacit permission of the Prime Minister of Canada.

The reign of terror began literally the day the troops arrived and it continued for two and a half years. Many people wrote in horror about what they were witnessing in Red River. It was even a headline in the *New York Times*. Macdonald knew exactly what he had set in motion and what was happening.

The lottery and the selection of lands was taking so long (15 years) that nobody was getting anything. Also, there was a wave of Protestant settlers coming from Ontario who were literally squatting on Métis lands, and because the settlers could be armed and the Métis couldn't, the settlers were successful in dislodging Métis off their own lands.

Many Métis started to leave Red River. There were about three waves of people leaving over a three to five year period. Because their lands were not protected and because of the extreme violence in Red River and the horrible prejudice that they were beginning to encounter on their own lands. It's an ugly story, implemented by Prime Minister John A. Macdonald. He used his administrative arm through the delays in handing over the land. He used military might and he used the act of bringing in the settlers. All of these were ways of destroying the Métis lands and the people in Red River. All of it was deliberately done. It was a plan.

Mounting a Legal Challenge
The Manitoba Métis Federation was created in 1967. One of their immediate concerns was about the *Manitoba Lands Act*. It was part of their opening agenda.

By 1979, Canada was starting to get into the constitutional discussions and the push was to get constitutional protection for Aboriginal rights in the constitution. The Métis National Council established a Métis commission to hold community discussions with their people. The Commission travelled throughout the Prairies. But in Manitoba, there was a whole different take on the issue than there was in Saskatchewan and Alberta. The Manitoba position was: Why would we bother protecting our rights in the constitution when nobody's done anything about s. 31 of the *Manitoba Act* of 1870, that was supposed to provide the Métis with 1.4 million acres of land? That was already in the constitution, and we didn't get any land. Why would we spend our time doing that, negotiating another constitutional provision that would not be honoured?

They weren't saying: Don't bother. They were saying that the Manitoba Métis were not going to put their energy into that task. The Manitoba Métis leadership was more and more of the opinion that this was just a waste of time. They wanted to focus on getting implementation of s. 31's promise of 1.4 million acres of land.

They launched the Manitoba Métis Federation case in 1981 because they hoped it would have some influence on the constitutional discussions. But it had none. Still they put it in abeyance while the constitutional conferences went on: 1983, 1984, 1985. They had filed the case, but they sat back and waited to see whether anything would come of the conferences. As we all know, nothing did come out of those conferences. And so after 1985, that's when they got serious about the case. That's when Tom Berger came on, that's when they went into full swing.

~

A CONVERSATION WITH DAVID CHARTRAND, PRESIDENT, MANITOBA MÉTIS FEDERATION

David Chartrand has had a 35-year career as a political leader. Twenty-seven of those years were spent as President of the Manitoba Métis Federation. He has led the Red River Métis to win several critical court cases, including the 2013 Supreme Court case described here.

"The Métis have been called 'the forgotten people'. At one time we owned this territory. Back in 1870, the West had a population of 12,000 and 10,000 of them were Métis. We were the dominant force. But after 1885, the last battle at Batoche, we disappeared from history.

We were in the way, according to John A. Macdonald. In the agreement, Section 31 gave us 1.4 million acres of land. But that land was never given to us. You see that in our documents; the land was sold, stolen. That's why we were economically in despair. But we never gave up. This land claim, we pursued it.

Growing up, we knew Canada robbed us of our future. We always hoped that one day we could take this case forward. That started in 1979, when finally we said: we've got to take the government to court. We knew it would cost a lot of money. But one community raised $10,000, that was the catalyst. The lawyer who originally filed the case in 1981 was Dale Gibson.

Tom Berger was brought on in 1985. We looked for a lawyer who was seasoned, who could argue a complicated case. Tom, in his cleverness, because of his his past experience, was able to design an argument about how to go forward, putting the government on trial, making our case through the voices of John A. Macdonald and Cartier from the documents in the archives.

The government of Canada's argument was that we didn't have the right to bring this case forward. So we went all the way to the Supreme Court of Canada in the first round. It took five years, that issue. Then we had to start over as the case found its way back into the court. It's as slow as molasses.

We needed the tag team of lawyers, Tom Berger and Jim Aldridge, to come and defend the case. I flew to Vancouver and told Tom Berger: 'We'll pay you every cent. We just need you to believe in us.' I talked to Tom for about an hour and a half, back and forth, and he said he'd take the case.

I told our people: 'We are going to win either way. If we bring our evidence all the way to the Supreme Court and the court rules against us, we'll get our story told. And if we win the case, it will change the Métis for generations into the future. We won't be in the muskeg, watching everyone else prosper on our land.'

When I took over the federation, all funding from the government was cut off. We had a $750,000 debt. So we remortgaged our houses. We did fundraising. We started earning money from businesses. We phoned our creditors and said: 'We'll pay you back if you give us some time.'

The government of Canada was smart. They knew what their game plan was: they were throwing red herrings at us constantly. Tom Berger and Jim Aldridge would support our case with statements in the historical documents and the government lawyers would argue. We had to go to court to fight that. It took years and a lot of money. They were on the brink of breaking us. Finally, Justice Jeffrey Oliphant made a ruling, told the federal government: you've had enough time, years already. You're going to trial now.

One of the arguments the government made was that it had to be a class action. Tom was worried that we would have to get all the Métis signed up. By the time we finish that, we'd all be dead and gone. Tom was able to convince the court that we should move forward. That was lucky. We were paying for this from our back pockets.

After Oliphant ruled, I was rejoicing, Tom was rejoicing. We were finally going to argue this case, after 32 years of waiting. Then, all of a sudden an emergency meeting was called. What was going on? No one was told. As I walked into court, I was nervous. Did the government find a way to stop this case? If they did, we were finished. There was nothing left to mortgage.

Tom was called into the judge's chambers. When he came out, I was staring at Tom's face. Give me a clue. What happened? No smile. Judge Oliphant said: 'I regret to inform you that I must recuse myself from this case.' Oh no! One of the reasons we liked Judge Oliphant was that he was a history buff. We knew he would read all the documents in our case.

But we lost Judge Oliphant because his wife was Métis. She had her citizenship card so it would be seen as a conflict if he heard the case, given the potential benefit for his family. The judge we got was dragged out of another courtroom to take over the case.

In December, 2011, Tom argued the case at the Supreme Court of Canada. He was so meticulous. He had been a judge so he knew the skill set. He took the judges through the case with him. He took them through the story. That's a superior legal skill. That's why it was unanimous. Such a powerful day for all of us. 〞

A CONVERSATION WITH JIM ALDRIDGE,
LAWYER

One day in 1985, Tom Berger walked into the office of his old law firm to meet with Jim Aldridge, who was a partner in what had been Tom's former law firm and to which he had returned as associate counsel. Jim said:

> "After Tom left the bench, he was required to take a couple of years before he could start practicing law again. He came into my office and said: 'Jim I've got this case I'm working on for some folks in Winnipeg. I wonder if you have a couple of months to help me with it?'"

The case, for the Manitoba Métis, took 28 years to work its way through the courts, ending in the Supreme Court of Canada in 2013.

❝Part of my work with Tom on the Manitoba Métis case was to research the history of the *Manitoba Act*, 1870 and its implementation. Professor Doug Sprague, who had been hired by the MMF to undertake research into Métis land claims, and Professor Thomas Flanagan who had been retained by the federal government, had both written articles and books on the subject. So my starting point was the footnotes for those works, gathering all the documents they referred to. That required going to the Archives in Ottawa, digging out those documents and finding new documents.

I would bring back a massive amount of documentation and Tom and I would work through it together. We would settle on what materials we wanted to have before the court. Then the next part was putting together a list of evidence with the lawyers for Canada and for Manitoba, because they had their lists too, each with a different emphasis. We ended up collaborating on a final list of documents that we all agreed were relevant and should be before the court. But that took a long time. Then each of us culled down the documents into a smaller set that we wanted to use to bolster our particular cases.

One of the interesting aspects of the case was that Tom and I made the decision not to call an expert witness. We put the documents before the court. It was our view that the documents speak for themselves and that the court was able to look at them and interpret them as an expert would. That was a controversial decision but it's one that turned out I think.

When we headed to the Supreme Court, we felt like we had the correct arguments. We felt that the law was on our side and that justice ought to prevail by giving the Manitoba Métis Federation a decision in their favour. But we had also thought that at trial and at the Court of Appeal and we had not succeeded in those two courts. So there's always trepidation.

By the time you finish your arguments in the Supreme Court of Canada, the books are closed. There is nothing you can do. You just sit and wait.

That morning of the decision at the Supreme Court, the Red River Métis were there in force with their flags. The leadership was there. We went up into the court registry and they handed everyone a copy. Tom and I were still looking at the early parts of the decision but President Chartrand went right to the end of it. So he was on his way out the door with his arms in the air: We won! Meanwhile, Tom and I were still saying: 'Let's just get a handle on this.'

At the end of the day the court ruled that the government had breached the honour of the Crown and had failed to diligently implement the promises that had been made to the provisional government and the leaders of the Red River Métis at the time in respect of the 1.4 million acres that were promised to the children of the so-called 'half-breed heads of families' resident in the province at the time. The court said that failure has left a 'rift in the constitutional fabric,' which remains unremedied, and '[t]he unfinished business of reconciliation of the Métis people with Canadian sovereignty is a matter of national and constitutional import'. x

The Court's declaration vindicated many decades of legal work, and the many decades before that during which the Red River Métis advanced their position. So we felt jubilation. And relief.〞

EDITORIAL WITH THOMAS R. BERGER

In August of 2013, five months after the Supreme Court decision in the Manitoba Metis case, an editorial criticizing the decision appeared in the Winnipeg Free Press under the headline: "Canada: Resist the Money Grab by Manitoba Métis Federation." Thomas Berger fired back with an editorial of his own, demanding to know: Who was cheated?

"The Métis case was all about a promise made by Canada to the Métis. When Manitoba entered Confederation in 1870, the children of the Métis, numbering about 7,000, were promised 1.4 million acres of land. So what happened? Was the promise kept? The complete story is compelling.

When, after Confederation in 1867, John A. Macdonald wished to extend Canada westward, he had to deal with the Métis. The Métis were a new nation that had arisen in the West. The Red River Settlement (now Winnipeg), the largest (12,000) community on the Prairies, was a Métis settlement.

In the fall of 1869, when Canada moved to acquire the West without consulting or considering the interests of the people of the Red River, the Métis resisted. They turned back Canadian road builders and surveyors. Métis riflemen refused to allow Macdonald's newly appointed lieutenant governor, sent out from Ottawa to establish Canadian sovereignty, to enter the territory. Led by Louis Riel, the Métis formed their own provisional government, and governed Red River until the summer of 1870.

At first Macdonald dismissed the Métis. He wrote in October 1869:

> ...it will require considerable management to keep these wild people quiet. In another year the present residents (the Métis) will be altogether swamped by the influx of strangers who will go in with the idea of becoming industrious and peaceable settlers.

Macdonald wanted to send British troops to Manitoba together with Canadian militia to put down the Métis, but the troops could not reach Red River until the late spring or summer of the following year.

So he had to negotiate with the Métis if he was to bring Manitoba peacefully into Confederation. Riel's government sent delegates, led by Father-Joseph-Noël Ritchot, to Ottawa to negotiate and in May 1870 they reached an agreement with Macdonald and his principal colleague, Sir George-Étienne Cartier.

Thus, the *Manitoba Act* provided that the children of the Métis would receive 1.4 million acres of land "for the benefit of the Métis families" so that the next generation of Métis would have a secure place in the new province. Macdonald told the House of Commons that the purpose of the land grant was to enable the children to become settlers, that the land was not to go to speculators. Cartier told the House that Ottawa would act as "guardians" of the children's land.

In the recent litigation, the trial judge held that the purpose of the land grant was to give the Métis a head start, to enable them to become landowners in the new province. The Manitoba Court of Appeal agreed. Did the Métis get a "head start"? No, they didn't even get to the start line for a decade, and deeds were not distributed for 15 years.

After the soldiers and settlers arrived there was a 'reign of terror' against the Métis. Within 10 years, the population of Manitoba had risen to 60,000 (a five-fold increase). Land was distributed to everyone, but the Métis did not receive their 1.4 million acres.

The Supreme Court summed up what occurred: "The Métis did not receive the intended head start, and following the influx of settlers, they found themselves increasingly marginalized, facing discrimination and poverty."

The Manitoba Métis Federation had to prove its case in court. And did. The Supreme Court held that the promise to the Métis had not been implemented "in accordance with the honour of the Crown." The Supreme Court described it as a case of "repeated mistakes and inaction that persisted for more than a decade." The Supreme Court concluded that a "persistent pattern of errors and indifference that substantially frustrates the purposes of a solemn promise may amount to a betrayal of the Crown's duty to act honourably."

The federal government had every opportunity to answer the Manitoba Métis Federation's case. They had the legal resources of the department of

Justice, as well as outside counsel. And they had two experts, an historian and a political scientist, on the federal payroll for many years. And they lost in the Supreme Court, 6 to 2.

The Supreme Court described the promise of 1.4 million acres of the land for the next generation of Métis as "the central promise the Métis obtained from the Crown in order to prevent their future marginalization." The Métis, after years of struggle, have now established that a solemn promise made to persuade them to lay down their arms and enter Canada was never kept.

In the Manitoba courts it was held that Manitoba's statute of limitations was an absolute bar to the Métis suit. But the Métis claim was no ordinary claim.

Macdonald's promise is contained in Sec. 31 of the *Manitoba Act*, the constitutional instrument that brought Manitoba into Confederation. It is still there, still unfulfilled. The Supreme Court held that "the courts are the guardians of the Constitution and cannot be barred from issuing a declaration on a fundamental constitutional matter. The principles of legality, constitutionality and the rule of law demand no less."

The Supreme Court described the failure of the Crown to carry out the solemn constitutional promise it made to the Métis as "a rift in the national fabric." It can only be mended through negotiations, by the federal government, the government of Manitoba and the Métis. A negotiated settlement will take time, but it is the means to reconciliation. The work of nation-building is not yet completed. "

CHAPTER FIFTEEN

THE PEEL WATERSHED CASE

Drew Ann Wake

⌐○

THE PEEL WATERSHED is a magnificent wilderness. Six wild rivers—the Ogilvie, the Hart, the Blackstone, the Wind, the Bonnet Plume, and the Snake—tumble out of the Richardson Mountains to join the Peel. That river flows into the Mackenzie, across the Delta and enters the Beaufort Sea.

As remote as this land is, it has been crossed for centuries by the Indigenous hunters and trappers. Since ancient times, Gwich'in people, east and west of the mountains, have travelled to visit with one another. Elder Robert Alexie, now in his ninetieth year, describes a journey he made many times since the 1940s, from Fort McPherson through the mountains to Old Crow, 215 kilometres away. He makes it sound like a walk in the park.

> Once you cross the river you go up the first hill and follow a trail. From there I don't think you can get lost. When you get to LaChute, you head through the mountains until you hit the Bell River. Then you build a spruce boat and head down the Bell River to Old Crow. Not that hard.

In the 1970s, when the Mackenzie Valley Pipeline Inquiry visited communities in Yukon and Northwest Territories, the

Peel Watershed was one of the primary concerns of Gwich'in communities. Gladys Netro had just finished high school when Judge Berger began the community hearings. After three years in a residential school in Whitehorse, she had been keen to get back to the land so she went to her family's fish camp to harvest salmon:

> I was busy non-stop, making salmon strips and watching out for bears. When I had time to rest I read Thomas Berger's books. Then, when I went back to cutting salmon strips, I would think. The ideas were resonating with me.

At the fish camp, Gladys listened to the news from the Berger Inquiry on the radio each evening. When the hearings reached her home community of Old Crow, she listened as her people described their profound attachment to the land. "The Judge empowered people. He was making a difference right in front of us."

Years later, when Gladys was in Whitehorse, she spotted a sign announcing a meeting where respected Gwich'in leaders from Fort McPherson would discuss the Yukon government's plan for mining in the Peel Watershed. "They invited me into the circle," Gladys said in an interview. "Chief Johnny Charlie and Charlie Snowshoe took turns talking about the Peel Watershed where their ancestors came from."

Juri Peepre, a leader of the Canadian Parks and Wilderness Society, Yukon Chapter (CPAWS-YT), also attended the meeting. Together, the Gwich'in and the environmentalists examined a map to identify the areas that the government was planning to protect: critical habitat for caribou and migratory birds. "The protected areas looked like postage stamps on the map," Gladys recalled. "So we decided to make a slide show and take it to the communities, to see what they thought." In each village, they visited Elders and schools as well as the chiefs and councillors. "It took work, but we had time and patience."

The visits cemented the collaboration between the four First Nations and the two conservation groups, CPAWS and the Yukon Conservation Society. Chris Rider of CPAWS believed that the strength of the collaboration came from the historic connection of the Gwich'in First Nations with the watershed. He had travelled the rivers with the Gwich'in and remembered that they could point to places where their ancestors were buried, places their families had lived for millennia. "They were the ones who had the vision of what they wanted to see happen," he said. "We were there to support that vision."

Flipping the Final Agreement

The Peel Watershed had been a priority during the 1980s and '90s, when First Nations on both sides of the mountains settled their land claims. The Yukon claim included a chapter that ensured that the Peel Watershed would remain protected. The agreement allowed for a commission that would hold public hearings to decide the future of the watershed. Tom Berger said:

> The fascinating feature of the 1991 land claims agreement was that it provided that when the First Nations and the government were locked in controversy about the future of this land, everybody would be heard, including Yukoners, people who had nothing to do with the government or First Nations. It was a remarkable document.

Accordingly, in 2004, the government of Yukon established a five-person panel to recommend a plan for the Peel Watershed. Tom Berger noted:

> This wasn't like looking at whether someone can mend their sidewalk. This was an area as large as Scotland or New Brunswick. The question was: should it be protected or should it simply be made available for industrial development at any time at the wish of the Yukon government?

The panel took five years to study the options. They called witnesses from across the territory. Consultations were held with four First Nations in Yukon and the Northwest Territories.

"In Fort McPherson, we wanted 100 percent protection," remembered Charlie Snowshoe's daughter, Elizabeth Vittrekwa. "But that couldn't happen because some of the mining operations were grandfathered in." At the end of five years, the panel wrote a 300-page report, concluding that approximately 80 percent of the watershed should be preserved as protected land.

In the summer of 2011, shortly after the Final Recommended Plan had been released, an election was called in Yukon. Throughout the campaign, the environmental groups tried to bring a discussion about the Peel Watershed into the political debate, but candidates from the Yukon Party were vague about their approach to the Final Recommended Plan. "The politicians stayed quiet," said Joti Overduin of the Canadian Parks and Wilderness Society. "They didn't take a stand on it during the election."

But when the Yukon Party was elected, the new government announced that it was no longer bound by the agreement that had been concluded the year before. The legislators were going to establish their own plan and enact it into law.

Joti Overduin observed:

People felt that the government's approach went beyond the environmental issues, it was an attack on democracy and Indigenous rights. It was a very dark time. We were up against a powerful government that was not listening. They had endless financial resources, our tax dollars in fact, to keep going. They had lawyers and they had time.

Joti recalled a time when the Premier and Ministers met with the four Chiefs of the Peel Nations. Minutes after the meeting ended, and without the approval of the Chiefs, the government's press release went out, announcing the new guidelines for the Peel planning process. "The decisions were made unilaterally, without any input," Joti said. "There were many times it felt easy to be overcome with despair."

The sudden reversal of the plan drew the environmental organizations and the affected First Nations into a closer alliance. They concentrated on building a united grassroots movement. Large protests were held outside the Yukon Legislature. Voices and drums were so loud that they could be heard by the politicians inside the building. Citizens lined up to add their names to a banner called 'River of Names' outside the Legislature. Eventually it stretched for a city block. Others dipped their hands in paint and stamped their handprints on a Peel Unity Wall.

The leaders of the movement travelled around the North to meetings where they explained their case. Wildlife photographer Peter Mather climbed a mountain above the watershed to capture images of the river, so that posters could be created. Protect the Peel stickers were suddenly in great demand, appearing on computers and guitars. The grassroots movement was inescapable.

To give greater visibility to the protest, the Canadian Parks and Wilderness Society designed a t-shirt. Supporters wore them to protests outside the Legislature or to the visitor's gallery inside, as a form of silent, but visible, protest.

At the same time, the Yukon government was also presenting its case to the public. Each year a geoscience forum is held in Whitehorse to encourage the mining and petroleum industries to consider new opportunities in the territory. In 2012, Yukon's Minister of Energy, Mines and Resources and the Minister of the Environment were invited to address the forum about the territory's new land use plan. The event had rules: audience members were not permitted to raise questions or debate the ministers, although they could submit written questions.

Joti Overduin recalled a remarkable rupture in the forum:

> The two ministers were up at the front with maps that
> were deceiving. They used green to colour huge areas
> that were actually open for development. I was sitting
> there feeling hopeless. Then, suddenly a loud voice
> said: 'Excuse me, my name is Charlie Snowshoe and I
> am from Fort McPherson. I am sitting here feeling like
> a student in a classroom. Why are you two up there
> instructing me, when I've been in this planning pro-
> cess since its inception?'

Joti Overduin further recalled that the Minister of
Environment was polite but didn't know what to say. "The
Minister of Energy, Mines and Resources went beet red and
tried to cut Charlie off. I was floored at Charlie's willingness to
speak up when they had tried to silence us all."

Hiring a Lawyer

Gladys Netro was relieved when the four First Nations and
two conservation organizations decided that they would take
the Yukon government to court. She hoped they would hire
Thomas Berger as their lawyer. "Who else could we ask? Tom
Berger had walked that journey along the Mackenzie Valley,
then into Alaska, listening to all those stories. Who else could
we ask?"

When Tom Berger was invited to speak at a meeting,
Gladys arrived wearing her traditional regalia and introduced
herself. "I said I had read his books and they had changed my
life. I explained that we were embarking on protecting the Peel
and I hoped we could be in touch."

A short time later, both Gladys and Tom Berger were
invited to speak at a conference of funders. Said Gladys:

> As Tom Berger left the stage I was at the bottom of the
> stairs. I said: 'Would you come and help us protect the

Peel?' He said, 'I don't know whether they'd have me. Let me work on that.' And he gave me the biggest smile.

Following Gwich'in tradition, the Elders participated in making the decision about the lawyer who should lead the case. Tom Berger was invited to meet with Elders at a traditional camp near Cache Creek. On his arrival, Gladys recalled that members of the audience were subdued; they were meeting Berger for the first time since the pipeline inquiry hearings more than thirty years before. "When Tom stood up to speak he joked that he was elderly, so some of them might worry that he would not be able to see the case through to the end. He chuckled. The Elders chuckled, too. That broke the ice."

The lawyers, Tom Berger and Margie Rosling, were hired. The chiefs and councillors began to hold meetings with the environmentalists to plan a joint strategy. Gladys Netro and Joti Overduin were given the task of keeping the First Nations and the environmental community in touch with developments. Gladys made presentations to the councils and home visits to Elders. Joti prepared bulletins for the news media. The battle for the Peel Watershed was underway.

To Court in Whitehorse

The case came up before Judge Ron Veale in Whitehorse in the summer of 2014. The staff of the Canadian Parks and Wilderness Society debated two possible legal strategies. Said Chris Rider of CPAWS:

> One option was to argue that there had been insufficient consultation. But Tom Berger said, 'If we do that they'll do more consultation and we'll end up back where we are.' Instead, Tom said we had to look at the case from a treaty perspective. The Yukon government derailed this process; Yukon did not uphold the honour of the Crown. Everyone ultimately got behind Tom's vision.

By the time the hearings opened, Elders from across Yukon had expressed a desire to attend in person. Gladys Netro organized buses to bring the Elders to a hotel across the street from the courthouse.

On the morning the case opened, I dashed to the lobby. It was full of Elders. The Elders from Mayo asked to lead the procession. Traffic stopped as the long line of Elders crossed to the courthouse, where Thomas Berger greeted them at the door.

The courtroom was filled with leaders and their legal teams. An additional courtroom was opened so that the overflow crowd could view a live stream of the proceedings.

Thomas Berger summed up their position succinctly.

The whole procedure under the land claims provided that when the panel came down with its decision, the First Nations could object, Yukon could object, but they had to give reasons. The Yukon government simply wrote a letter saying: 'The land use plan has dedicated too much land to environmental protection and not enough to industrial development. And we want this revised.' The Yukon government then pressed ahead as if their objections had all been accepted. They enacted a land use plan that essentially devoted most of the land to industrial purposes and left very little protection. When the matter went to court, we said: 'They didn't give reasons, they just expressed an attitude.' It was like the old line in the Groucho Marx film: Whatever it is, I'm against it.

In contrast to the raucous demonstrations at the Legislature, the court hearing was dignified. First Nations representatives arrived in traditional dress. They held a water ceremony outdoors; visitors brought water from rivers across Yukon to pour into the Yukon River near the courthouse. On another day, people sat in a silent vigil outside the courthouse. "It felt more like a prayer than a protest," said Joti Overduin.

When Justice Veale released his decision, there was jubilation in the environmental community and the four First Nations. On point after point, the judge found in their favour. But over the following days, Chris Rider of CPAWS felt that a more somber attitude took over.

> There was an awareness that this wasn't going to end there. The Yukon government was not going to give up. We knew they would appeal. So we experienced a joy mixed with trepidation over what would happen next.

The concern was warranted. Yukon government appealed the case.

Paddle Politics

Activists in Yukon knew that it was critical to spark the interest of a wider swath of the public. But that was a challenge. Very few Canadians had any idea where the Peel Watershed was located, much less why it should be protected.

So northern activists mounted a campaign to bring the issue to a southern audience. They created a slide show with magnificent images of the Peel Watershed and gave presentations in cities across southern Canada. Then they hatched a more ambitious project, a documentary film. Over two months, a crew of six young men and two dogs made a 1,500 kilometre canoe journey that included crossing six rapids and making a gruelling portage. Audiences that viewed "Paddle for the North" were given a glimpse of the spectacular scenery of the Peel. But more importantly, the young paddlers projected a compelling commitment to saving the watershed.

A group of potential funders were invited to take a somewhat less arduous journey. Indigenous guides and scientists travelled with them, so funders could see the land from a range of perspectives. The strategy was a success: at the end of the trip the funders had made a commitment to backing the project.

These journeys encouraged young Indigenous men and women to experience the wilderness. One of them was Dana Tizya Tramm, who had moved from Whitehorse to his grandparents' community of Old Crow two years before. He got his first taste of the wilderness by volunteering to help local families in their hunting trips. He remembered with awe his first experience paddling through the Peel Canyon.

> It is an epic moment when you go through that canyon. The water picks up a little bit, a subtle cue. Dark clouds part, a rainbow hovers over the cliffs. There are boils, upswells of water, which can send you into the river's current, sideways. There are whirlpools the size of a car that drag you alongside the cliff and undercurrents that can suck you down. You're scared, but you've got to do it.

On one journey, Dana Tizya Tramm fell into a political conversation with five other Indigenous youths.

> As young adults, we were reconnecting with our families who had travelled through those lands for centuries. We were having discussions about cultural revitalization. We decided we couldn't be the last generation to go through that land, so we decided to set up a mentorship program, 'Youth of the Peel'. We would bring Indigenous youth to places their families had lived in history, back in the nomadic days. We would share our stories, taking them back through time.

Over the next few years, they built a cohort of young people who were committed to wrestling the Peel Watershed case through the Yukon courts, all the way to the Supreme Court of

Canada. Slowly, the movement began to gain a wider vision of its aspirations. Dana Tizya Tramm described the change this way.

> In 2016, we were four First Nations grappling with land use planning. We began to realize that these conversations are more about the principles of our relationship with the land. All our lands are at stake. We need to engage youth as the leaders we are going to need them to be.

Court of Appeal

When the case reached the Court of Appeal, the First Nations and the environmental groups mobilized their supporters in Whitehorse. Activists were marching in the street in front of the courthouse. There was a barbecue attended by a mixture of supporters from across Yukon and Northwest Territories. But the decision from the court was a disappointment.

After some discussion, the First Nations and the environmentalists reached the conclusion that they had no choice but to appeal the case to the Supreme Court of Canada. But would the court agree to take the case? Only a small percentage of the submitted cases are accepted for review.

On the day when the Supreme Court was to make its announcement, Chris Rider and his colleagues gathered in front of a computer in their office. "We kept refreshing the Supreme Court website. I remember feeling such a sense of relief when they said they would take the case—even though it meant we had a lot of work to do."

The Supreme Court of Canada

The Yukon First Nations and the environmental groups wanted their presence to be felt in Ottawa when the case was heard at the Supreme Court. Flights to the south were booked solid with activists. Elders were escorted by their children and grandchildren. A class of high school students travelled with their teachers to witness the proceedings.

Support was offered by chiefs and councillors from across Canada. The Kitigan Zibi Anishinabeg First Nation travelled to Ottawa from Maniwaki, on the Quebec border, to conduct a water ceremony on the steps of the Supreme Court of Canada. They were joined by the First Nations from Yukon and Northwest Territories, in full regalia.

Entering the courtroom, Gladys Netro was hit by a wave of emotion. "We filled the Supreme Court. I was touched when I saw the nine judges sitting up there.

But the delegation from the Canadian Parks and Wilderness Society was on edge. The government of Yukon had hired a high profile Toronto law firm to handle their case. So Chris Rider was relieved when the Chief Justice interrupted with his first question and the Bay Street lawyer seemed flustered.

When Tom Berger rose to make his case, the visitors from Yukon watched every flicker of emotion crossing the faces of the judges. "It was a roller coaster of emotions," said Chris Rider.

After the hearing, the visitors from Yukon headed back to their home communities. The wait for a decision was hard. But Gladys had learned an important lesson. "We are not doing enough. We have to engage with others to speak up for our special places. We need more fighters."

On December 1, 2017, the Supreme Court was due to announce its decision. In Whitehorse, representatives of the First Nations and environmental groups boarded flights to return to Ottawa. In Vancouver, Tom Berger's colleague, Margie Rosling, prepared to join them for the decision. Tom Berger, at 84 years of age, was not well enough to travel.

The Yukon activists rented a room so they could read the ruling, and consult over the phone with Tom Berger, before facing the media. That day was etched in Chris Rider's memory.

We read the ruling, but with all the legal language we weren't sure. As we waited for Margie Rosling to join us, we were saying to each other: I think this looks good. Are we reading this right? It seemed like an eternity before the lawyers came into the room and Margie threw her arms up in the air. We won.

Tom Berger reached his colleagues by phone from the other side of the country. He pointed out that the ruling ensured that modern land claims agreements, like the 1992 agreement, had assumed a vital place in the Canadian constitutional fabric. "Negotiating modern treaties, and living by the mutual rights and responsibilities they set out, has the potential to forge a renewed relationship between the Crown and Indigenous Peoples."

This meant that the Yukon government's unilateral attempt to impose its plan was halted, and the process would resume from the point where the government had derailed it, with all parties involved. But the Supreme Court of Canada also said that Yukon's changes to the final recommended plan of the 5-person commission did not respect the land use planning process and its conduct was not becoming of the honour of the Crown. Therefore, the Yukon's plan must be quashed. In Berger's view:

The concept of 'the honour of the Crown' is a test that the courts impose on governments now in these disputes by saying: Did government act honourably? Yukon had trashed this plan, developed after five years by agreement of all parties, and then said: We have the authority to do whatever we want. That was a clear violation of the honour of the Crown and it was the basis on which the Supreme Court said: No, we can't allow this behaviour.

After the unanimous decision was announced, Joti Overduin summed up:

We couldn't have hoped for a better decision. It identified where the federal government had gone off the rails. Also, the decision left room for improvements because it allowed for a joint implementation of the plan. The First Nations were to be treated as equals. The government would never run roughshod over them again.

~⌒

A CONVERSATION WITH BOBBI ROSE KOE, GUIDE

"I have travelled on the Peel River for most of my life but I didn't see the watershed until 2015, when I paddled the Wind River. Since then I've paddled the Snake River and the Ogilvie River a dozen times. There's no other place in the world like it. It's beautiful, pristine, no roads, nothing has been disturbed.

Knowing that my grandfathers, my great-grandfathers, travelled these rivers is a great connection. In some of the rivers you can see the fish. There are caribou and Dall sheep, bears, and peregrine falcons. It's like a storybook.

When the hearings came for the Peel court case, my jiijii (grandfather) Robert Alexie encouraged me to speak. We had travelled the land together and he encouraged me to speak because I knew the land and the people who live there. What I had to offer as a young person was my voice and my energy. I was able to navigate what was happening, share our voices and our stories.

We created 'Youth of the Peel', trips on the river for young people, to shine a light on the Peel court case. With five or six youth from Gwich'in communities, we went down the river for seventeen days. When I was getting ready, Elders in my community were telling me stories about the watershed. My jiijii said that it was a once-in-a-lifetime trip. Neil Colin said to watch the land, the mountains where I was going, and to be thankful each day.

Then I went on the trip. Half way along the Wind River there is a beautiful hike. The comments from my grandfather and Neil Colin came back to me. I told the youth: these trips should not be once in a lifetime. We made a promise to the land that we were going to bring more people to see this land.

I was honoured to travel, to speak on behalf of my people. But it was hard to go to the court cases and hear them talk about this land as if our people are not living here. It was hard to walk in protest and raise our voices to say this land has to be protected. No young person should have to sacrifice that time in their life to protect their land. At the end of the day I was proud to do that, but it was hard.

When our case went to the Supreme Court, many of us went to Ottawa. I went with my grandfather. We had travelled together before, by boat and snowmobile, but we'd never travelled in the air. We'd never gone to a big city together so that was a huge experience. There were a lot of people from the northern communities. When we went to the court it was exciting, that huge building. But we had a lot of anxiety. We were stressed. What would come out of today?

Then we went in, me and my jiijii, and we sat in the front, right behind Thomas Berger. All the judges were there. Each side spoke. The judges asked questions. It was hard for my grandfather, knowing that his great-grandparents are buried on that land. At the end of the day, everyone felt good about it. Thomas Berger thought it was a success.

Then, it was a waiting game. My grandfather said: 'If they start building roads, we're going to go up there and lay our bodies down to protect the land.' But it turned out for the best.

That court case really changed my life. I thought: people have to know this land. It made me think about what I should do to have an impact on this world. So I became a guide, to build the future. "

EPILOGUE

WEIGHING JUSTICE

Drew Ann Wake and Thomas R. Berger

A FEW MONTHS AFTER the Peel Watershed case concluded, Tom Berger and I sat down to chat. He was in
good spirits. He had recently returned from Whitehorse,
where the environmental groups and First Nations had
gathered on the banks of the Yukon River to celebrate victory in their years-long battle to protect the Peel.

I as curious how, in retrospect, he evaluated the case
made by the Yukon government. Tom didn't hold their
argument in high regard. When he answered, there was a
touch of disbelief in his voice.

> "This was a government, for God's sake, not some
> lonely taxpayer befuddled by bureaucratic jargon.
> They were determining the future of an area of
> land the size of Scotland! Give your reasons for
> thinking the plan is not adequate. But they didn't
> give reasons. It was a failure on their part to recog-
> nize the significance of the case."

I was curious about the risk that the First Nations and
environmental organizations had taken by appealing the

case to the Supreme Court. The Yukon Court of Appeal had given them the opportunity to return to the negotiating table instead. Was there ever a moment when he thought: "Gee, maybe it wasn't a good idea for us to appeal the case. Maybe we'll lose."

. Tom said that he had not been guided solely by weighing whether the case would win or lose. Principle was paramount.

> "If you believe in the argument you are making, if you feel you're right, you proceed. I think that it is important that the justice of your case be apparent, to the judges, to everyone who listens to you. It often moves the court to a greater extent than delineating a point of law if you can persuade them: there's been an injustice here."

That seemed to sum up Tom's legal career. He not only had a profound belief that justice must be served; he believed that others—lawyers, judges and his fellow citizens—could see and act upon these principles. It was this belief that had sustained him through the challenging cases that, over the course of more than sixty years, had altered the legal landscape, transforming Indigenous rights from 'a historical might-have-been' to a foundation of Canadian law.

BETWEEN TWO WORLDS

Drew Ann Wake and Shaznay Waugh

A RE YOUNG PEOPLE TODAY propelled forward by the legal battles of previous generations? Or do those struggles seem dated and arcane? To find out, I passed a few chapters on to a gifted young Dene scholar, Shaznay Waugh, who dreams of becoming a lawyer. She says

“The stories in this book about Indigenous leadership make me think about how our tactics in this collective struggle must be enduring, adaptive, and just that: collective. More than that, it evokes questions as to what might be the most effective and meaningful way to enter into political and legal debates over Indigenous rights when such rights are still not wholly recognized, or understood, in their distinct cultural contexts. This reminds me of the concept of walking between two worlds by which we, as young Indigenous peoples, have the responsibility of learning how to navigate the colonial world while honouring and asserting the right to our own worlds. **"**

It appears that the younger generation continues to draw on the lessons from the battles fought by their Elders. I hope that this book, with the stories of Tom Berger and his many Indigenous collaborators and friends, will encourage young people to continue steering this country on its journey toward Indigenous rights.

RESURCES

Against the Odds: The Indigenous Rights Cases of
Thomas R. Berger was written using more than
four hundred audio and video interviews that were
recorded by Drew Ann Wake between 1975 and 2024.
The earliest recordings, on reel-to-reel and cassette
audio tapes, have been digitized.

Over the last decade, a number of interviews with
Thomas R. Berger and Indigenous leaders were
captured on video. These have been edited into more
than 20 short video documentaries featuring people
who testified in the court cases discussed in this book.

Some readers may be interested in following the step-
by-step development of Tom Berger's legal cases and
commissions. Before he passed away in 2021, Berger
assembled an archive of his legal documents and
correspondence. It is available through Rare Books and
Special Collections at the Library of the University of
British Columbia. The Berger family is continuing to
add to this collection so that it will reflect the long and
remarkable career of this legal pioneer.

Reference materials can also be found in the books and
reports that Thomas Berger wrote over the course of
his career.

Berger, Thomas R., (1977). *Northern Frontier, Northern Homeland, Report of the Mackenzie Valley Pipeline Inquiry, Volumes 1 and 2*. Government of Canada. The report, published in two volumes, deals with the social, economic, and environmental impacts of a proposed natural gas pipeline in the Mackenzie Valley and the Western Arctic, Northwest Territories.

Berger, Thomas R., (1981). *Fragile Freedoms: Human Rights and Dissent in Canada*. Clarke and Irwin. This book discusses human rights and the role of dissent in Canada, reflecting on Berger's experiences as a judge and his advocacy for Indigenous rights and other civil liberties.

Berger, Thomas R., (1985). *Village Journey: The Report of the Alaska Native Claims Review*, Hill and Wang. In this book, Thomas Berger reviews the implementation of the *Alaska Native Claims Settlement Act* and its impact on Alaska Indigenous communities.

Berger, Thomas R., (2002). *One Man's Justice: A Life in the Law,* Douglas and McIntyre and University of Washington Press. This is an autobiographical account detailing Berger's legal career and his involvement in significant cases and inquiries related to Indigenous rights and environmental justice.

Additionally, these books by other authors provide insights into Thomas Berger's life and career:

Swayze, Carolyn, (1987). *Hard Choices: A Life of Tom Berger*, Douglas and Macintyre. This biography covers Berger's life, emphasizing his legal career and his role in significant legal and social issues in Canada.

Scott, Patrick, (2007). *Stories Told: Stories and Images of the Berger Inquiry*, The Enzo Institute. This book offers a narrative and visual account of the Berger Inquiry, highlighting its impact on Indigenous communities and Canadian society.

Follow this QR code for additional references, resources, and information for *Against the Odds*. There, you will find links to the audiobook and ebook, documentaries, and full interviews with Thomas Berger and the Indigenous rights activists he worked with.

INDEX

OTHER TITLES IN THE DURVILE TRUE CASES SERIES

SERIES EDITOR: LORENE SHYBA | ALSO AVAILABLE AS AUDIOBOOKS AND E-BOOKS

PUBLISHING AUTHORS WHO HAVE THE AMBITION TO BRING KNOWLEDGE ABOUT LEGAL ISSUES TO THE WORLD

TOUGH CRIMES
Eds. C.D. Evans & L. Shyba
ISBN: 9781988824031

SHRUNK
Eds. L. Shyba & J. T. Dalby
ISBN: 9781988824055

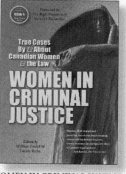

MORE TOUGH CRIMES
Eds. W. Trudell & L. Shyba
ISBN: 9781988824635

WOMEN IN CRIMINAL JUSTICE
Eds. W. Trudell & LShyba
ISBN: 9781988824215

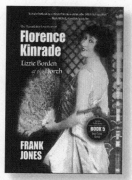

FLORENCE KINRADE
By Frank Jones
ISBN 9781990735493

GO AHEAD AND SHOOT ME
By Doug Heckbert
ISBN: 9781990735103

OTHER TITLES IN THE DURVILE TRUE CASES SERIES

SERIES EDITOR: LORENE SHYBA | ALSO AVAILABLE AS AUDIOBOOKS AND E-BOOKS

PUBLISHING AUTHORS WHO HAVE THE AMBITION TO BRING KNOWLEDGE ABOUT LEGAL ISSUES TO THE WORLD

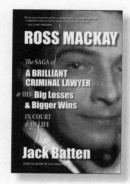

ROSS MACKAY
By Jack Batten
ISBN: 9781988824277

BENCHED
By Nancy Morrison
ISBN: 9781988824277

AFTER THE FORCE
Ed. Debbie Doyle
ISBN: 9781988824826

PINE BOX PAROLE
By John L. Hill
ISBN: 9781988824833

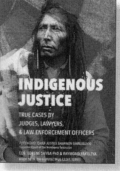

INDIGENOUS JUSTICE
Eds. L. Shyba & R. Yakeleya
ISBN: 9781988824833

AGAINST THE ODDS
By Drew Ann Wake
ISBN: 9781990735127

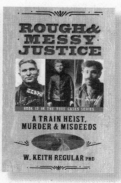

ROUGH & MESSY JUSTICE
By W. Keith Regular
ISBN: 9781990735301

POLARIZED
By Lorene Shyba
ISBN: 9781990735431

OTHER TITLES IN THE INDIGENOUS SPIRIT OF NATURE SERIES

SERIES EDITORS: RAYMOND YAKELEYA & LORENE SHYBA

PUBLISHING AUTHORS WHO HAVE THE AMBITION TO BRING TRADITIONAL KNOWLEDGE TO THE WORLD

**THE TREE BY THE
WOODPILE**
By Raymond Yakeleya

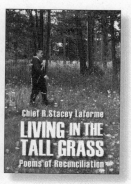

**LIVING IN THE
TALL GRASS**
By Chief R. Stacey Laforme

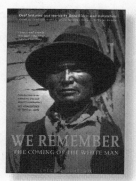

**WE REMEMBER
SPECIAL EDITION**
Eds. Stewart & Yakeleya

**STORIES OF
METIS WOMEN**
Eds. Oster & Lizee

**NAHGANNE TALES OF THE
NORTHERN SASQUATCH**
By Red Grossinger

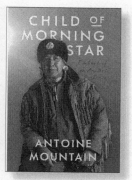

**CHILD OF MORNING STAR
EMBERS OF AN ANCIENT DAWN**
By Antoine Mountain

OTHER TITLES IN THE INDIGENOUS SPIRIT OF NATURE SERIES

SERIES EDITORS: RAYMOND YAKELEYA & LORENE SHYBA

PUBLISHING AUTHORS WHO HAVE THE AMBITION TO BRING TRADITIONAL KNOWLEDGE TO THE WORLD

**LILLIAN & KOKOMIS
THE SPIRIT OF DANCE**
By Lynda Partridge

**WHY ARE YOU STILL
HERE?: A LILLIAN MYSTERY**
By Lynda Partridge

**SIKSIKAITSITAPI: STORIES
OF THE BLACKFOOT PEOPLE**
By Payne Many Guns *et al*

**THE RAINBOW, THE
MIDWIFE, & THE BIRDS**
By Raymond Yakeleya

**ÎETHKA: STORIES FROM
STONEY NAKODA COUNTRY**
By Trent and Tina Fox

**MIDNIGHT STORM
MOONLESS SKY**
By Alex Soop

**WHISTLE AT NIGHT
AND THEY WILL COME**
By Alex Soop

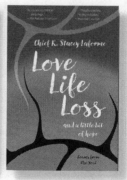

**LOVE LIFE LOSS
AND A LITTLE BIT OF HOPE**
By Chief R. Stacey Laforme

DREW ANN WAKE

D rew Ann Wake is a filmmaker and new media producer who began her career with CBC North and the National Film Board in Yellowknife. She covered the Berger Inquiry from 1975-1977 and then worked on the independent documentary, *The Inquiry Film,* which won the Canadian Film Festival award for Best Documentary. Drew Ann also works as a museum designer, developing exhibitions in Canada as well as in the US and the UK.